12/02

ROOF GARDENS

. . . .

THEODORE OSMUNDSON FASLA

W.W. NORTON & COMPANY
NEW YORK · LONDON

ROOF GARDENS

HISTORY, DESIGN, AND CONSTRUCTION

All photographs by the author unless noted.

For information about permission to reproduce selections from this book,
write to Permissions, W. W. Norton & Company, Inc., 500 Fifth Avenue,
New York, NY 10110

The text of this book is composed in Minion
with the display set in Casablanca
Manufacturing by Chroma Graphics Pte. Ltd.
Book design by Gilda Hannah

pages 2–3: Newton Vineyard, Saint Helena, California
page 6: Ghirardelli Square, San Francisco, California
page 8: Grosse Schanze Park, Bern, Switzerland
page 10: Kaiser Resources, Vancouver, Canada

Library of Congress Cataloging-in-Publication Data

Osmundson, Theodore.
Roof gardens: history, design, and construction / Theodore Osmundson.
p. cm.
Includes bibliographical references (p.   ) and index.
ISBN 0-393-73012-3
1. Roof gardening.   I. Title.
SB419.5.075   1999
635.9'671—dc21   98-50595
                                                          CIP

W. W. Norton & Company, Inc., 500 Fifth Avenue, New York, NY 10110
http://www.wwnorton.com

W. W. Norton & Company Ltd., 10 Coptic Street, London WC1A 1PU

2 4 6 8 0 9 7 5 3 1

To two loving women:

my mother, who gave me my life and later saved it;

and my wife, Lorraine, who made it a pleasure to live.

CONTENTS

....

FOREWORD

This long-awaited treatise on rooftop landscape architecture is far more than a book about "greening the skyline." It is an authoritative work on transforming thousands of acres of neglected urban rooftop into valuable real estate, benefiting not only surrounding apartment dwellers, but even more, the building occupants, who can thus enjoy aerial gardens, premium living space, and convenient outdoor recreation.

Inexplicably, while city land at street level—with its traffic, friction, fumes, and attendant hubbub—is exorbitantly expensive, the same building space aloft, open to the sun, sky, fresh breeze, and dramatic views, remains underutilized. Worse, too often in summer it weaves with the heat of asphaltic surfacing, and in winter it lies windswept and frigid, adding immensely to the cost of year-round air conditioning and heating of the supporting structure and surrounding buildings. Then, too, vacant rooftops have traditionally become the repository of dilapidated water tanks, rusty air-conditioning units, and a random accumulation of trash, which detracts immensely from the whole upper-story field of view.

This need not be. Theodore Osmundson provides a generous array of examples of handsome rooftop treatments, ranging from sheltered sitting and dining spaces to extensive garage-top plazas. Illustrated are such upper-deck structures as pergolas, raised planting beds, and shade canopies. Shown too are plazas with tubbed foliage plants, benches and chairs, sculpture, and a wide range of paving. Of added interest are the possibilities of reflecting pools or moving water, as in wall fountains, waterfalls, splashing jets, and sprays. Such planted or shaded areas can ameliorate ambient air temperatures by as much as fif-teen degrees in the heat of summertime and greatly reduce the winter chill factor.

A distinguishing feature of *Roof Gardens* is the wealth of technical construction data provided. Typical sections and details cover such aspects as raised planters, walls, paving, drainage, and lighting. Of special interest are the discussions on planting soils and drainage and the examinations of new techniques for constructing roof gardens from abroad.

Widely recognized as a leading exponent and designer of rooftop places and spaces, Theodore Osmundson has shared his knowledge in courses at Harvard's Graduate School of Design and in lectures throughout the country. His pioneering Kaiser Center in Oakland, California, remains a highly successful prototype of an extensive roof-deck park. It has greatly enhanced the experience and lifestyle of workers in the surrounding office towers and dramatically increased the adjacent property values. In addition to the succession of upper-story gardens and recreation areas of his own design, he has included in this work graphic description of many other examples in the United States and abroad.

Building upon an absorbing historical background, *Roof Gardens* presages a new order of upper-level landscape that will transform vast desolate areas of urban rooftop into veritable hanging gardens. They will become in effect terraced, and often interconnected, garden parks, bringing dimensions of comfort and delight to city dwellers and visitors. The visual, social, and economic yields will be manifold.

Here is a practical, creative, and stimulating book that is bound to make a difference.

JOHN ORMSBEE SIMONDS FASLA

PREFACE

· ·

Over the past fifty years, a great many new roof gardens have been built around the world, ranging from intimate private enclaves to enormous public spaces. Yet little formal research into the systems that support successful roof gardens has been conducted. The sparse literature that does exist consists primarily of glowing newspaper and magazine articles focusing on crowd-pleasing features. Not much has been written about the technical requirements of a long-lived, healthy roof garden, nor of the costly failures that can result when such requirements are ignored. With so little hard information available, it is not surprising that building professionals—from developers and financiers to architects, engineers, and contractors—are reluctant to include roof gardens in their projects. Nor is it particularly surprising that many of the roof gardens that have been undertaken are poorly designed and constructed.

As a practicing landscape architect, I too have been frustrated by the lack of practical information available to professionals on the techniques of roof garden design and construction. Over the past thirty years, I have traveled all around the United States and the world, visiting and photographing roof gardens and corresponding with landscape architects and product manufacturers, in an effort to learn more about successful roof garden design. I have tried, with mixed success, to learn which construction techniques have been used and why design decisions were made. The results of these studies have been disheartening at best. (The one exception to an otherwise bleak picture is the very thorough research that has been undertaken in Germany over the past fifteen years to determine the value of every material and system used in that country. But almost all the data are available only in German, which is not very helpful to most American landscape architects.) Despite the increasing number of roof gar-

dens and the apparent success of many of them, a disturbing lack of knowledge about or even understanding of the simplest problems continues to exist. With little to rely on but word of mouth, roof garden designers must continually "reinvent the wheel." As a result, many roof gardens will almost certainly fail; indeed, some of the gardens featured in this book are already experiencing problems. The overloading of roof structures, the penetration of the roof membrane by roots, the deterioration of galvanized steel pipe in irrigation lines, the obstruction of drain lines and loss of soil caused by water drainage, and the leaching of organic material from soil—all of these problems and more could be avoided with appropriate design and maintenance. That is what this book is all about.

The first two chapters of this book provide an overview of roof gardens past and present. The book opens with an introductory look at the state of roof garden design today, exploring different kinds of roof gardens, discussing the advantages of including a roof garden in a project, and differentiating roof garden design from garden design. The second chapter looks back at roof gardens throughout history, from the legendary Hanging Gardens of Babylon to early-twentieth-century masterpieces of design and imagination. The four chapters that follow guide you through the process of roof garden design and construction, examining site considerations, construction techniques (including three case studies of actual construction projects), design features (such as plants, paving, furnishings, sculpture, and the like), and critical maintenance procedures. Included herein are the results of years of professional practice, travel, and research, including information on state-of-the-art European technology that is virtually unknown in the United States. The appendixes include a list of suppliers and their addresses, as well as tables and charts of data commonly used in roof garden design.

Despite the limited amount of information available to landscape architects, some magnificent roof gardens have been designed, both in the United States and abroad. Three portfolios showcase some of these gems, providing case studies of over fifty roof gardens in the United States, Canada, Mexico, Europe, Japan, and Australia. The scores of color photographs, as well as plans, black-and-white photos, and a detailed discussion of each garden, are intended as an illustration of what has been done and, more important, as an inspiration for what could be done.

ACKNOWLEDGMENTS

The creation of this book, like most others, has depended on the help and encouragement of a number of people who generously supplied information, photographs, drawings, comments, access for photography, and other assistance. First, thanks go to my wife, Lorraine, for her endless patience in waiting for me to photograph many gardens and graciously enduring my countless hours in the darkroom to produce most of the photographs in this book and for giving me encouragement and the very best of company in my travels.

My son Richard spent much time and effort researching roof garden literature from all over the world at the University of California at Berkeley library. I am also grateful to Ralph Wilcoxen, architect and accomplished researcher, for his early work and knowledge about what to look for and how to credit his finds.

I am beholden to the German landscape architect Arno Schmid, a loyal friend, who shared his broad personal knowledge of the techniques used in Germany and throughout Europe and who provided invaluable help by introducing me to other landscape architects in major German cities, all of whom have taken me to visit their work. Special thanks goes to his brilliant daughter, Ilka Schmid, whose sleuthing revealed where the "green roof" ordinances now prevalent in Germany's larger cities are in force.

To American landscape architects Sasaki, Inc.; Carol Johnson and Associates; EDAW, Inc.; to John Whalley in the United Kingdom, and to others, I extend my appreciation for providing information and photos of their work. In Japan I could not have visited roof gardens in Tokyo, Osaka, and Kitakyushu without the generous help of Haruto Kobayashi, Shintaro Sugio, and the late Yoshiko Arata and Kenzo Ogata, all master landscape architects.

I am also grateful to the researchers of roof garden materials, Dr. Hans-Joachim Liesecke of the University of Hannover in Germany and his team, and Dr. Francis R. Gouin of the University of Maryland, for their pioneering work, and to Robert Wilkinson, good friend and world-class structural engineer. Thanks to Warner K. Hobart and John van Wagoner, roofing experts, for reviewing the discussion of waterproofing.

To all of the manufacturers of products used in roof gardens, for generously providing me with information on their products, I extend my gratitude.

Finally, my gratitude goes to the editor, Nancy Green, who oversaw the publication process and kept it moving, and to Linda Venator, the copy editor, a very knowledgeable and skillful critic with the right questions and suggestions to improve the content and flow of my writing and the meaning of my message.

CHAPTER ONE

. . . .

INTRODUCTION

oof gardens can be delightful substitutes for natural landscaped areas at ground level, with all of the amenities of gardens on the ground. Indeed, a roof garden can be virtually indistinguishable from a garden planted directly in the earth (fig. 1-1). Although commonly envisioned as gardens in the sky, atop the roofs of multistory buildings, roof gardens are just as often found at or just above grade, atop the roofs of underground structures. A roof garden is any planted open space, intended to provide human enjoyment or environmental enhancement, that is separated from the earth by a building or other structure. It may be below, level with, or above the ground. While it may serve other functions—as a means of circulation or access or as a dining space, for example—a roof garden's primary purpose is to provide a place to be among or to view plants. Utilitarian structures, such as parking lots, paved recreation courts, swimming pools, and storage areas, however incidentally ornamented by plantings, are not considered to be roof gardens for the purposes of this book. Nonetheless, a wide range of structures are topped by roof gardens, in a variety of styles, conveying a host of benefits. This

1-1. Roof gardens are often indistinguishable from gardens at ground level. This roof garden, part of a bank building in Phoenix, Arizona, makes a grand three-dimensional mural when viewed from the mezzanine of the lower-level shopping arcade.

chapter will look at where roof gardens can be found and why they are built.

SPACES FOR ROOF GARDENS

Although site considerations are discussed in detail in chapter 3, a brief look at the great variety of structures on which roof gardens are built demonstrates the range of possibilities available to the building professional.

Where are the best places to construct roof gardens? Certainly they should be built only on the roofs of buildings that are structurally strong enough to support them. In the past, some stone buildings with arched masonry ceilings in the rooms below were capable of supporting flat surfaces above, upon which roof gardens were built (for example, the garden at Pienza, Italy; see chapter 2). Although it is possible to construct them on wood-frame structures, the reinforcement needed to support the extra load of the garden, including saturated soil before drainage occurs, often makes such sites cost-prohibitive. Roof gardens are more ideally suited to steel-frame and reinforced-concrete structures, on which strong support platforms can be provided at reasonable cost. With the technological advances in this type of construction over the last fifty years, such gardens have been built atop many types of structures.

Underground Buildings

The development of roof gardens, in the form of parks or plazas, atop underground parking garages has become commonplace (figs. 1-2, 1-3, 1-4, and 1-5). Indeed, such multiuse development can often justify the purchase of land for open space, which would be too expensive if purchased for that purpose alone. Parking fees then cover the expense of the garage as well as the installation and maintenance of the garden on the roof. Pioneering examples of such gardens include Union Square and Portsmouth Square in San Francisco and Mellon Square in Pittsburgh (figs. 1-6, 1-7, and 1-8).

Historical or environmentally sensitive sites often require special consideration when buildings are added to them. One technique architects have used to preserve such sites is underground,

1-2 (top). The roof of the parking structure for the Utah State Capitol and its offices was developed into a park, with a living map of the state as its central feature; Karsten Hansen, landscape architect.

1-3 (bottom). The garage for the Prague InterContinental Hotel is located in front of the building. To avoid placing mechanical structures in the plaza at the entrance to the hotel, a raised planted area was built atop the roof of the garage.

or earth-sheltered, building. These structures can be configured in a number of ways, but they often have earth on the roof as well as earth berms that hug all of the walls except one (to allow access and egress). Earth-sheltered buildings are frequently built into the sides of slopes. They have been successfully constructed using "cut-and-cover" techniques, as well as by underground mining. Underground buildings are ideally suited for functions that do not require much human oversight, such as parking garages and storage facilities (see the discussion of Newton Vineyard in the portfolio of American gardens as an example). But this technique has also been used for libraries, schools, prisons, convention centers, and even monasteries. Although many earth-sheltered buildings are not covered with plantings, their roofs can become roof gardens, often planted in such a way that the garden camouflages the building, blending it into its site. Such roof gardens help to preserve the character of the site. The Nathan Marsh Pusey Library at Harvard University, shown in figures 1-9 and 1-10, and the Enid A. Haupt Garden at the Smithsonian Institution exemplify the successful incorporation of a building into its historically sensitive site through the use of underground construction and roof gardens (see also the American gardens portfolio).

Office Buildings

The roof gardens of office buildings are designed for a variety of users, in a variety of spaces. Some, with restricted access, are reserved solely for the private use of executives, while others are open to all building employees and visitors—some even to the public at large—as a space for eating, socializing, and relaxing. Because the roof gardens share structural space with a workplace, consideration must be given to separating the recreational activities of the roof garden from the conduct of business, to avoid conflict, particularly when the public has unrestricted access to the garden. Roof gardens associated with office buildings may be many stories above the ground, or they can be at or just above grade (figs. 1-11 and 1-12).

Roof gardens atop office buildings may also serve solely as a visual amenity, where the drab

1-4 (top). A children's playground was included on the roof of the underground garage serving this apartment complex in Stuttgart, Germany.

1-5 (bottom). In need of additional parking space, the owners of the Grand Hotel Villa d'Este on Lake Como in Italy burrowed beneath an existing garden to avoid adding an ugly parking lot to the hotel's grounds.

1-6. Union Square in San Francisco was the first combination plaza/subterranean garage in the United States. Built in the early 1940s, it has served as a successful model for other cities around the world.

1-7. Portsmouth Square in San Francisco was one of the original town plazas, created by the early Spanish settlers of the city. The original park was removed in the 1950s and replaced with this underground garage topped by a newly designed park.

1-8. One of the first major public plazas built atop a downtown parking structure, Mellon Square in Pittsburgh was inspired by San Francisco's Union Square and in turn inspired many other cities to create similar plazas.

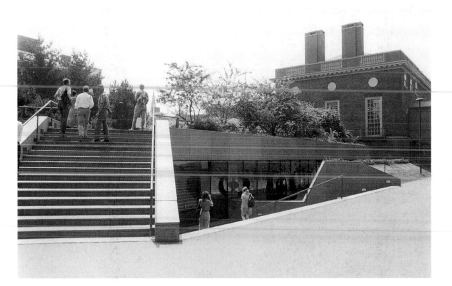

1-9. The entrance to Harvard University's Pusey Library is below grade. Steps lead up to the lawn on the library's roof.

1-10. A cross-campus walk traverses the roof of Pusey Library at Harvard University. Only the protective railing around the library's atrium, visible at left, indicates the building's presence below.

1-11. The quiet pleasures of a roof garden are readily apparent in this garden atop an office building in Lillehammer, Norway. Smooth paving blocks in the sitting area, comfortable movable furnishings, transparent fencing for safety, and handsome planting beds between the fence and roof edge combine to make a pleasant and useful open space with lovely views.

1-12. The Champion Paper Company in Stamford, Connecticut, opened one of its office buildings' floors onto the roof of an adjacent garage to create an outdoor lunch area for employees. The greenhouse in the mid-ground is also atop the roof of the garage.

ugliness of roofs—with their glut of vents, pipes, mechanical equipment, and miscellaneous storage—would detract from the value of any interior space that looks out onto the roof. In addition, such roof gardens, especially those with strong planting patterns, offer a pleasant alternative to the usually unattractive views of urban roofs from neighboring buildings; the gardens atop Rockefeller Center are perhaps the most well-known example of this type of roof garden (fig. 1-13; see also the portfolio of historical gardens).

1-13. Looking down at the Palazzo d'Italia and the International Building North in New York's Rockefeller Center, one can easily see how roof gardens enhance the view from neighboring buildings. (Photo © The Rockefeller Group 1996)

Hotels

As early as the late 1800s, hotels such as the Astor and the Waldorf-Astoria in New York City, as well as many others, had extensive roof gardens. After World War II, hotel owners in the United States soon recognized the value of their roofs in providing space for outdoor gardens that could also be used for parties, special events, dining, and other activities. Today new hotels in the downtown areas of American cities can again boast of rooftop decks or terraces rivaling the quality of any roof gardens in the United States (figs. 1-14 and 1-15).

Residences

As America's suburbs continue to multiply, so too do the most common manifestations of the roof garden, the ubiquitous suburban deck and garden apartment balcony (fig. 1-16). Though usually not atop a true roof, gardens on a deck or apartment terrace require some of the same considerations as roof gardens do, on a smaller scale: plants are container-grown, furnishings are essential, loads are a concern, access must be convenient, orientation affects both user comfort and plant survival, and maintenance must be meticulous. The small scale of such gardens, however, eliminates some of the major concerns common to the larger roof garden: irrigation and fertilizing are simpler, soil is generally not in contact with the structure, waterproofing is usually not part of the deck structure, and plantings are generally less extensive and more easily replaced. Consequently, although decks and terraces technically fit within the definition of roof gardens that opened this chapter, they will not be addressed specifically in this book, though some of the advice about roof gardens can certainly apply to them as well.

More in keeping with the traditional notion of roof gardens is the community garden atop an urban apartment building. Such a garden may be ornamental, designed as a comfortable place for residents to use as an outdoor room. More commonly, however, these gardens are productive vegetable or herb gardens planted and maintained by resident gardening enthusiasts in the building. The recent trend promoting the use of the freshest vegetables and herbs has made such rooftop gardening quite popular in urban areas, where the lack of available space precludes ground-level gardening. Because rooftop gardens rise above nearby buildings and trees, they generally receive more sunshine than ground-level plots, a condition necessary not only for plant growth and the production of vegetables, but for

1-14. The Hilton Palacio del Rio in San Antonio, Texas, built its roof garden atop the porte cochere at the entrance in 1984, sixteen years after the hotel itself was built. Like most hotel roof gardens, it can be entered only from the hotel's interior.

1-15. Shade structures and well-designed planting areas make the roof garden atop the Hilton Palacio del Rio in San Antonio a popular space for cocktail parties and small receptions. The garden is open only for hotel-sponsored events; it is inaccessible to guests otherwise.

the comfort of the gardener as well. Such gardens offer an easily accessible, private area that can also provide pleasant opportunities for social contact with others who have a common interest in growing plants (figs. 1-17 and 1-18).

Bridges

Although not truly on a roof, a garden or park atop a bridge does have the same scale and many of the same structural requirements as a garden atop a building. Such spaces can be used to preserve a valuable connection from one side of a project to the other. An outstanding example of this technique is Freeway Park in Seattle, where a portion of a large park extends completely above and across a six-lane freeway, linking the park to the densely developed opposite side. While in the park, one is hardly aware of the freeway's presence (see the American gardens portfolio).

Connected Podiums

A roof garden can be singular, and it can be plural. The most noticeable roof gardens are those that serve as the elevated forefront of a single building. This concept has been expanded to produce connected roof gardens, located just above street level, on high-rise buildings that often have different owners. Such gardens are linked by bridges over adjacent streets (figs. 1-19 and 1-20). The interiors of the buildings open directly onto the elevated roof decks, which lead to other roof decks, forming a gigantic podium level designed for human use and enjoyment. The high towers spill their human contents into these planted spaces for a few hours, concentrated during lunch time and gradually ebbing as the end of the work day approaches.

The idea of connecting roofscapes is a modern one, growing from the close proximity of new buildings in the city core. The first appearance of this concept seems to have been in Rockefeller Center in New York, one of the first building complexes developed in a modern, highly dense central city. Although its entire open space at street level is on the roof of a vast underground concourse, its garden glory is the series of roof gardens atop four of its towers (fig. 1-21). These towers are separate, but their original plan called for the towers to be linked by bridges above the

1-16. Small terrace and deck gardens, like this one outside a New York City apartment, are roof gardens on a smaller scale.

1-17. Community roof gardens can look quite messy, as this garden at Woolf House in San Francisco demonstrates. During the height of the growing season, a vegetable or herb garden may not have the orderly beauty of an ornamental garden, but that is not its purpose. No one sees this space except the resident gardeners who enjoy working the soil.

1-18. The basics for a productive community garden are raised planter beds with good soil and drainage, seeds or plants, hand tools, a wheelbarrow, a few buckets for hauling, stakes or support structures for climbing plants, and access to water. The ladderlike 3-foot (91-cm) steel railing at right is barely adequate for adults and unacceptably dangerous for children.

1-19 and 1-20. Connected-podium roof gardens are a modern development in which roof gardens are connected by bridges over streets. The roof gardens then become one long podium above street level, as shown here in San Francisco's Embarcadero Center (left) and Hartford's Constitution Plaza (right).

1-21. Early renderings of New York's Rockefeller Center show it was one of the first roof gardens planned with connected podiums. Financial setbacks during the Great Depression prevented the completion of the links. (Rendering © The Rockefeller Group 1996)

streets. With the advent of the Great Depression, these plans were abandoned, and the towers were left separate. Nonetheless, the seeds of the idea to connect towers above the street had been planted. Beginning with the construction of Constitution Plaza in Hartford, Connecticut, in the early 1960s, followed by Embarcadero Center in San Francisco and the Stamford Center in Stamford, Connecticut, the idea blossomed wherever the opportunity presented itself (figs. 1-22 and 1-23).

One of the most outstanding podium developments in recent years is in the Bunker Hill area of downtown Los Angeles, where three city blocks of high-rises have been connected at similar podium levels by bridges over city streets: Union Bank Square, the Westin Bonaventure Hotel roof deck, and 444 South Flower, all of which have roof gardens (fig. 1-24). A fourth building, occupied by the First Interstate Bank, does not have a podium but can be entered at the common podium level via the Bunker Hill Steps, a huge staircase leading up from the street (fig. 1-25). This staircase, an outstanding design feature in itself, allows access to the connected roof spaces of the three adjacent high-rise towers. (See "Union Bank Square" and "Bunker Hill Steps and 444 South Flower" in the American gardens portfolio for further discussion of this project.) The connection of large developed roof spaces offers a whole new opportunity for the development of usable open space for people in crowded urban areas.

Building Edges

All buildings cannot have gardens on their roof decks, but some owners have chosen to modify the edges of their structures with luxurious plantings for a more attractive street façade, as figures 1-26, 1-27, 1-28, and 1-29 show. Edge planting is analogous to an enormous window box; it is strip planting on the edge of a building, rather than on the roof itself. This addition is particularly appropriate on parking garages in downtown areas, creating a far softer appearance than that conveyed by the sterile concrete structures found in many cities. An irrigation system controlled by an electric clock and the use of freely growing, nontrimmed plants can dramatically reduce the labor required for such plantings.

1-22 (top). Constitution Plaza in Hartford, Connecticut, one of the first connected-podium roof gardens, comprises a number of discrete spaces linked by walkways. The entrance shown here, from a major thoroughfare, is via a grand stairway broken by landings.

1-23 (bottom). The bridges linking connected-podium gardens can be gardenlike themselves, as is the case at San Francisco's Embarcadero Center.

1-24 (right). Pedestrian bridges, such as this one between the Westin Bonaventure Hotel and 444 South Flower in the Bunker Hill section of Los Angeles, are key elements of podium development.

1-25 (below). The most grandiose way of gaining access to a roof garden is this monumental stairway at Bunker Hill in downtown Los Angeles. Landings connect to the steps and ramps of roof gardens at left and to the side entrances of the building at right.

1-26. Well-designed and carefully maintained plantings on elevated building edges can make a striking difference in their appearance, as can be seen on this garage at Harvey's Resort on Lake Tahoe in Stateline, Nevada.

1-27. Trailing plants, such as this ivy at San Francisco's Embarcadero Center, require little maintenance and work well on building edges.

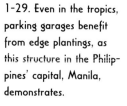

1-28. With plantings surrounding it at ground level as well as spilling over the edges of the upper-story parking decks, this parking structure at Stamford Center in Stamford, Connecticut, looks nothing like the typical sterile concrete parking garage.

1-29. Even in the tropics, parking garages benefit from edge plantings, as this structure in the Philippines' capital, Manila, demonstrates.

ADVANTAGES OF ROOF GARDENS

The decision to incorporate a roof garden into the plans for a new or refurbished building should be based on many factors. Clearly, not every structure can support the extra loads generated by a roof garden. The configuration of the roof itself also plays a role: obviously, it must be flat, with enough open space to hold the garden.

Such issues as climate, access, and local building codes also help determine whether a roof garden is appropriate for a particular space. (All of these factors are discussed in more detail in chapter 3.) But even if a particular building is an ideal site for a roof garden, its addition must offer advantages to those involved in its development. Roof gardens are not incidental ornaments that can be added on a whim and forgotten. They involve a significant initial expense, in that experienced professionals must be consulted, materials must be purchased, and plantings, paving, and other design elements must be installed. But start-up costs are only part of the story. To be truly successful, a roof garden requires meticulous maintenance. It is a living space that will change over time. Plants will shed assorted leaves, seeds, and flowers, outgrow their containers, and eventually die. Soil will lose its organic content through leaching. Paving, furnishings, sculpture—all will wear with use and exposure. Even assuming that the garden's critical systems, such as waterproofing and drainage, are well designed and do not fail, the costs of constructing and maintaining a roof garden can be substantial.

The advantages successful roof gardens convey, however, can far outweigh the hefty financial outlays. They can generate tangible benefits, in the form of financial returns, as well as less quantifiable social and environmental benefits. Some of these advantages have been touched upon in the preceding discussion of sites, and many of them are related to one another. For example, roof gardens convey economic advantages precisely because of their underlying social and environmental benefits. Although these benefits are discussed separately below, keep in mind that they are not mutually exclusive; indeed, a single roof garden can offer a number of different advantages.

Economic Advantages

The most obvious advantage of a roof garden is as a valuable amenity that enhances the worth of the structure it occupies. The building owner can charge higher rates for rental space because the garden is an attraction. Similarly, hotel owners can charge more for buildings with roof gardens and for rooms with direct access into or views onto roof gardens. Businesses that own or rent space in a building with a roof garden can showcase the garden as an amenity to attract and keep valuable employees as well as to impress clients.

A roof garden can also contribute to the renewal of an urban area, particularly if it is designed in conjunction with another project. Office complexes, convention centers, theaters, shopping complexes, and other urban projects all require parking to ensure their success. Instead of simply including a parking lot or garage on or near the site, planners can incorporate a roof garden or plaza atop an underground garage. Such an addition increases the value of both the parking area itself and the project with which it is associated, enticing visitors to stay longer and convincing retail merchants and businesses to locate near the project. The result is an increase in tax dollars for the municipality and greater business volume and revenues in the neighborhood. Examples of this kind of coordinated development are many: Hartford's Constitution Plaza and Pittsburgh's Mellon Square, both associated with office complexes; Kansas City's Allis Plaza and San Francisco's Yerba Buena Gardens, with convention centers; San Francisco's Ghirardelli Square, with a shopping mall; and most recently, Newark's Military Park, associated with the New Jersey Performing Arts Center. These are but a few of the roof gardens that have played a role in both reclaiming a dilapidated city neighborhood and attracting visitors to a nearby project.

Roof gardens can also enable developers to meet the requirements of local municipal land-use ordinances in less costly ways. As cities and towns everywhere recognize the need to alleviate congestion and provide open space to make their confines more livable, they are adopting ordinances that require the provision of open space near new construction. In some places a roof garden can be used in place of costly ground-level land to help meet this requirement. In San Francisco, for example, a city ordinance stipulates that a certain amount of open space for public use must be left around new commercial office buildings, based on the building's square footage of floor space. If such land is not available, space can be purchased for this purpose within a 900-foot (275-m) radius of the building site. Developed roof areas, accessible to the public, can also be substituted, but with a lesser exchange per square foot. If the roof garden option is chosen, access for the public from the street must be included, as must a retail commercial food outlet at roof level.

Similarly, many municipalities have adopted

restrictions on building height, square footage, and lot size for new construction. The inclusion of public open space as part of a project can often be traded off for greater height, square footage, or density. Particularly in a city, where open land is so scarce and its cost is so high, such a trade-off might be impossible, or at least cost-prohibitive. A public roof garden could conceivably be used instead of ground-level land to achieve similar results at a far lower cost.

Another benefit roof gardens may convey is lower energy costs. One of the main reasons earth-shelter technology advanced so rapidly in the 1970s was the sharp rise in the cost of heating fuels during that decade. As scientists, architects, and individual home owners searched for alternative energy sources and ways to reduce fuel consumption, one method they explored was earth-sheltered, or underground, building. Earth-sheltered buildings are not subject to the same fluctuating air-temperature extremes that aboveground buildings are; surrounded by the more stable temperatures of the earth, they require less energy to maintain comfortable temperatures. Hence, the roof garden atop an earth-sheltered building can contribute to lower energy costs for years to come. Even aboveground buildings may gain some advantage in reduced energy costs, as the roof garden does provide some additional insulation for the roof. Roof gardens can also help to protect waterproofing materials from degradation caused by exposure to sunlight and rapid temperature changes.

Social Advantages

Any well-designed open space amid the chaos of a modern city can provide some respite from the noise and bustle all around. But a roof garden, particularly a roof garden located above ground level, is like a peaceful island within the urban jungle. A feeling of isolation from the traffic, noise, dust, and general confusion of the typical downtown city street can be sensed in most roof gardens above ground level. It is one of their major attributes, and one which a downtown park at street level can rarely achieve. One of the most notable qualities in almost all above-grade roof gardens is their quietness. Street sounds seem to rebound off building walls and bypass

the roof level. Moreover, distant views from the garden can give the impression that one is in the country or suburbs. One of the most common reactions of those first visiting a roof garden is pleased astonishment that such a quiet, natural place can exist in a busy city. This initial feeling of pleasure seems to remain as they continue to enjoy the garden over time.

Yet, inasmuch as roof gardens give a sense of isolation from the urban environment, they can also promote community within a city. Residential gardens atop apartment buildings bring together neighbors whose only other contact might be a brief nod in an elevator. Roof gardens associated with office buildings provide a place for employees to mingle in a more relaxed setting. Public roof gardens serve a myriad of community functions, as spaces to meet, to socialize, to attend special events. In the suburbs, ground-level parks, plazas, and gardens could fill such needs, but in built-up cities, roofs are often the only spaces available.

Roof gardens can also enable city dwellers to maintain a connection with nature that might not otherwise be possible. Over the last thirty years, efforts have been made to insert nature into the urban landscape by placing potted plants on sidewalks, planting street trees, and landscaping center islands and median strips of streets. Many existing plazas have been redesigned and rebuilt, including Pioneer Park in Portland, Oregon, Copley Plaza in Boston, and Pershing Square in Los Angeles, which is now a roof garden (fig. 1-30). These are all worthy components of a many-faceted effort to make our cities more livable. Much has been done to provide open space in the new developments around the perimeters of our cities, where land has never been built on before. But land costs are so high in heavily developed downtown areas that little land has been purchased for open space, and urban areas are thus as congested and unattractive as they have always been. Indeed, many downtown areas are so crowded with buildings, streets, and parking lots that scraggly weeds and urban pests are the only reminders that there is more to the environment than concrete and asphalt. Roof gardens can bring a patch of country back into even the most overdeveloped urban space. Such a

reminder of our place within nature is vital to our sense of well-being.

In less crowded places, roof gardens can be used to retain historically or culturally significant spaces. As noted previously, when new buildings must be constructed on sensitive sites, roof gardens can camouflage their presence; such buildings may even be almost completely below grade, hidden by the garden on the roof. Retaining the character of such spaces, even with a new addition, maintains connections with tradition and the past that often enrich the activities taking place there.

Environmental Advantages

From an aesthetic standpoint, roof gardens clearly help to improve the environment. But adding such green space can do more than simply improve the looks of a space. When developed on a greater scale, roof gardens can play a significant role in maintaining a healthy ecosystem, especially in heavily built-up areas (fig. 1-31).

The role of plants in maintaining air quality is well established. By absorbing carbon dioxide and releasing oxygen via photosynthesis, plants recharge the atmosphere that enables all animal life, including human life, to exist. Forests, farms, and lawns can accomplish this task in suburban, rural, and undeveloped areas. Ironically, in the city, where air pollution is heaviest because of traffic and industry, the limited land available for plants helps compound an already difficult problem. By making optimal use of available space for plantings, roof gardens can play an important role in maintaining air quality in urban areas.

Roof gardens can also help to moderate the climate of urban areas. Cities do not only seem hotter than outlying areas do in the summer; they actually are warmer, by as much as twelve degrees Fahrenheit (seven degrees Celsius) at night and five degrees Fahrenheit (three degrees Celsius) during the day. Urban areas are hotter because most of the land area is covered by materials, such as asphalt and concrete, that have a low albedo, or reflective power. These surfaces absorb

1-30. The pond, waterfall, and clock pylon are strong design elements in Pershing Square in Los Angeles, which has been newly designed, replacing the original plaza over a huge underground garage; Hanna/Olin, landscape architect.

1-31. This bird's-eye view of Oakland, California, is typical of many modern cities, with parking lots, hard-wall surfaces, asphalt streets, freeways—and barren roofs. All contribute to higher air temperatures and excess storm runoff.

1-32. The costs of rights-of-way, construction, and maintenance of storm channels that carry water away from buildings, streets, and parking lots could be reduced by the installation of rooftop planting.

and retain heat energy from the sun, rather than reflecting it. Consequently, built-up areas get hotter and stay hotter than outlying areas, where plant cover reflects more sunlight. An extensive network of roof gardens in an urban area could reduce the temperature by several degrees by covering heat-retaining spaces with more reflective plant cover, as well as by increasing the evaporation of moisture, which helps cool the air. In addition to making urban areas more comfortable, such a temperature reduction could result in a significant reduction in energy usage, as less energy would be needed for air conditioning.

As noted earlier in the discussion of earth sheltering, roof gardens can also help reduce energy usage by protecting a structure from air-temperature fluctuations if it is below grade or by acting as an insulating layer, thus restricting heat transfer, if it is above grade. Lower heating and cooling requirements result in energy savings.

Water retention is another advantage of roof gardens in urban areas. When rain falls on hard surfaces such as pavement and bare roofs, most of it runs off into storm drains that carry it to nearby bodies of water (fig. 1-32). Heavy rains tax these runoff systems, sometimes resulting in flooding. More problematic, however, in many older cities, such as New York, the sewer system serves as a collection facility for storm runoff. A heavy downpour of a half inch (a centimeter) or more causes sewage to overflow into the storm tunnels leading directly into nearby waterways. Hence, with every heavy rainstorm, New York sends raw, unprocessed sewage directly into the East River and Flushing Bay. Roof gardens can help to alleviate this problem by serving as a kind of water-retention system. The soil in roof gardens can hold as much as 15 to 20 percent of the rain falling on planted areas for up to two months, releasing it more slowly into a city's storm system. An extensive network of roof gardens could greatly decrease the load on a city's storm-runoff system, reduce flooding, and dramatically improve the quality of surrounding waterways.

Most of these environmental benefits cannot be achieved by the occasional planting of a roof garden here or there. Improving air quality, moderating climate, and reducing storm runoff require a concerted effort to increase green spaces in urban areas, with the inclusion of a network of roof gardens constituting one part of the program. Such a plan might seem impossible, given the costs involved, and in the United States, where roof gardens are viewed as merely aesthetic improvements, that conclusion might be valid. But in several European countries, such programs are already underway. In Swiss cities, for example, laws require that 25 percent of all new commercial construction areas be "greened" following completion of the buildings, in an attempt to restore the original climate. In Stuttgart, Germany, a city of a half million, the city government has adopted a program of subsidizing one-half the cost of greening the city's roofs. Stuttgart has thus far spent over 3 million Deutsche Marks on the subsidy program (fig. 1-33). The League of Cities in Germany supports the idea because it saves on air-conditioning and heating costs, and the cities of Mannheim and Frankfurt have similar programs.

Indeed, according to figures published by ZVG (Germany's central horticultural society), by GALK (the park administrators in the German League of Cities), and by FLL (the research society for landscape construction and development), 43 percent of German cities offer financial incentives for roof greening, 37 percent under a financial aid program for "general greening" and 17 percent as part of their water-management program. Of 193 larger cities in Germany, 29 give direct financial support to roof gardening, ranging from 10 to 100 Deutsche Marks per square meter, or 25 to 100 percent of the installation cost. (Some cities have a ceiling for financial support, ranging from 500 to 20,000 Deutsche Marks.) Cities providing such financial aid include Berlin, Karlsruhe, Kassel, Stuttgart, Böblingen, and Leonberg.

In addition, thirteen cities, including Berlin, Dortmund, Kassel, and Mannheim, give indirect financial aid to roof-greening projects by allowing deductions in the calculation of sewage disposal fees. Forty-one cities accept roof greening as a measure to counterbalance the ecological impact of building construction, which is mandatory under the country's Federal Nature

Conservation Act. Twenty-seven cities, including Düsseldorf, Hamburg, Karlsruhe, Kassel, and Stuttgart, will issue building permits for buildings with flat roofs only if greening of the roof is stipulated. Moreover, it is standard practice in German zoning and development to require that flat roofs and roofs with up to 10-degree slopes (almost 20 percent of all roofs) be greened, at least to some degree.

As technological underpinning for all of the above, intense research into the strength, durability, resistance to root penetration, drainage, and protection of the roof has been conducted under controlled conditions by Dr. Hans-Joachim Liesecke of the University of Hannover and a group of dedicated landscape architects both in the universities and in the field. This group, the Research Society for Landscape Construction and Development, has researched roof garden technology for over fifteen years, and many of its research papers have been published in German and Swiss landscape-design journals; several are in English. Dr. Liesecke and his colleagues have produced one book as well as research summaries covering their findings (see the bibliography). An effort is being made to have this material translated into English in the United States by the American Society of Landscape Architects.

The Germans and Swiss have divided their studies of roof greening into two types: intensive

1-33. This roof garden on the Allianz building in Stuttgart, Germany, is one result of that city's effort to "green" its roofs.

1-34. An example of extensive greening. Roof gardens do not have to be fancy to convey environmental benefits, as this garden in Stuttgart shows.

and extensive. *Intensive greening* applies to gardens similar to most of those found in the United States, Japan, and the rest of the world, that is, complete gardens or parks like those found at natural ground level. *Extensive greening* usually involves using a thin layer of growing medium (about 6 inches [15 cm] or so) or small plant containers above a drainage layer; it is often irrigated by an overhead water system. The plants in such spaces are shallow rooted, such as wildflowers, low hardy succulents (such as *Sedum acre*), or grasses (fig. 1-34). This type of garden is seldom entered except for maintenance. Its primary purposes are adding insulation, addressing ecological issues, and improving views from nearby office windows.

An example of extensive greening can also be found in Paris, where the largest expanse of roof greening in France is on the international school complex of Lyon-Gerland. A continuous area of 70,000 square feet (6,503 square meters), planted in clover, poppies, and a mixture of alpine wildflowers, is supported by an automatic sprinkler system; there is no mowing. Maintenance is limited to removing dried vegetation annually. The system used in this space, Vegetoit, developed by the Nature Company, ensures soil adhesion and wind resistance of the 1,200 tons of special growing mix used in the garden.

The argument for planting the cities of the United States has been largely based on aesthetics, with little thought given to the broader effects of overall environmental quality. We would do well to take note of the European experience and to adopt similar corrective programs to improve the environment of our cities.

A WALK THROUGH THE GARDENS
A PORTFOLIO OF AMERICAN ROOF GARDENS

FEDERAL RESERVE BANK
BOSTON, MASSACHUSETTS

LANDSCAPE ARCHITECT: Robert Fager ASLA
ARCHITECT: The Stubbins Group, Boston

This 18,000–square foot (1,672–square meter) garden atop the Federal Reserve Bank of Boston, built in the mid-1970s, is on the roof of a three-story portion of the thirty-three-floor office tower. The garden adjoins the fourth floor, with the cafeteria on that floor opening onto it; access is also possible from each room at the ends of the garden. Large floor-to-ceiling windows provide ample views. The glass-enclosed inner courtyard, Japanese in style, may be viewed from inside the building only.

The maintenance of the plantings, so necessary in roof gardens, has been impeccable. The landscape architect wisely selected hardy plants that could withstand the wind and bitter cold of New England's winters. Even the trees were chosen for their dwarf and weeping characteristics, to withstand the wind; they include Canadian hemlock, golden threadleaf cypress, Japanese maple, weeping Norway spruce, and contorted beech. Low-growing shrubs and ground covers include Bar Harbor juniper, English yew, Baltic ivy, and low cotoneaster. Potted flowers provide color in the garden throughout the summer.

The entire paved area is finished in dark, tightly jointed paving bricks, which complement the plantings as well as the precast curbs and seat-high concrete edging bordering some of the greenery. Raked pea gravel is used next to the windows of the cafeteria.

Three clearly defined sitting areas, protected from breezes, are furnished with comfortable outdoor chairs; less formal seating is available on the precast-concrete edgers. Inconspicuous containers for trash are located throughout the space. This well-maintained garden has easily retained its freshness over twenty years.

This inviting garden, with three separate seating areas, offers an excellent view of Boston's harbor. The walking surface is hard brick paving.

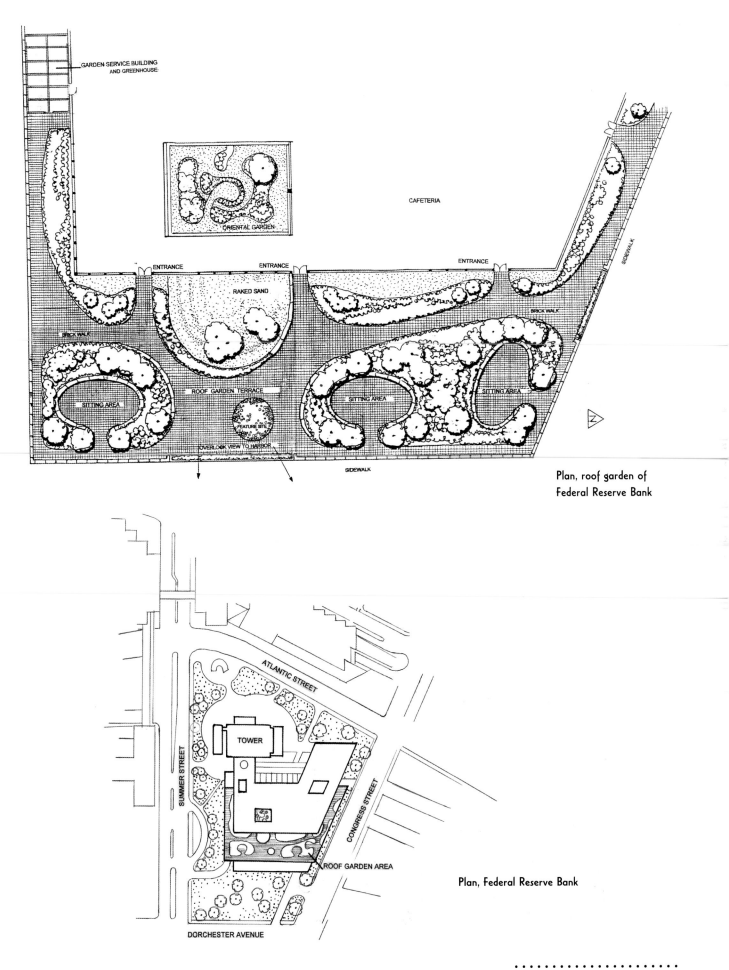

GARDEN SERVICE BUILDING
AND GREENHOUSE

ORIENTAL GARDEN

CAFETERIA

SIDEWALK

ENTRANCE   ENTRANCE   ENTRANCE

RAKED SAND

BRICK WALK

BRICK WALK

SITTING AREA   ROOF GARDEN TERRACE   SITTING AREA   SITTING AREA

FEATURE SITE

OVERLOOK VIEW TO HARBOR

SIDEWALK

N

Plan, roof garden of
Federal Reserve Bank

ATLANTIC STREET

SUMMER STREET

TOWER

CONGRESS STREET

ROOF GARDEN AREA

Plan, Federal Reserve Bank

DORCHESTER AVENUE

The interior-court design comprises dwarf evergreen shrubs, large pebbles, and raked pea gravel in the Japanese style. The flowing curves of the raked gravel are intended to simulate the ripples in a body of water. The building walls buffer any wind that might blow the gravel.

This seating area overlooks the docked replica of one of the Boston Tea Party ships and other historical vessels in the harbor.

Below: The primary seating areas are well furnished, with the chairs carefully arranged when not in use. Unfortunately, there are no tables to complement those in the cafeteria.

NEW ENGLAND MERCHANTS NATIONAL BANK

BOSTON, MASSACHUSETTS

LANDSCAPE ARCHITECT: Shurcliff, Merrill and Footit
ARCHITECT: Edward Larrabee Barnes
CLIENT: New England Merchants National Bank

Built in 1969 as part of the office building on which it rests, this 52- by 172-foot (16- by 52-m) roof garden lies atop offices on the floor below. The interior uses of the upper floor on which the garden is located strongly influenced its design. A reception room and a dining room are located at the opposite ends of the building. Each has access outside to a paved terrace; walkways from each end terrace lead to a smaller central terrace, which is slightly raised. This smaller terrace can be entered from an interior hallway as well as from the two end terraces.

The terraces are all paved in brick. The brick paving pattern of the end terrace near the reception room is echoed in the tile-lined pool. Stationary granite benches and raised planter boxes border the central terrace. Portable furniture is moved into the end terraces during warm weather. The principal plants throughout the space are rows of flowering crab apple trees, with evergreen ivy used as a ground cover. (The fruit from the trees falls into the ivy, rather than onto the pavement, thus avoiding stains on the pavement.) Seasonal annuals planted in portable round concrete plant tubs add color throughout the space.

The entire garden is surrounded by a 7-foot-tall (2.1-m) plate-glass windbreak and parapet, providing a view of downtown Boston and Logan International Airport.

In recent years, root penetration of the tar waterproof membrane on the north terrace has resulted in leaks into the ceiling of the offices below.

The coordinated patterns of the paving and pool bottom are clearly visible in this view through the fountain's metal arch.

Above: The central terrace is almost surrounded by plantings of crab apple and ivy.

Top right: This end terrace, adjacent to the dining room, is very similar to the terrace outside the reception room except for the design of the pool.

Right: The circular paving of the fountain and pool outside the reception room mirrors the granite paving of the terrace.

Plan, roof garden of New England
Merchants National Bank

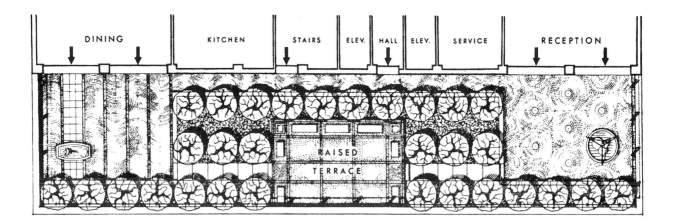

DINING   KITCHEN   STAIRS   ELEV.   HALL   ELEV.   SERVICE   RECEPTION

RAISED
TERRACE

SCALE IN FEET

8   0   8   16   24   32   48

CAMBRIDGE CENTER

CAMBRIDGE, MASSACHUSETTS

LANDSCAPE ARCHITECT: SWA Group
OWNER: Boston Properties

This 1-acre (0.4-hectare) garden, built in 1984, is located on the roof of a five-floor parking garage adjacent to a hotel and office buildings in Cambridge's Kendall Square, at the rear of the Massachusetts Institute of Technology. Access is via the elevator from the garage. A total load limit of 150 pounds per square foot (732 kg per square meter), along with high winds, severely limited the options for rooftop development. Trees and shrubs were ruled out because of the quantity of soil needed for root support. In their place, four large and five small pipe sculptures were arranged on the roof for vertical interest. A surface of finely textured mauve-colored gravel supports a grid of turquoise pavers. Low wooden planters containing colorful annuals and low-growing junipers form a permanent parterre bordering the sculptures. (These planters originally contained only junipers, which did not all thrive and so were replaced.) Permanent metal benches and raised concrete-block planters faced with dark wooden lattice edge the perimeter of the space.

Above: The strong pattern formed by paving, planters, and pipe sculptures is clearly visible from an upper floor of the hotel adjacent to the roof garden.

Left: An outdoor lounge area, accessible only from an adjacent office building, overlooks the roof garden.

Right: The surface of fine gravel is dotted with turquoise pavers and edged by low wooden planters, with colorful annuals forming a maze in the foreground. The hotel is in the background.

Below: Stationary metal benches are provided around the perimeter of the garden. Unfortunately, very little shade is available for protection from the heat and glare of the summer sun.

NATHAN MARSH PUSEY LIBRARY, HARVARD UNIVERSITY

CAMBRIDGE, MASSACHUSETTS

LANDSCAPE ARCHITECT: Robert Fager ASLA
ARCHITECT: Hugh Stubbins and Associates
OWNER: President and Fellows of Harvard College

Inserting a new building into a historical setting always requires great sensitivity: to be successful, the new structure must not overwhelm or detract from the character of its special setting. Such was the concern at Harvard University when its library collection required additional space. The new library would be located adjacent to three other libraries, on a sloped site that served as a major circulation route across campus. To maintain the open space considered crucial to the character of Harvard Yard, it was decided that the new library would be built underground, into the slope of the site.

The plantings that surround underground, or earth-sheltered, buildings are most often designed to blend into the existing surroundings rather than to serve as a respite from them. Here, with three sides of the building completely below grade, the rooftop landscape is simply a continuation of the existing landscape on campus. Lawns, shrubs, and flowering tress cover the roof, camouflaging the building mass, so that, when approached from the southeast, the library's pres-

ence can barely be perceived. The design maintains the pedestrian walkway across the landscaped roof. Only a fenced atrium courtyard that extends to the library below, to allow natural light into the building, hints that this space is more than a campus lawn; all of the building's vents and exhaust grilles are integrated into the landscape design.

The library's entry on the northwest side, though clearly visible to users, also blends into the setting. An earth berm on this side of the library shields its façade. A wide stairway leading to the entrance interrupts the berm; an adjoining stairway leads up the slope to the roof and walkway. Space remains between the berm and the building, creating a moatlike passageway that allows light to enter the upper floors of the library.

Completed in 1976, the structure has a cast-in-place reinforced-concrete roof. The entire roof is covered with 1 to 3 feet (30 to 91 cm) of soil over 2-inch-thick (5.1-cm) rigid extruded polystyrene and a waterproofing layer of mastic coating applied over neoprene sheet membrane.

The Pusey Library at Harvard University is completely underground on three sides. The fourth side, shown here, includes the building's entrance. Steps lead to the planted roof above.

The entrance side of the below-grade building is almost completely concealed by a grassy berm. Only the entrance itself (not shown here) is clearly visible.

Earth berms form a moatlike passage around the exposed end of the building. The wall of the structure is the same as the entry side.

The atrium of the library is open to surrounding rooms but is not a used space. The single small tree is a Japanese maple.

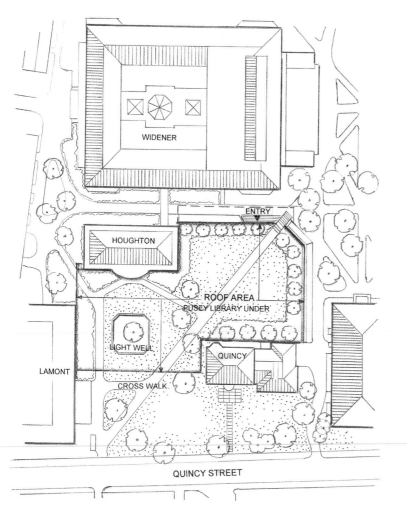

WIDENER

ENTRY

HOUGHTON

ROOF AREA
PUSEY LIBRARY UNDER

LIGHT WELL

QUINCY

LAMONT

CROSS WALK

QUINCY STREET

A cross-campus walkway traverses the roof of the library. The railing at left encloses the perimeter of the open atrium, which allows daylight to reach library rooms below grade.

UNIVERSITY GREEN

CAMBRIDGE, MASSACHUSETTS

LANDSCAPE ARCHITECT: Carol R. Johnson
Associates
ARCHITECT: Fales, Letendre and Ziobros
and Skidmore, Owings, Merrill, Chicago
OWNER: Harvard Real Estate

The herb garden, looking toward one of
the restored historical houses on the site.
(Courtesy Carol R. Johnson Associates)

About one-third of this 12,500–square foot
(1,161–square meter) garden was built over an
existing concrete slab atop an underground
garage. The garage was originally designed to
have a ground-floor condominium unit built
above it; the condominium was never built. The
roof garden, built in 1985, is part of the setting
for three occupied historical houses preserved on
the site, as well as a four-story condominium
building known as University Green.

The slab, which was at existing grade, was thus
too high to allow for the addition of soil and
drainage material if the garden was to be flush
with the surrounding grade. Moreover, the flat
slab did not provide the slope necessary for
drainage. The garden was therefore elevated atop
the slab using polystyrene fill; sloped cobblestone
walls bordered its perimeter. To provide drainage
and prevent water from leaking into the garage
beneath the slab, the landscape architects recommended that the slab have several holes cored
into it to accommodate roof drains and that a
rubber membrane waterproofing system and a
layer of lightweight Enkadrain plastic-wire mesh
be included in the garden design. To reduce construction costs, the developer decided to provide
only one drain in the slab's center and chose to
eliminate the rubber membrane waterproofing,
substituting a sprayed-on asphaltic system covered by a layer of tar paper and protection board.
The landscape architects warned them of the
potential failure of such a system; and indeed, ten
years later, water began leaking into the garage
below. Corrections for the problem are being
sought.

In addition to drainage concerns, the landscape architects had to contend with load limitations due to the relatively weak structural slab.
The live load limit was estimated to be 100
pounds per square foot (488 kg per square
meter); the superimposed dead load, 90 to 100
pounds per square foot (439 to 488 kg per square
meter); with a combined loading capacity in the
range of 190 to 200 pounds per square foot (928
to 976 kg per square meter). After calculating the
weights proposed for each garden area, they
worked to reduce loads throughout the space.
Plastic-wire mesh with attached filter fabric

(Enkadrain) was used for the drainage layer instead of gravel, polystyrene fill replaced part of the loam, trees were planted only at the outside edges of the roof slab, and shrub pits were carved out of the polystyrene fill. Lawn and perennial areas were covered by only 6 inches (15 cm) of loam. All of the polystyrene fill, ranging from only a few inches to 3 feet (91 cm) in depth, was cored on 12-inch (30 cm) centers and filled with sand to facilitate drainage from the soil to the mesh drainage layer beneath the polystyrene. The final loads ranged from 50 to 180 pounds per square foot (244 to 879 kg per square meter), well within the calculated limit.

Despite its structural difficulties, the garden is quite handsome. The design presented a challenge in that the historical buildings nearby are from different periods. Rather than choosing one or another, the designer instead decided to create a garden reminiscent of the mid-1800s. The space has some of the flavor of the Federal period, with its kitchen herb garden, which is trimmed with low boxwood and centered around a bird bath atop a pedestal. It also contains Victorian features, such as the trellised grape arbor, as well as plantings typical of the Victorian era, including Higan cherry, Sargent crab apple, zelkova trees, yews, mountain laurel, and viburnum. Springtime tulips and peonies, summer daylilies, and autumn chrysanthemums add color over the seasons, as do the herbs in the kitchen garden. The garden is fenced with two gates on Mount Auburn Street for privacy.

Top: This sculptural garden trellis has been carefully secured on the roof over columns of the underground garage. Vines will eventually cover it. (Courtesy Carol R. Johnson Associates)

Bottom: A later view of the herb garden indicates that plants thrive in the soil of this roof garden. (Courtesy Carol R. Johnson Associates)

The garden can be entered through one of two matching gates on Mount Auburn Street. (Courtesy Carol R. Johnson Associates)

Plan, University Green

Section, University Green

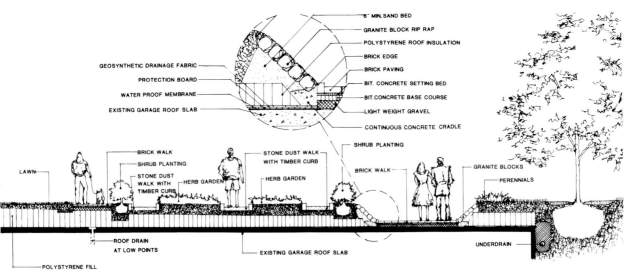

CONSTITUTION PLAZA
HARTFORD, CONNECTICUT

LANDSCAPE ARCHITECT: Sasaki Associates
COORDINATING ARCHITECT: Charles DuBose
CLIENT: Broadcast-Plaza

Constitution Plaza was hailed as a major breakthrough in urban redevelopment when it was completed in 1964. It comprises a group of office buildings, built above five levels of parking, connected aboveground by a continuous podium that includes bridges above the streets. The idea of lifting the common entrance of all buildings by incorporating a continuous podium above street level was unique and has since been copied by many cities in the United States and around the world. All buildings can be immediately accessed from the open plazas above the parking area below. The raised podium is accessible from the street via exterior stairways as well as by elevators from the underground garage.

Each space in the plaza has an individual character and scale. The two main open spaces, one containing a granite fountain and the other a clock tower, are paved. Although they are used primarily for circulation, public concerts, dances, art shows, and other performances, both formal and informal, are held here as well. The smaller courts and gardens are planted with evergreens and flowering trees; a garden of mounded beds featuring weeping willows, a rhododendron garden, and a crab apple orchard with a sitting area are special features of the development.

Like all gardens in downtown urban areas, security is a concern here. But the raised podium does limit access, especially immediate access via automobile, making the space a less easy target for the criminally inclined. Clear sight distances across much of the project enable better monitoring of the space as well.

The largest plaza, designed and used for public events, features a granite fountain that is in scale with this expansive area.

Top right: This quiet, shaded plaza includes seating on permanent benches. The pool on the top of the granite slab in the foreground reflects the feeling of repose in this area.

Bottom right: The bridges over the city streets function as continuations of the plazas.

Bottom left: Flags flying in the breeze add a note of gaiety between the two main plazas.

Top left: The willow court, at the far end of the clock-tower plaza, is planted with weeping willows, which offer a welcome respite from nearby sunny areas.

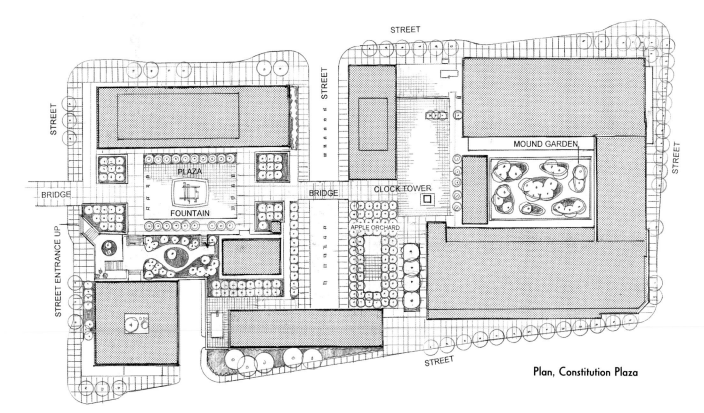

Plan, Constitution Plaza

The orchard of crab apples, which bloom profusely in the spring, includes a series of raised planters with flowering plants. It surrounds an atrium that supplies light to the building below. (Courtesy Sasaki Associates)

ENID A. HAUPT GARDEN, SMITHSONIAN INSTITUTION
WASHINGTON, D.C.

LANDSCAPE ARCHITECT: Sasaki Associates, with Lester R. Collins ASLA, consultant
ARCHITECT: Shepley, Bulfinch, Richardson and Abbott
CLIENT: Smithsonian Institution

These 4.2-acre (1.7-hectare) gardens, completed in 1987 and named for the donor who made them possible, are on the Independence Avenue side of the Smithsonian complex in Washington, D.C. They provide the setting for the entry pavilions to the Smithsonian's newer museums of African and Asian art, which are located beneath the gardens, and enhance the historical buildings that frame the site. The Asian art pavilion has a moon garden; the African art pavilion, a fountain and *chadar*. Surrounded by the "Castle," the Arts and Industries Building, and the Freer Gallery, the gardens preserve the historical setting of these older buildings and provide display space for the Smithsonian's extensive collection of plants and horticultural artifacts.

An overall Victorian theme is established by the central parterre, adapted from the floral beds at the 1876 Centennial Exposition in Philadelphia. The two subgardens complement the museum pavilions flanking this parterre.

In addition to the seasonal plantings of colorful flowers, the gardens house an extensive tree-planting program. Included are many *Magnolia soulangeana* (saucer magnolia), for spectacular spring color, along with *Malus zumi calocarpa* (Sargent crab apple), *Crataegus crus-galli* 'Inermis' (thornless cockspur hawthorn), and *Prunus*

The central parterre, as seen from the entrance gate, with the Castle in the background. It is planted seasonally with thousands of bedding plants in Victorian patterns. (Courtesy Sasaki Associates)

subhirtella 'Pendula' (weeping Japanese cherry). Other trees include *Magnolia grandiflora* (southern magnolia), *Tilia platyphyllos* (European linden), *Quercus phellos* (willow oak), *Ginkgo biloba* 'Princeton Sentry' (Princeton sentry ginkgo), and *Cedrus libani* (cedar of Lebanon).

A technical challenge in the garden design was the placement of plant material, ranging from bedding plants to almost fully mature shade trees, over structurally compatible roof areas of the subterranean museums, which have an overburden of 5 to 6 feet (1.5 to 1.8 m) of planting soil in some areas where large shade trees are planted. In other areas large trees or other heavy weights were located over structural columns. The engineered allowable weight limits for the ceilings below the garden were 140 pounds per cubic foot (2,242.5 kg per cubic meter), with a depth of 1½ feet (45.7 cm) at the parterre and 3-foot (91-cm) depths typical in other areas. Surface drainage comprises catch basins piped to the storm drain system. The building roof also has a continuous waterproof membrane with drains at the edges.

Top: The Arts and Industries Building, seen through a stone moon gate and across a sitting court in the Asian garden. (Courtesy Sasaki Associates)

Bottom: The axis of the African pavilion's garden is centered on the entrance to the Arts and Industries Building. The *chadar's* separate fountain is in the middle distance. The single jet of water, rising from a shallow depression in the pavement, provides a cooling effect for pedestrians on hot Washington afternoons. (Courtesy Sasaki Associates)

Plan, Enid A. Haupt
Garden, Smithsonian
Institution

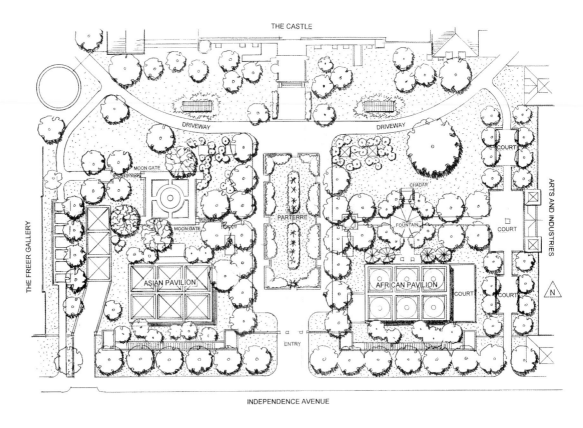

The garden's allées,
lined with pink- and
white-flowered saucer
magnolias, make a
spectacular show of
color in the warm
spring of Washington.
(Courtesy Sasaki
Associates)

From the African pavilion, the focal point of the garden is a *chadar:* a sloping wall of textured granite with water cascading over its sloped surface. This fountain is at the intersection of crosswalks, with the *chadar* in the background. (Courtesy Sasaki Associates)

One of the moon-gate entrances to the Asian garden, where a circular stone island in a square pool is featured. The 5- to 6-foot (1.5- to 1.8-m) mound at left has a greater depth to accommodate the extensive root system of a large shade tree. It is supported by extra strength in the structure below. The stone moon gate is a heavy weight in itself. (Courtesy Sasaki Associates)

EQUITABLE PLAZA

PITTSBURGH, PENNSYLVANIA

LANDSCAPE ARCHITECT: Collins, Simonds and
Simonds
ARCHITECT: Schell and Deeter, with Harrison
and Abramovitz, consultants
CLIENT: Equitable Life Insurance Company of
America

From the roof garden, other parts of downtown
Pittsburgh can be glimpsed between buildings.

This roof garden, at the forecourt entrance to Office Building Number Four in the Equitable Gateway Center, was part of the formerly rundown area known as the Triangle in Pittsburgh. One of the early major modern roof gardens, covering over 6 acres (2.4 hectares), it was built in 1961 atop the roof deck of a then-new multistory underground garage. The plaza can be accessed from the adjoining office buildings as well as via a recently built ramp bridge over an adjacent street that leads to a neighboring park. A superbly maintained and highly popular lunchhour meeting place for area workers, it is also heavily used by shoppers and tourists, who come to enjoy the fountains and colorful plantings, as well as more formal events, including the city's annual art festival.

The concrete retaining walls, planting beds, and tree boxes were lined with waterproofing and faced with green-gray sandstone. Ground covers, including grass, Baltic ivy, pachysandra, and ajuga, plus seasonal annuals and bulbs, are used extensively. A variety of trees and flowering shrubs provide additional color as well as shade. Included among the trees are sweet gum, honey locust, weeping purple beech, ginkgo, white ash, pyramidal European beech, little-leaf linden, sweetbay magnolia, zumi crab apple, Washington hawthorn, Lemme magnolia, glossy hawthorn, weeping cherry, kousa dogwood, hopa crab apple, tea crab apple, saucer magnolia, and star magnolia. Shrubs and flowering shrubs include privet, small-leafed yew, Hick's yew, dwarf winged euonymus, Brown's yew, rock cotoneaster, purple-leaf euonymus, forsythia, Marie's viburnum, roses, wisteria, Burkwood viburnum, and tree fuchsia.

The plaza is paved with a ¾-inch (1.9-cm) layer of two-color Venetian terrazzo, which lies atop a 3¼-inch (8.25-cm) reinforced-concrete slab, which in turn rests atop the structural slab of the garage roof. The fountain basins are of polished dark green terrazzo laid over concrete. The pumps for the fountain are in the garage below.

Top: This recent photograph of Equitable Plaza provides an overview of the garden space. The bridge over Fort Pitt Boulevard, added some years after the garden's construction, is visible at the top. The garden can also be entered via a stairway from Liberty Street, not shown here, as well as from the office buildings surrounding the plaza. (Courtesy John Simonds)

Bottom left: Flowers are changed throughout the summer to provide color and human scale.

Bottom right: The fountains are a delight to see and hear in an urban center. The basin slabs are of polished dark green terrazzo, formed over a concrete shape. The fountain's pumps are located in the garage below.

MELLON SQUARE

PITTSBURGH, PENNSYLVANIA

LANDSCAPE ARCHITECT: Simonds and Simonds
ARCHITECT: Mitchell and Ritchey
CLIENT: City of Pittsburgh Parking Authority

One of the first public garages with a park on its roof built after World War II, Mellon Square was conceived by R. K. Mellon after visiting Union Square in San Francisco. Three Mellon foundations made a combined grant of $4 million to launch the 1.37-acre (0.5-hectare) project in 1948. The plaza was dedicated to two deceased Mellon brothers who had advanced the family fortunes from steel and whose philanthropy had aided the city of Pittsburgh. The five-story thousand-car underground garage and plaza were completed in 1955.

The project had three aims: to rehabilitate the urban area, to ease parking problems, and to increase the surrounding property's value tenfold. Before the garden's completion, Alcoa and U.S. Steel began to build two major high-rise buildings located on the square in anticipation of the plaza. Although the project itself generated $2.3 million less in taxes than the buildings it replaced, it indirectly added $20 million to the city's coffers because of the higher assessments on the new developments surrounding it.

During the design stage, the landscape architects conducted a thorough analysis of the site and its environs, including its topographical features, open space and structural framework, pedestrian generation factors and point sources, and projected traffic flow, even suggesting a loca-

Above: The edge of a raised planting bed, at a height conducive to sitting, provides additional space for visitors to enjoy the profusion of greenery in the square.

Right: A view of Mellon Square from above. The placement of heavier elements above the structural columns is clearly visible. The diamond paving pattern visually links the various parts of the space.

The fountains in the raised basin and its bronze saucers are a major attraction.

Below: A typical fountain bowl.

tion for a below-grade rapid-transit station, now completed. Undertaking such a comprehensive study was practically unheard of at that time.

The square was designed to work with the structural grid of the columns supporting the garage roof beneath. The slab was elevated above street level to reduce the noise and views of traffic; the buildings surrounding the plaza, rather than the vehicles rushing by, thus form the plaza's visual boundaries.

The roof has three layers of waterproofing, a layer of gravel, plus 4 inches (10 cm) of concrete topped with Italian terrazzo containing a built-in snow-melting system. The fountains flow from nine bronze basins, each 9 feet (27 m) across and weighing 3,500 pounds (1,588 kg). All benches, raised planters, and other facing trim are Minneapolis granite. The paving finish is modeled after a rustic Venetian terrazzo, with four colors of marble chips, from Belgium, Italy, and Maryland, set in mortar. Mature American sweetgum (*Liquidambar styraciflua*) and black locust (*Robinia pseudoacacia decaisneana*) trees, chosen for their longevity, were used throughout. Ground covers include grass, English ivy (*Hedera helix*), and common periwinkle (*Vinca minor*).

Plan, Mellon Square

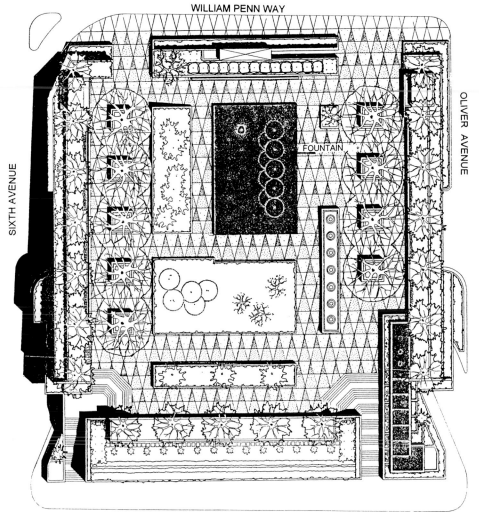

WILLIAM PENN WAY

SIXTH AVENUE

OLIVER AVENUE

FOUNTAIN

SMITHFIELD STREET

At plaza level, the effect is of dense planting, adding to the comfortable human scale of the plaza.

MAYOR OGDEN PLAZA

CHICAGO, ILLINOIS

LANDSCAPE ARCHITECT: Jacobs/Ryan Associates
ARCHITECT: Lohan Associates
CLIENT: Chicago Dock and Canal Trust

Mayor Ogden Plaza is just north of Chicago's Loop, along a busy downtown street. Its 1.2-acre (0.5-hectare) sloped site does double duty as park and multistory public garage, although few would realize this while in the park, as the plaza has no entrances into the garage to indicate its presence below.

Ogden Plaza begins at street level with a paved space directly across from the Sheraton Hotel at the high end of the site. From this vantage point, one can look down along the entire length of the paved and planted areas below.

The remaining plaza consists of three distinct areas. The first is depressed more than 10 feet (3 m) below the overlook grade. It is surrounded on three sides by high white precast-concrete walls that are relieved by a horizontal stripe near the top; these walls, along with rows of pin oak trees at street level, screen the park from urban noise outside the space. This level meets the slope's grade at the central area, where a huge metal-sculpted working clock, 70 feet (21 m) in diameter, is located. The clock, which is difficult

to read at ground level, has no plantings around it, enabling it to be read easily from surrounding high-rise buildings. The third area is stepped down from the clock area to the level of the street

Above: The upper and lower levels both have a pair of stairways for access, as well as direct access from surrounding streets.

Left: Striking raised beds on a grid pattern, planted with Bradford pears, constitute the principal design feature of the plaza.

at the opposite end of the plaza. It too is surrounded by high walls.

The plazas at each end of the long, narrow site feature a formal grid of 10- by 10-foot raised planters of granite and white precast concrete planted with Bradford pears (*Pyrus calleryana* "Bradford") and seasonal flowers. The planters are insulated from cold and irrigated by overhead sprinklers. Planters along the perimeter walls contain perennials, ornamental grasses, and climbing vines. Low light fixtures attached to the planters reinforce the grid pattern used in the space.

Left: View into the plaza from the overlook.

Right: A wall in the lower level at the far end of the plaza features a "picture frame" in which the image is always changing.

Plan, Mayor Ogden Plaza

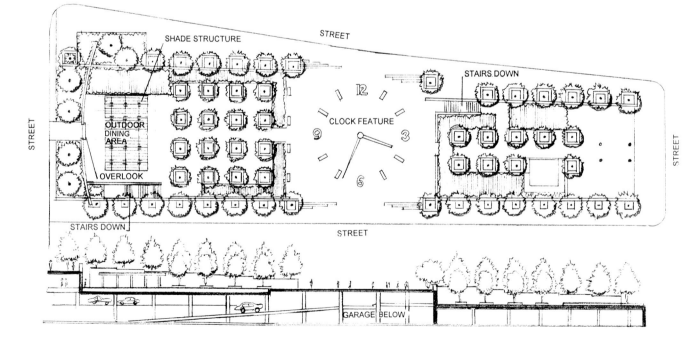

From this overlook at the upper street level of the plaza, one can see the whole space. Lighting bubbles attached to the raised beds and other concrete elements are decorative by day and provide a low level of light by night.

A planter along the plaza's edge contains perennials and vines climbing up the walls.

The upper level of the plaza, below the overlook, has an area of paving shaded by a trellis for outdoor dining.

BARNEY ALLIS PLAZA

KANSAS CITY, MISSOURI

LANDSCAPE ARCHITECT: The SWA Group
ARCHITECT: Marshall and Brown
CLIENT: City of Kansas City

Built in the mid-1980s, Allis Plaza occupies one city block across the street from the Kansas City Convention Center, resting on the roof of a three-story underground garage that serves the convention facility. The financially viable parking structure not only provides parking convenience for eleven hundred cars below ground, but it also supplies a 2½-acre (1-hectare) site for a fine open park, both of which have increased the use of the convention center. A change in grade from the northern end of the plaza to the southern end allows automobiles access to the parking structure without intruding on the serenity of the plaza above. The park itself can be accessed at grade on its east side and via stairways on its west side and on its southeastern and southwestern corners.

The roof development has several unusual features. Despite its great size and substantial structural supports, its shade trees are planted in relatively small 6-foot (1.8-m) circular openings surrounded by concrete curbs. About half of its surface is paved with compacted "decomposed granite," broken stone that has a high content of fines. After it is wetted and rolled, this material forms a hard, smooth walking surface that is easy to maintain and repair. Its color and textured

Above: The entire plaza is open for the casual pleasure of its visitors. The thornless locusts (*Robinia*) have tempered the glare and heat as they matured.

Right: Inside the concrete shade structure, the shadow patterns are dramatic. These have softened as the vines on the columns grew.

look provide a far more pleasing appearance than concrete does. A huge concrete shade structure offers protection from the sun; its great height and depth are in keeping with the scale of the plaza and surrounding buildings. Perhaps most notably, lightweight plastic-covered metal furniture is provided throughout the space during the spring, summer, and fall. The plaza also features a life-sized replica of a Frederic Remington equestrian sculpture and a long pool with splashing water jets facing Allis Hotel. A permanent stage, accessible via both stairs and elevator at its rear, is available for plays, concerts, pageants, and other public performances.

The space below the paving and above the structural roof slab is filled with as much as 6 feet (1.8 m) of Styrofoam blocks, which establish the plaza's grade. Drainage is achieved via surface drains and through the slope of the space.

The managers of the plaza evidently decided to defy the long-held belief that the public cannot be trusted with movable furniture. Perhaps heavy usage protects it from theft and vandalism. Certainly the people in the park seem to love it, flocking there during the day. With garden furnishings astonishingly inexpensive, what is an occasional loss compared to the comfort and pleasure they give to the public? Kansas City is to be congratulated for providing practical comfort in its Allis Plaza.

Plan, Barney Allis Plaza

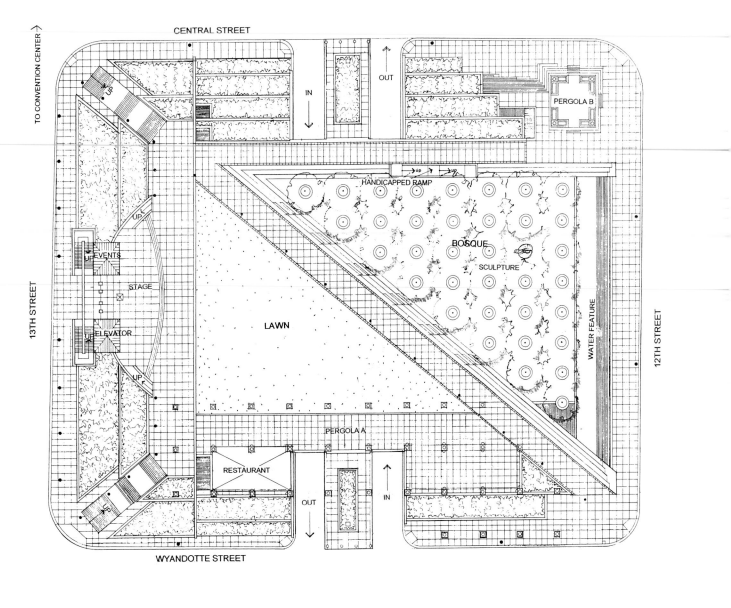

NORTH   0 5 10 20 30 40 50

The fountains offer a pleasant visual and aural backdrop for the park

At the southern end of the level plaza, over the garage entrance, it is necessary to enter the plaza via a high stairway.

The provision of comfortable garden furniture invites small groups to gather for lunch and conversation. The fountain and sculpture are in the background.

GRIZZLY CREEK REST AND RESTORATION PROJECT

GLENWOOD CANYON, COLORADO

LANDSCAPE ARCHITECT: Phillip Flores Associates (project director)
ARCHITECT: Davis and Brandeberry Associates, Denver
CLIENT: Colorado Department of Transportation

W hen highway rest areas and, particularly, scenic overlooks are located in undeveloped areas, their designers may strive to blend the structures into the landscape, leaving the surroundings as undisturbed as possible. An earth-sheltered structure that is built into an existing slope is one way to achieve this goal, and several examples of such rest areas exist along the inter-

Top: The native plantings on the roof have become established, so that the top of the skylight for the building below is all that is visible. The interstate passes above and beyond the building.

Bottom: On the upper level, the overlook is backed by the densely planted roof, which conceals the excavation into the slope and helps to camouflage mechanical equipment and the building's skylight.

At the entrance level is a small plaza with concrete pedestals for seating. The overlook is directly above the entry.

state highway system. This one, alongside Interstate 70 in Colorado, is especially notable. The handsome entry to the building extends out from the slope; on its roof is a paved overlook with views of the swift Colorado River flowing through magnificent Glenwood Canyon below. The remainder of the concrete structure, which contains an information area and rest rooms, has been built into the slope. Its roof has been landscaped with native flowering plants, a technique that successfully incorporates the building into its natural surroundings.

The entire building, except its entrance, is waterproofed. The roof also has a layer of drainage material covered with filter fabric, which is topped with 18 inches (45.7 cm) of topsoil. All plants were watered by a drip irrigation system for the first three years after planting; this system was then removed after the plantings were established.

Section, Grizzly Creek Rest and Restoration Project

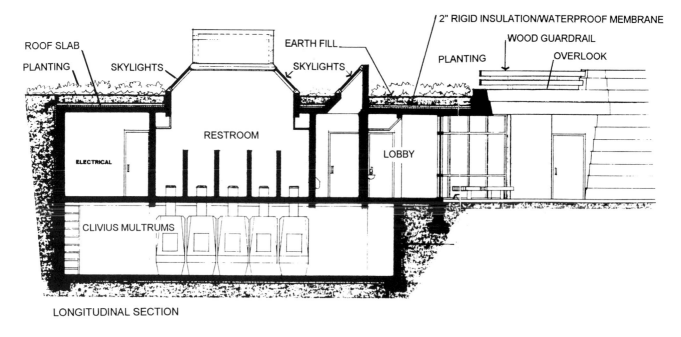

LONGITUDINAL SECTION

UNION BANK SQUARE

LOS ANGELES, CALIFORNIA

LANDSCAPE ARCHITECT: Eckbo, Dean, Austin and Williams
ARCHITECT: Harrison and Abramovitz
CLIENT: Union Bank of California

This roof garden, atop a large garage on Fifth and Figueroa streets in downtown Los Angeles, occupies approximately 120,250 square feet (11,172 square meters) of its 150,000–square foot (13,935–square meter) building site. Built in 1967, the adjacent office tower was the first of three high-rise buildings located on Fifth Street across from the Central Library, Bertram Grosvenor Goodhue's 1926 landmark structure. The podiums of all three are connected by bridges across major streets (the other two buildings are the Westin Bonaventure Hotel and 444 South Flower; see next portfolio entry).

The roof garden's hardscape is largely concrete, which is used throughout in appropriate paving patterns, as well as for raised beds, a bridge, and ramps. The dominant trees used in the raised beds are exceptionally well shaped specimens of coral trees (*Erythrina americanum*).

Access to the plaza is via the office tower entrance, the podium bridge from the Westin Bonaventure, the garage below, and by steps and an escalator leading up from street level. The plaza is very lightly used even during the lunch hours, when many employees emerge from the on-site office building and surrounding structures. Such light usage may result from the lack of building entrances opening directly onto the main part of the plaza; moreover, few intimate

The center of the garden is highlighted by a low overlook onto a pond with water jets, which can also be viewed from a walkway and ramp that bridge it.

The garden occupies the entire roof of the large underground garage, beneath the continuous podium of the building.

A small area near the building entrance is furnished with tables and chairs, but foodservice is not conveniently close by.

spaces with suitable furnishings for informal gathering are available. Tables and chairs are provided near the building entrance and connecting bridge to the Westin Bonaventure Hotel podium; these, however, can be assumed to be an afterthought, as there is no foodservice inside the building at that location. The edges of the huge planters are too high to sit upon; the benches near the fountain have no backs, and outdoor furniture has not been provided in the primary garden area. This space would surely benefit from the installation of comfortable garden furniture that would add human scale to the imposing features now in place. Incorporating more movement into, and so, producing more sound from, the water feature might also attract more visitors to its central location. Nevertheless, the plaza is a pleasant landscaped public space, and the maintenance is impeccable.

Plan, Union Bank Square

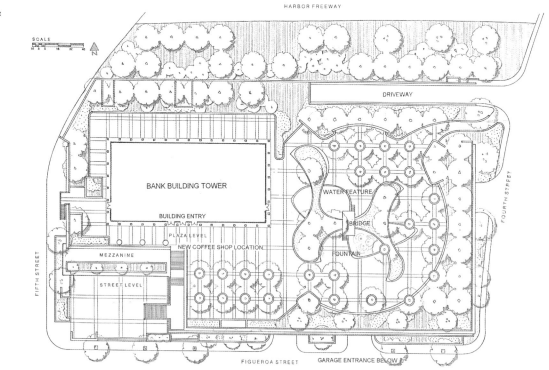

BUNKER HILL STEPS AND 444 SOUTH FLOWER TERRACE

LOS ANGELES, CALIFORNIA

LANDSCAPE ARCHITECT: Lawrence Halprin and Associates, with Omi Lang Associates
CLIENT: Maguire/Thomas Partners

Built atop a public garage in downtown Los Angeles, the Bunker Hill Steps rise from Fifth Street, across from the Central Library, to Hope Place, the site of a huge aboveground garage. The landings of this monumental precast-concrete staircase (as well as to the escalators that parallel them) provide access to the First Interstate World center on one side and the podium of 444 South Flower on the other. The podium at 444 South Flower leads, via a pedestrian bridge over Flower Street, to the podium of the neighboring Westin Bonaventure Hotel; the hotel's podium, in turn, is connected to the podium that forms Union Bank Square via a pedestrian bridge over Figueroa Street. The Bunker Hill Steps thus can provide access to four major high-rise buildings in the downtown area. Because they serve as such a major pedestrian point-of-entry during the day, the steps and the adjoining podium are alive with people—socializing, resting, sunning, or simply moving from place to place.

From the podium, one can take an escalator or stairs to the upper-level terrace garden of the building, which, like the podium of 444 South Flower, was designed to coordinate with the steps. (The steps actually extend above both the podium and the terrace garden. Entrance to the garden from the steps is through an arched opening and down a short flight of stairs.) The garden features an outdoor eating area, a reflecting pool that flows to a waterfall flanking the escalator, and plenty of wooden benches with tables for comfortable seating.

Plantings in the space include *Eucalyptus ficifolia* (red-flowering gum), *Erythrina caffra* (Kaffirboom coral tree), *Prunus cerasifera* (flowering plum), *Pittisporum undulatum* (Victorian box), *Olea europea* (olive), *Jacaranda mimosifolia* (jacaranda), and *Magnolia grandiflora* (southern magnolia), as well as wisteria, espaliered bougainvillea, gardenia, sun azaleas, and bird-of-paradise.

The steps, which form the entrance to the building at right and the podium at left, are reminiscent of the Spanish Steps in Rome. The terrace garden at 444 South Flower is behind the wall at the left.

Although the imposing steps, dramatic waterfalls, and majestic palms provide a grandiose setting, the space is successful in part because human scale has not been neglected. Smaller flowering plants and shrubs in concrete containers, ample foodservice with plenty of seating, and cozy protected nooks that give people a place to relax out of the mainstream—all invite people to use this space as more than just a means to get from here to there. The steps and their adjoining garden spaces have become not just a means of access but a destination themselves, a well-integrated, strikingly handsome design success.

Top left: The escalator leading from the main podium of 444 South Flower to the terrace garden is flanked on its right by a waterfall, fed by the ornamental pool above.

Bottom left: The ornamental pool in the terrace garden overflows to a waterfall on its far side

Top right: A fast-food stand on the first level provides lunch and snacks.

Bottom right: An intimate furnished area opposite the food counter is very popular.

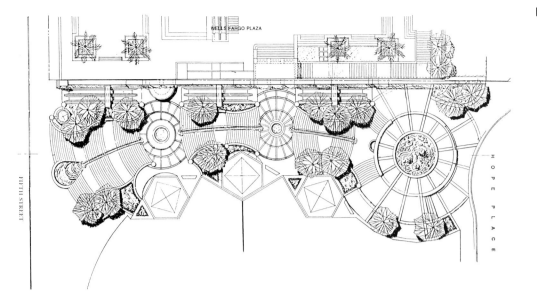

Plan, Bunker Hill Steps

EAST ELEVATION SCALE: 1/8"=1'-0"

WEST ELEVATION SCALE: 1/8"=1'-0"

Elevations, Bunker Hill Steps

Below left: Halfway up the Bunker Hill Steps, one can walk from the landing, through the arches, and down these steps to the terrace garden of 444 South Flower.

Below right: A long view of the terrace garden, which parallels and can be entered from the Bunker Hills Steps at left.

PORTSMOUTH SQUARE
SAN FRANCISCO, CALIFORNIA

LANDSCAPE ARCHITECT: Royston, Hanamoto, Abey and Alley

OWNER: The City and County of San Francisco

Portsmouth Square is San Francisco's original plaza, established as the town square by Spanish settlers who built the small settlement of Yerba Buena here in the late eighteenth century. In 1846 Captain John B. Montgomery sailed into San Francisco Bay and claimed the whole area for the United States; he renamed the plaza Portsmouth Square after his ship, the USS *Portsmouth*. Once the busy center of San Francisco, it is now considered part of the city's Chinatown. In the late 1950s, the local parking authority received city approval to replace the original plaza with an underground garage that would have a new park on its roof.

The square, which covers a full city block, slopes evenly down from west to east. Cars enter the garage beneath via Kearny Street at grade. Access to the park is via walkways at street grade from east and west as well as by stairs on the northern and southern edges. A children's playground, at a lower level than the plaza, can also be entered at grade. A number of years after the plaza was finished, a wide pedestrian bridge was built above Kearny Street, connecting the nearby Chinese Cultural Center, in a local hotel, to the square. Although this bridge carries little pedestrian traffic, its permanent benches provide additional spaces for sunning, resting, and conversation.

Top: The adult area, with wooden sun shelters, has become an informal outdoor senior citizens' center.

Bottom: From the upper floors of the Holiday Inn on Kearny Street, which houses the Chinese Cultural Center, the park displays all the characteristics of an urban roof garden, with an entrance to the garage below from a main street, a children's play area immediately above it, and the adult garden area adjacent, separated from the playground by a change of grade. The elevators leading down to the garage are at the top center of the picture. The footbridge over Kearny Street connects the cultural center with the park and also serves as a quiet area to take sun.

Most of the park enjoys full, warm sun on clear days. It is protected from the prevailing east-blowing winds off the Pacific Ocean by the multistory buildings to its west. A retaining wall along the western edge of the playground provides additional protection to the lower level. Italian poplars (*Populus italica nigra*) provide some shade, as do wooden sun shelters. Some shrubbery buffers the park along its perimeter, but its use is limited for security reasons, so that visibility is not impeded.

Special features of Portsmouth Square include a monument to the author Robert Louis Stevenson. In response to requests from area residents for a neighborhood park, the square was recently redesigned to include additional play equipment as well as a wooden pagoda-like structure.

Right: The playground is a unique—and popular—feature of this roof garden. The wooden shelters on the upper level shade visitors from the sun's glare.

Below: Plan, Portsmouth Square

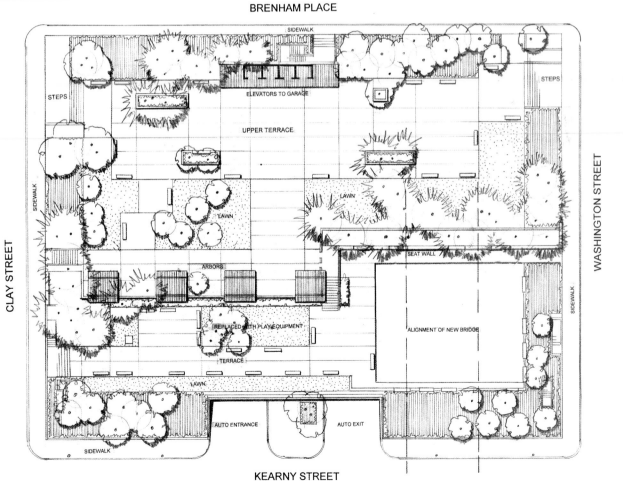

Top: The upper part of the park, at the same grade as the street, serves as a convenient crosswalk and neighborhood gathering place.

Bottom: Heavy usage is a clear indication of successful design. The playground, which features this fanciful climbing apparatus, clearly contributes to the enjoyment of the garden.

BANK OF CALIFORNIA
SAN FRANCISCO, CALIFORNIA

LANDSCAPE ARCHITECT: Royston, Hanamoto, Abey and Alley
ARCHITECT: Anshen and Allen
CLIENT: Bank of California

When the Bank of California decided to construct a new building in the late 1960s, they chose to build it beside the original structure. The old building's upper floors were removed, and a 9,100–square foot (845–square meter) garden was put in their place, with its base on the ceiling level of the first floor of the original building. Although rather sparsely planted, the space has enough greenery to give one the sense of being in a garden.

The garden, protected by the new building from the prevailing westerly winds, is a pleasant space. Although some outdoor furniture is provided, more would improve the scale and diminish the impression of emptiness conveyed by the bare expanses of brick paving. The addition of potted perennials and colorful annuals to the simple ivy, shrubs, and trees (primarily *Ficus rutusa nitida*, Indian laurel) now in place would also improve the scale of and brighten the space.

Once open to the public, the garden and its adjacent coffee shop can now only be used by the bank's occupants. Access is limited; one can enter the garden only through an upper level of the bank. The space is used primarily during lunch hours.

Above: Changes of grade provide a variety of places to eat and view the rest of the terrace.

Left: The availability of foodservice just inside the building is convenient for people who want to order hot food, as well as for "brown baggers."

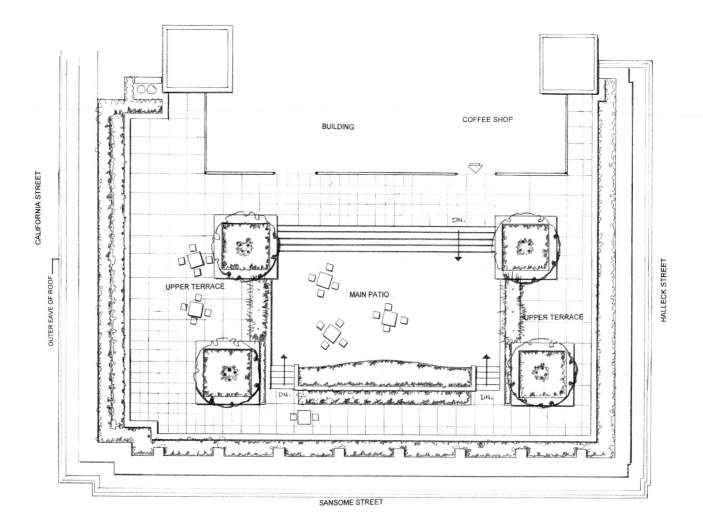

BUILDING

COFFEE SHOP

CALIFORNIA STREET

OUTER EAVE OF ROOF

HALLECK STREET

DN.

UPPER TERRACE

MAIN PATIO

UPPER TERRACE

DN.

DN.

SANSOME STREET

Above: Plan, roof garden of Bank of California

Right: From the upper level, one can look into the garden, which compensates for the closeness of surrounding high-rise buildings.

GHIRARDELLI SQUARE

SAN FRANCISCO, CALIFORNIA

LANDSCAPE ARCHITECT: Lawrence Halprin and Associates (plaza design)
ARCHITECT: Wurster, Bernardi and Emmons (building renovation)
CLIENT: William Matson, Matson Steamship Lines

Ghirardelli Square is one of the earliest and most successful examples of adaptive reuse in the country. It is named for Domingo Ghirardelli, a chocolate maker who bought an 1864 brick factory building and moved his chocolate-making operations here in 1897. Ghirardelli expanded the factory complex over the next twenty years, and his company continued to make chocolate here until 1962. Saved from demolition, the complex was then transformed into a premier shopping mall housed in the original factory buildings. Its success has been duplicated in cities around the country: Boston's Faneuil Hall/ Quincy Market, New York's South Street Seaport, and Baltimore's Harborplace, as well as the nearby Cannery complex in San Francisco, are but a few examples of adaptive reuse that have their roots in Ghirardelli Square.

Few of Ghirardelli's visitors realize that the plaza they traverse as they move from shop to shop actually rests on the roof of an underground garage. This 1¼-acre (0.5-hectare) space, with its magnificent views of San Francisco Bay, was completed in 1968. Its design was key to the

Above: The focal point of the square is this fountain with a bronze mermaid sculpture.

Left: The lower level of the roof development includes shops at the left, an open plaza, and a ramp in the foreground to a higher level, with more shops and terraces overlooking the space below.

successful renovation of the complex, for it set the tone for the space, transforming old brick factory buildings into a modern, exciting place where people want to congregate. An important consideration in its design was the need for access, not only to the plaza but to the multiple levels of the mall. In addition to stairs, ramps were constructed to permit access for baby strollers and wheelchairs. To facilitate access for visitors from nearby Fisherman's Wharf and other attractions, the plaza has entrances from the garage below and at a number of points around its perimeter, both at street level and by stairs to the upper levels. The plantings in the space are limited to small, easily maintained areas, also to allow free and unobstructed movement of visitors.

Because the property had little ground-level space open to the street, it was natural to face all rental space inward, toward the plaza, making it the center of the project. This design also provided protection from westerly winds and enabled the creation of more intimate spaces throughout the plaza.

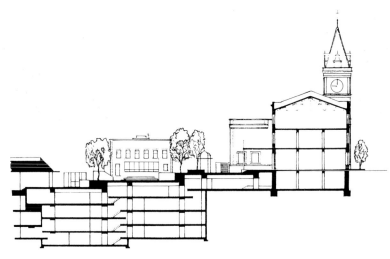

Top: Although the square has a direct entrance at grade, this stairway takes one from Fisherman's Wharf directly into the square above.

Middle: Section, Ghirardelli Square

Right: Plan, Ghirardelli Square

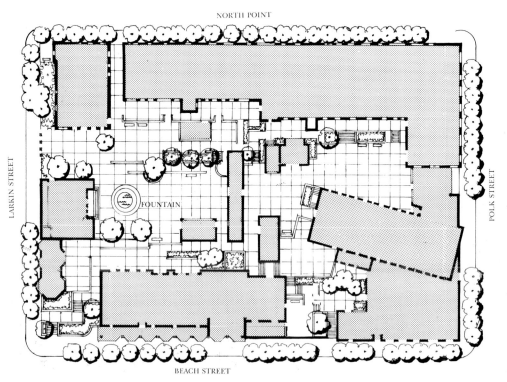

FAIRMONT HOTEL AND TOWER
SAN FRANCISCO, CALIFORNIA

LANDSCAPE ARCHITECT: Lawrence Halprin and Associates
ARCHITECT: Mario Gaidano AIA
CLIENT: Fairmont Hotels

Slated to open in 1906, the Fairmont Hotel survived the great San Francisco earthquake and resulting fires, albeit with gutted interiors, which the architect Stanford White then redesigned. In 1962 the landmark hotel added an adjoining twenty-four-story tower and other facilities, including a 72- by 120-foot (22- by 36-m) garden on one of its new roof decks. The garden, directly over the main convention auditorium, has walks, lawns, lighting, a fountain, and full-grown Canary Island date palms (*Phoenix canariensis*). The garden is immediately accessible from the hotel's Pavilion Room, enabling guests to use both the room indoors and the garden for the same event. This is an ideal location for an outdoor public space.

Above: The Pavilion Room, entered from a long gallery adjoining the main lobby level, is at the southern end of the garden, which includes lawn, walks, flower beds, fountains, and three full-grown Canary Island palms.

Left: The smaller adjoining garden provides outdoor space next to the Fountain Room, at the same level as the lobby. A 6-foot (1.8-m) fence and plantings buffer this smaller space from the main garden, providing privacy for both.

Along the perimeter of the main garden are walks, permanent benches, and plantings, all facing the central fountain.

Plan, roof garden of Fairmont Hotel and Tower

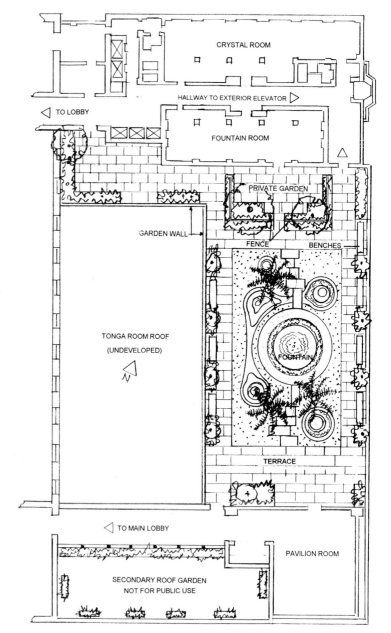

CRYSTAL ROOM

HALLWAY TO EXTERIOR ELEVATOR ▷

◁ TO LOBBY

FOUNTAIN ROOM

PRIVATE GARDEN

GARDEN WALL

FENCE   BENCHES

TONGA ROOM ROOF
(UNDEVELOPED)

FOUNTAIN

TERRACE

◁ TO MAIN LOBBY

PAVILION ROOM

SECONDARY ROOF GARDEN
NOT FOR PUBLIC USE

WESTIN SAINT FRANCIS HOTEL

SAN FRANCISCO, CALIFORNIA

LANDSCAPE ARCHITECT: Theodore Osmundson and Associates
ARCHITECT: William L. Pereira and Associates
CLIENT: Westin Hotels

Located on Union Square in downtown San Francisco, the Westin Saint Francis is one of the grand old hotels in the United States. Built in 1904, it weathered the earthquake of 1906 but was damaged sufficiently to require extensive repairs. In 1972 a new thirty-two-story tower was connected to the rear of the old hotel. One of the more spectacular features of the addition was the inclusion of five glass-enclosed elevators on the exterior of the tower. The elevators would provide breathtaking views of the downtown area, but they would also reveal a far less stunning vista: the roof of the single-story portion of the hotel, a space cluttered with the concrete structures needed for the mechanical operations of the reception rooms below. To camouflage this space, a roof garden was planned.

The structurally weak roof had already required exterior ceiling bracing just to support it

Above: At roof level the planting containers are clearly visible. However, from the fourth floor, where the elevators emerge, the angle of view successfully obscures them.

Left: The passing view from the elevators, as passengers rise from the floors below. Air vents, concentrated in one location, form a base for ornamental plant containers with colorful flowers and junipers.

over the rooms below. Hence, a load limit of only 25 pounds per square foot (122 kg per square meter) was established for the roof garden. Such a severe load restriction meant the garden would have no public access; perhaps needless to say, it also seriously limited the design options available for the space. With plant selection so limited, the garden relies on strong patterns of lightweight colored gravel, laid in layers 1½ inches (3.8 cm) thick, for design interest. Plantings are restricted to small terra-cotta containers.

To maintain the garden, one of the first drip irrigation systems in the San Francisco area was designed by the landscape architects to provide water for each individual plant container. It was chosen because piping and spray heads were not practical in the gravel areas. During the recent seven-year drought, all water for the roof garden was cut off. The plantings were replaced after the drought ended.

Although the load restrictions did impose constraints on the garden design, the decision to restrict access to the space did have some advantages. Because visitors did not need to be accommodated, easy access, furnishings, circulation, and shelter from weather did not require consideration, allowing more freedom in the design of the garden itself. The load restrictions also indirectly helped to reduce the cost of the garden, since large trees and plants simply could not be included in the space.

Top: Ventilation equipment and light wells are camouflaged by their new color and by the surface gravel. Post Street can be seen at the top of the photo; Geary Street is at its opposite end.

Bottom: Plan, roof garden of Westin Saint Francis Hotel

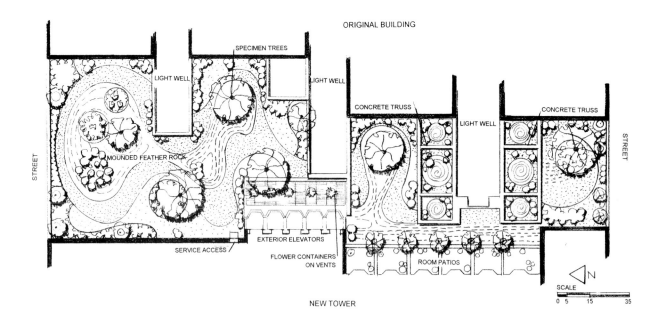

555 MARKET BUILDING

SAN FRANCISCO, CALIFORNIA

LANDSCAPE ARCHITECT: Theodore Osmundson and Associates, David Arbegast, associate
ARCHITECT: Hertzka and Knowles AIA
CLIENT: Chevron Corporation

This roof garden was built in 1965 for the sole use of the employees in the building. As such, it is used primarily during lunch hours, for short periods of time. Located at the rear of a twenty-eight-story office building, on the roof of a six-story portion of that structure, it faces south and away from the noise of Market Street, the city's main artery. Access is limited to a single building entrance (such a design would violate today's more stringent code restrictions).

Durable concrete is used for paving, plant containers, and seating throughout, with hardy and wind-resistant trees, shrubs, and ground covers chosen for minimal maintenance. Wind resistance is an important consideration in San Francisco, where heat and cold are rarely problems but strong winds can wreak havoc on plantings. Included among the plants are the ground cover *Hedera helix* 'Hahn' (Hahn's ivy); the low-growing shrubs *Raphiolepis indica rosea* (Indian hawthorn), *Phormiun tenax* (New Zealand flax), and *Rosmarinus officinalus prostratus* (rosemary); and the wind-resistant tree *Melaleuca decusatta* (lilac melaleuca). Seating consists of integral benches permanently attached to the broad tops of the raised planters. Although ideally suited for flexible seating arrangements, no comfortable movable furniture has been provided.

The garden is lighted and is irrigated by overhead spray heads on automatic timers set for the very early morning hours, when wind spray is usually not a problem. The entire paved surface slopes to the rear of the building for drainage. A permanent but movable window-washing gondola mounted on tracks parallel to the roof's parapet is concealed behind a permanent screen when not in use.

Top: The screen at right conceals the storage space for window-washing equipment.

Bottom: Careful selection of plant materials has kept this roof garden flourishing for many years, despite its windy microclimate.

Above: The entrance to the roof garden is at deck level (to the left), flanked by potted plants. Small broadleaf trees are in permanent concrete boxes.

Right: Permanent benches are attached to the tops of the concrete raised planters.

Plan, roof garden of 555 Market Building

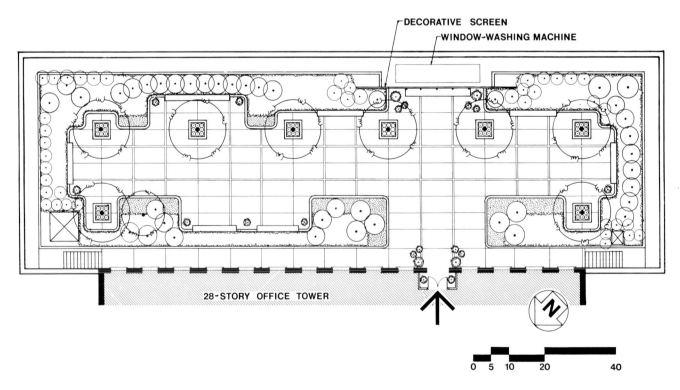

DECORATIVE SCREEN
WINDOW-WASHING MACHINE

28-STORY OFFICE TOWER

0 5 10   20   40

CROCKER TERRACE

SAN FRANCISCO, CALIFORNIA

LANDSCAPE ARCHITECT: Richard Vignola ASLA, consultant
ARCHITECT: Skidmore, Owings and Merrill
CLIENT: Crocker Bank (now owned by Wells Fargo)

Crocker Terrace is on the roof of a truncated, formerly seven-story office building in downtown San Francisco. Its design was part of a master plan developed for several parcels of land and existing buildings in the area. The project included building a multilevel indoor shopping mall, the Crocker Galleria, patterned after a similar structure in Milan, Italy, in an alley running through the block, adding a new high-rise office building with a small roof garden, and removing the top five floors of the old office building to make way for a roof garden of about 7,500 square feet (697 square meters). The first and second stories of the original office building, designed in the classical style, were considered worthy of preservation; these two floors remain in use by the bank. Although this garden was retrofitted onto the existing structure, no problems involving load restrictions were encountered. The northern part of the old roof remained undeveloped. A wall with hedges was installed on the terrace to block the view into this area.

Access to the roof garden is via an elevator from the street as well as by an outdoor stairway leading up from the third floor of the Crocker Galleria shopping mall next door.

At the eastern end of the garden, as one exits the elevator from the street, is an intimate plaza with a central sculptural sundial in a round planter, backed by an ornamental trellis on the parapet. The heavily used roof garden has a formal layout, with a central allée bordered by large pots containing specimen crab apple trees. A wall fountain, framed by the galleria's glass dome, is

Access to the roof garden is primarily via an elevator from the street-level bank entrance. The strong patterns created by the paving, plantings, seating, and structural elements are clearly visible here. Access to the galleria is via steps at the far end of the garden.

featured at the western end of this open space. Flanking the central area on each side are semicircular sitting areas, providing ample comfortable seating; individual benches provide additional seating. Throughout the space, round concrete containers are filled with flowers for seasonal color. The very striking paving is of brick outlined by light-colored double strips of 6-inch (15-cm) tile. Its pattern has been correlated to the location of every major element in the garden and is integral to the garden's overall design.

Above: Emerging from the elevator, one encounters a small plaza with a sundial and trellis.

Right: The central allée is formed by a double row of crab apples in huge planters. The glass-vaulted Crocker Galleria is in the background.

CALIFORNIA STATE COMPENSATION INSURANCE BUILDING

SAN FRANCISCO, CALIFORNIA

LANDSCAPE ARCHITECT: MPA Design
ARCHITECT: John Carl Warnecke and Associates
CLIENT: California State Workers Compensation Fund

This garden plaza is atop an underground garage at the rear of an office building. It can be accessed both from the building and via a gated entrance on Fifth Street. Sheltered by the building from two busy streets, this ½-acre (0.2-hectare) space provides a quiet haven for visitors and office workers, who can purchase food in the building and eat outdoors either on the second-floor dining terrace overlooking the plaza or in the garden plaza itself at ground level. The addition of movable outdoor furniture on the plaza would greatly increase its comfort and convenience.

The focal point of the plaza is a 20–square foot (1.9–square meter) pool lined with blue ceramic tile, which is recessed into the brick-and-granite plaza floor. A two-tier fountain flows into the pool. From the upper fountain, water flows beneath granite slabs that form stepping-stones over it. It then descends via a shallow waterfall into a lower pool, from which it is recirculated back to the pump in the garage below and then to the fountain. Additional water is added to the system only to compensate for evaporation. The water effects are achieved with a minimal addition of weight to the garage roof. Granite walls surrounding the pool and plaza have embedded strip lighting, which provides a wash of indirect light over the plaza floor.

Above: The planted areas south of the pool contain a rich selection of plants. This small garden is next to the shallow waterfall.

Left: The view from one of the building's second-floor terraces encompasses a wide variety of water features, colored masonry paving, and plantings.

Next to the plaza is a small informal garden of perennials, low shrubs, and ground cover, which provides a pleasing contrast to the open space. Redwood trees have been planted in the background (not on the roof) to shield the plaza from glare produced by the highly reflective wall of a neighboring building, and tall-growing trees have been planted along the plaza's southern border to provide more shade in the future. *Pyrus kawakamii* (evergreen pear) and *Robinia* 'Idaho' (pink Idaho locust) trees serve as accents. *Hedera helix* 'Hahn' (Hahn's ivy) provides a bright green carpet for pink *Raphiolepis indica* (Indian hawthorn), *Nandina domestica* (heavenly bamboo), and butterfly iris.

Above: The building and plaza were designed to complement each other, with planted terraces overlooking the rooftop plaza below. (Courtesy MPA Design)

Right: Water overflowing from the fountain basin forms a shallow waterfall leading to a lower basin.

Below right: Plan, roof garden of California State Compensation Insurance Building

Below left: The terraces of the building overlook the plaza. Their edges are planted with vines.

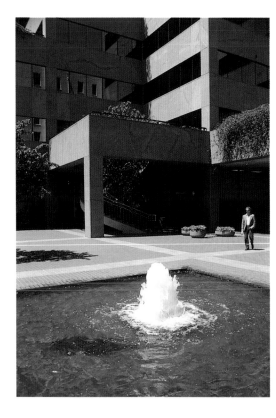

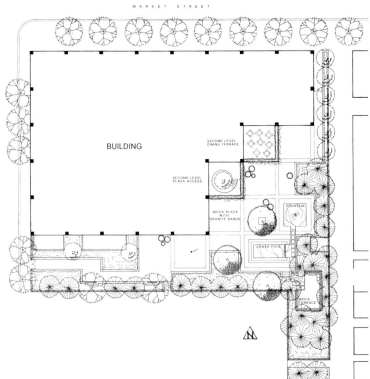

YERBA BUENA GARDENS

SAN FRANCISCO, CALIFORNIA

CONSULTING LANDSCAPE ARCHITECT: Omi Lang Associates
ARCHITECT: Mitchell, Giurgola and Associates
CLIENT: Redevelopment Agency of the City and County of San Francisco

The development of Yerba Buena Gardens, part of an enormous redevelopment effort known as Yerba Buena Center, was almost thirty years in the making. In the 1960s the city of San Francisco purchased 87 acres (35 hectares) of rundown neighborhoods one black south of Market Street and east of Fourth Street, with the intent of building a sports arena, convention center, and multiple high-rise buildings. Lawsuits involving the rights of displaced citizens, financial problems, changing public attitudes, and continuous design changes fragmented the project's development into a piecemeal affair. The ground-breaking below-grade George Moscone Convention Center, south of Folsom Street, was built in the 1970s; its underground space was later extended north of Folsom, and this extension is what lies below Yerba Buena Gardens. Development of the Yerba Buena area continues today. Complete are the Center for the Arts and the Performing Arts

Center, which border the gardens to the east, on Third Street, and Mario Botta's very popular San Francisco Museum of Modern Art, also to the east, across Third Street, which opened in 1995. In the planning and construction stages are a Jewish museum and a Mexican museum, north across Mission Street; a huge retail and movie complex to the west, bordering Fourth Street; and a children's complex atop the original convention center, south of Folsom Street; as well as several high-rises and hotels.

At the center of this gargantuan undertaking are the 5½-acre (2.2-hectare) Yerba Buena Gardens. The grassy slopes of the large lawn area were created by stacking 2-foot (61-cm) blocks of Styrofoam, used as fill to reduce weight, then covering the blocks with 2 feet (61 cm) of planting soil. The ramps, walkways, and plazas, paved with Sierra granite, were also built over Styrofoam fill. The trees, fountain, and restaurant

View from the upper level of the great lawn, which slopes down toward the Center for the Arts and its outdoor stage. This entire landscape, including its soil, rests on Styrofoam blocks.

Above: The waterfall, dedicated to the memory of Dr. Martin Luther King, Jr., plunges over a granite face to the basin below.

Below center: The edges of the festival stage also serve as perches for lunching and chatting.

Below right: Tall, slim lighting columns, a striking walkway, and colorful flowers enliven the walk from the restaurants to Mission Street at the northern end of the great lawn.

structure rest on the columns of the convention center extension below. The trees are anchored by guy wires attached to concrete deadmen. Drainage across the building's roof is through a 2-inch-thick (5.1-cm) layer of Grass-Cel covered with filter fabric, which permits water to drain while retaining the soil.

The highlight of the gardens is the Dr. Martin Luther King, Jr., memorial waterfall, which rivals that of the New Otani Hotel in Tokyo in size and spectacular effect. The marble walls of this walk-through waterfall are inscribed with quotations from Dr. King.

Two restaurants at the south end of the garden provide easily accessible foodservice. The numerous ramps and generous seating make Yerba Buena a comfortable space that everyone can enjoy.

The fountains and plaza on Third Street are the designs of Omi Lang Associates.

Above: The fountains in the East Garden fronting the Center for the Arts face onto Third Street, a busy thoroughfare.

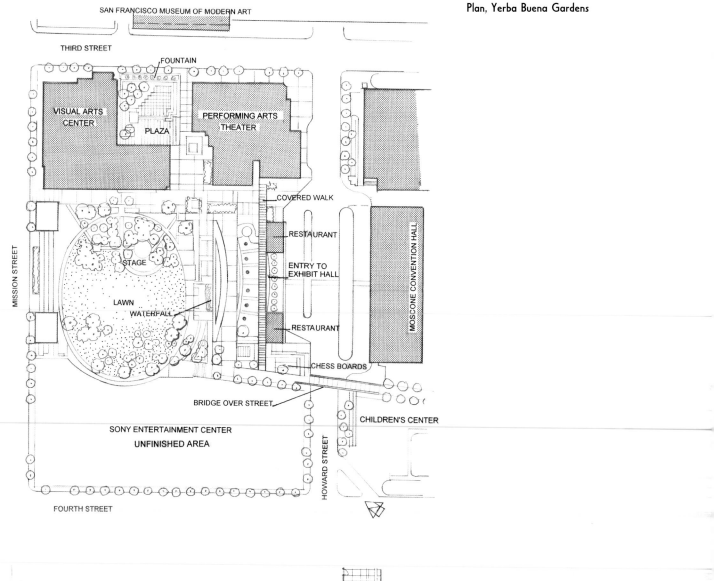

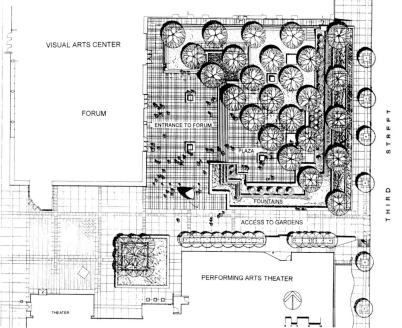

Plan, East Garden of Yerba
Buena project

KAISER CENTER

OAKLAND, CALIFORNIA

LANDSCAPE ARCHITECT: Osmundson and Staley
ASLA, with David Arbegast, associate
ARCHITECT: Welton Becket and Associates
CLIENT: Kaiser Center

The first major privately owned roof garden built after World War II, the Kaiser Center's 3-acre (1.2-hectare) roof garden was the largest continuous roof garden in the world when it opened in 1960. Highly acclaimed, this internationally renowned garden inspired the creation of many public and private roof gardens for years to come. The idea for the garden was conceived by Edgar Kaiser, Sr., the head of Kaiser and son of Henry J. Kaiser, the shipbuilding genius of World War II. Edgar Kaiser decided to make this roof a semipublic park, open to the public but controlled and maintained by Kaiser.

The materials for the garden were raised up to the solid concrete slab atop the roof bit by bit from the ground below to form a detached piece of landscape, independent of the ground, with its own irrigation and drainage system. The roof garden provides the foreground view to the west from the twenty-eight-floor glass-and-aluminum Kaiser Building, complementing the splendid view of Lake Merritt to the east.

Although 90 percent of the land at the Kaiser Center is covered by buildings, 60 percent of that same area is also covered with plantings, proving without question that high density need not preclude a green environment.

The primary challenges in constructing a roof garden are drainage and weight. The drainage of this roof garden relies on the basic drainage of the roof slab itself, consisting of a downspout at every alternate column to drain its individual area of roof. As with most large, flat roofs, water flows across the gradual slope of the concrete slab into a catch basin or roof drain, down the downspout through five floors of the building, to a storm sewer in the basement and thence to the city storm sewer system.

All garden water is directed toward these roof drains. Wherever possible, these existing drains were extended upward until their surface was flush with the new grade of the roof garden level. If it was not possible to slope the roof garden surface to the location of an existing drain, a new

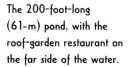

The 200-foot-long (61-m) pond, with the roof-garden restaurant on the far side of the water.

catch basin was installed at the low point, and the water was carried through a 4-inch (10-cm) galvanized iron pipe under the soil to the principal roof drain.

As an additional aid to drainage and to prevent souring of the soil (which might occur if underground drainage were not present), a 4-inch (10-cm) layer of coarse, lightweight expanded shale was installed over the entire surface of the roof. In the early 1960s, when this garden was built, polypropylene filter fabric had yet to be developed. The landscape architect was aware of the need for some type of barrier between the soil and the drainage system, however, and covered the layer of exposed aggregate with rice straw. Although it would soon decay and wash away, it lasted long enough to allow the soil to develop a structure to hold it in place. Soil, concrete paving, and all structures were then installed on top of the drainage and filter material, thereby permitting continuous subsurface drainage over the entire roof.

The weight between columns was limited to 135 pounds per square foot (659 kg per square meter) dead load, with 15,000 pounds (73,236 kg) over the columns below. This placed severe limitations on the amount and kind of soil and construction materials to use. When the soil did not have to be deep, as in the 6-inch (15-m) depth for general lawn areas, ordinary topsoil was used. Where the soil mounds up and over the 30-inch-high (76-cm) boxes for the specimen trees, a lightweight soil mix of fine expanded shale, peat moss, and various fertilizers was used. All paving and structures are made of lightweight concrete, and all rocks or boulders are lightweight pumice stone. The forty-two specimen trees (olive, holly oak, Japanese maple, and southern magnolia), which were originally as tall as 15 to 20 feet (4.6 to 6.1 m) and weighed up to 3 tons (2,722 kg), were placed over columns at carefully chosen locations in the design.

Top: In this aerial view, one can see the Kaiser Center with its roof garden, as well as the newer Ordway Building to its left and Lake Merritt at the upper right.

Bottom: The shape of the garden is determined by flowing curved walkways for casual strolling with ever-changing views.

In good weather, visitors relax, meet with friends, and enjoy the large reflecting pond with its small fountains.

Lighting is provided below eye level along all walks; in addition, separate mercury vapor lights are embedded in the soil to direct light upward into the branches of all specimen trees. The lights turn on automatically when the light level drops enough to activate a photoelectric cell.

The large pool has 8,800 square feet (818 square meters) of water surface and is kept in motion by jets around the perimeter, turned at a thirty-degree angle to the surface of the vertical face of the pool wall. The water is circulated through filters and is returned through these underwater jets. In addition, swimming-pool-type surface scum collectors are installed at separate locations around the inside edges of the pool to collect surface debris. Three bubbler jets are used to agitate the water in the center of the pool, but mechanical equipment and piping were also installed to accommodate a more elaborate water effect if desired. The free-form pool edge was widened in places to hold planting boxes and movable pots. The pool is 16 inches (40.6 cm) deep, with a black interior to give an impression of greater depth.

All of the trees have a fibrous root system, and all have performed well in their new environment. All trees were left in the 2-inch (5.1-cm) plank boxes in which they were delivered. The box formed part of the subsurface bracing, which eliminated the need for visible guying. Ultimately, the boxes and braces decomposed, and the roots of each tree now provide its support.

The entire garden is watered by a fully automatic underground irrigation system, controlled by an electric timer. Lawns and shrub areas are controlled separately because of their different watering requirements.

Since its completion, the garden has been open to visitors during working hours Monday through Friday.

For more details about the construction of this garden, see the discussion near the end of chapter 4.

Undulating lawns provide space to sit or even lie down to talk with others in the quiet garden.

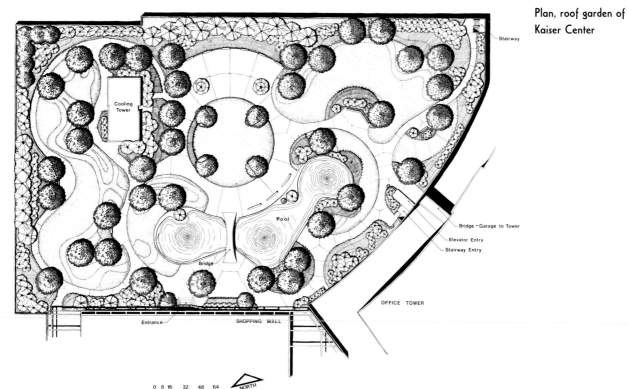

Plan, roof garden of
Kaiser Center

Stairway

Cooling
Tower

Pool

Bridge - Garage to Tower

Elevator Entry

Stairway Entry

OFFICE TOWER

Bridge

Entrance   SHOPPING MALL

0 8 16   32   48   64

NORTH

Left: Section, roof garden of Kaiser
Center

Below left: Access from the shopping mall is through doors on the same level as the roof and via covered stairs from the floor below.

Below right: A wooden bridge across the pond permits easier passage from one part of the garden to another. Although a bridge here was originally planned, it was not initially installed. This bridge was constructed for the convenience of visitors to a conference later held in the building and was allowed to remain.

HEAVY LOADS OVER COLUMNS

POND 16" DEEP

PARKING

PARKING

DRAINS ON ALTERNATE COLUMNS

PARKING

STREET

STEPHEN D. BECHTEL ENGINEERING CENTER, UNIVERSITY OF CALIFORNIA AT BERKELEY

BERKELEY, CALIFORNIA

LANDSCAPE ARCHITECT: Royston, Hanamoto, Abey and Alley
ARCHITECT: George Matsumoto AIA
CLIENT: Regents of the University of California

Stationary game tables and seats are located under the pergola.

This 44,570–square foot (4,141–square meter) engineering center houses not only the discipline's library but also student and faculty lounges, offices, a conference center, and a 270-seat auditorium. To maintain open space on campus, part of the building extends one floor above grade, while the remainder is below, built into a slope. The above-grade portion of the roof is used as a social and study center; the below-grade portion, as a lawn space. Included on the roof above grade is a foodservice building with an adjacent outdoor dining area, sheltered study carrels, built-in game boards with seating, and lounging space. The paving of the terrace contains a patterned grid produced by contrasting shades of concrete and brick.

Access to the roof garden is from the podium of the building next door and from the ground level via exterior stairways. A border of trees and a stone retaining wall provide a visual buffer between the roof garden and the taller neighboring building.

The foodservice building is located at one end of the roof, with permanent tables adjacent. A sense of separation from the rest of the roof is suggested by the overhead shade structure.

The building is partly above and partly below ground. The transparent dome at left is a skylight that provides natural light to the rooms below grade. The above-grade part of the building includes a plaza, plantings, and study carrels on the roof.

The view looking toward the foodservice building. The study carrels are at the left; at the right is a wooden pergola that provides shade. The expanse of paving is made more interesting by its surface pattern.

Study carrels, sheltered by a roof and a glass windbreak, offer pleasant places to read, study, or converse with others.

Plan, Stephen D. Bechtel Engineering
Center, U.C. at Berkeley

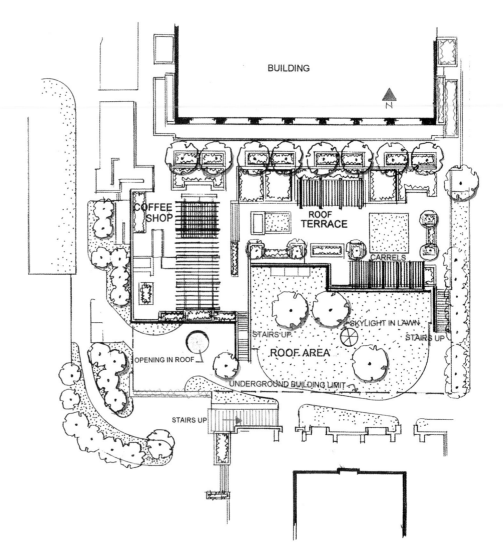

Most of the roof is
designed open space.

NEWTON VINEYARD

SAINT HELENA, CALIFORNIA

LANDSCAPE DESIGNERS: Peter Newton and Su Hua
ARCHITECT: William Turnbull Associates
STRUCTURAL ENGINEER: T. Y. Lin and Associates
OWNER: Newton Vineyard

Roof gardens on industrial structures are not only possible but can completely change the appearance and function of roof areas, making them useful, even beautiful, open spaces. This outstanding garden is on the roof of a building used to store and age barreled Chardonnay. From the outset the owners, Peter Newton and his wife, Su Hua, envisioned their winery set amidst gardens (it now has eleven separate garden spaces, covering 5½ of 560 acres [2.2 of 227 hectares] of property). They wanted the vineyard's buildings to be as visually inconspicuous as possible, blending into the hillsides.

The earth-sheltered barrel-storage building, which covers 60 by 200 feet (18.3 by 60.1 m), was the first structure built for the winery. It sits on a shelf excavated from the long dimension of a downward-sloping ridge. The upper portion of the hill remains, rising steeply above the building, while the opposite cut-away end provides a wide space for an access road at the building's floor level. The access road rises on both sides of the building to the upper end of the structure at roof level, providing vehicle access to bottling and packaging facilities. The floor of the long, rectangular concrete structure is at grade with the base of the hill, providing an entrance to the surrounding access road at that point.

Originally, rainwater could drain only through a layer of drain rock spread over the waterproofing. Because this system did not allow rainwater to drain through the soil quickly enough, the soil became water laden and unsuitable for growing plants. In the center of each star-shaped planting area formed by trimmed boxwood, the owner installed a 4-inch (10-cm)

From the terrace of the wine-tasting building, called a pagoda by the owners, the view extends beyond the garden into the valley, through spiraled juniper and Italian cypresses.

vertical drainpipe with a perforated metal grille at the surface, which penetrated the full depth of the soil, draining water to the gravel layer on the surface of the structural slab below. Water then drains through the drain rock and across the roof to the soil around the perimeter of the building. (This system of drainage is generally not recommended.) Excess water from the soil embankments on the north and south sides then flows into storm drains on the access road.

The long formal parterres of sheared boxwood, accented by Cinderella miniature roses and framed by spiral-shaped junipers, are difficult to appreciate fully at ground level. Such gardens in Europe are usually viewed from above, through high windows or elevated terraces, for

The side slopes leading up the hill are covered with heavy-flowering bank roses used as ground cover, surrounded by juniper topiary.

The barrel-storage building emerges at its full height at the east end of the roof garden. This is the driveway access for trucks and other vehicles. The exterior finish of all structures is wooden lattice facing, to make them seem less intrusive in their garden setting.

example. Such a vantage point is provided here in a small pagoda-like building, used for wine tastings, which has an upper terrace immediately adjacent to the formal garden.

This elegant garden is a far cry from the park atop the roof of a waste-water treatment plant in Tokyo (see the portfolio of international gardens), but the principle is the same. Almost any steel-and-concrete building can accommodate planting on the roof. The additional costs can be well worthwhile, as was the case in this garden.

Left: The central fountain, a feature reminiscent of formal Renaissance gardens of the fifteenth century, and the pagoda form an integrated scene in the garden.

Right top: At ground level, the garden becomes a "stroll garden," with perennials growing in horizontal boxwood frames.

Right bottom: The high hills to the west of Napa Valley are the setting for Newton Vineyard and its 5½ acres (2.2 hectares) of gardens.

Below: Elevation, roof garden of Newton Vineyard

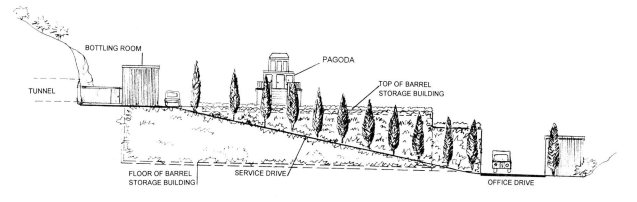

THOREAU HALL, UNIVERSITY OF CALIFORNIA AT DAVIS

DAVIS, CALIFORNIA

LANDSCAPE ARCHITECT: Theodore Osmundson and Associates, Gordon Osmundson, Associate
ARCHITECT: Backen, Arigoni and Ross
CLIENT: Regents of the University of California

Thoreau Hall provides student housing, but there its similarity to the typical college dormitory ends. Built in 1989, the housing in this residence complex consists of two-student suites, which each contain sleep/study rooms, a bath, closets, and a living room. Access to the suites is via wraparound terraces on the upper two floors and via a garden court at ground level. All of the suites look out onto this courtyard, which rests atop a garage for sixty cars. Access to the courtyard is via an elevator from the garage below and through a central building that houses common areas for the students. A ramp from a secondary street provides access for the disabled, and two fire exits lead to the main street.

Above: The pattern of the plaza is integrated with the fenestration of the main lounge building. This photo, taken seven years after installation, shows how the garden has matured. Even the growth of the wisteria on the trellis softens the look of the small plaza.

Right: Two years after installation, the roof garden's geometry is clearly visible; the garden still looks new and somewhat barren. Balcony entrances to the apartments allow students to experience the garden at all times.

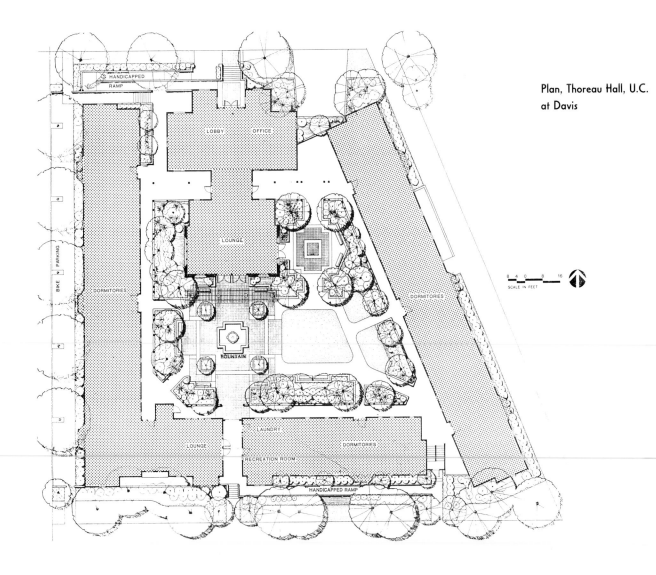

Plan, Thoreau Hall, U.C.
at Davis

The secondary garden off the main lounge offers a quiet place for study. After seven years' growth, this patio is beginning to be dappled with cooling shade. However, sun-loving perennials, installed during the garden's early years, have been shaded out and need to be replaced with plants for shade. The space also needs additional garden furniture.

The ¼-acre (0.1-hectare) courtyard comprises two principal areas. The fountain area is on axis with the interior hallway and lounge of the central common building. Its paving, in a pattern of warm varicolored brick, provides a backdrop for the fountain (whose cruciform shape mirrors the brick design), as well as for four earth-colored precast planters that hold pink oleanders. Heavily planted raised beds of split-faced concrete blocks surround the space. Permanent wooden benches with backs provide seating throughout the garden.

The secondary area, off to one side of the main lounge, has similar paving. Intended as a separate, more private area for students to use for studying and socializing outdoors, it was supposed to be furnished with garden tables, umbrellas, and chairs. The entire area is quiet except for the sound of the splashing fountain. The water and electrical supply lines, as well as drainage, are all carried in the ceiling of the garage below, penetrating the slab to the garden level where needed.

Plant materials include Chinese pistachios, Japanese maples, goldenrain trees, flowering cherries, oleanders, camellias, and ferns. Over time, wisteria has completely covered a trellis. A panel of lawn between the fountain and study areas is both decorative and provides a place to sunbathe. The soil mix throughout is 40 percent sand of various grain sizes (no silt), 40 percent expanded shale, and 20 percent organic humus, which was mixed, delivered, and placed while quite damp to prevent separation of its parts.

For more details about the construction of this garden, see the discussion near the end of chapter 4.

Top: The relationship of the trellis, fountain, and planter emphasize this featured area outside of the main lounge.

Bottom: Permanent benches, integral with their locations, provide places for quiet reflection and conversation.

PACIFIC BELL TELEPHONE COMPANY, NORTHERN CALIFORNIA HEADQUARTERS
SACRAMENTO, CALIFORNIA

LANDSCAPE ARCHITECT: Theodore Osmundson and Associates, David Arbegast, associate
ARCHITECT: Hertzka and Knowles AIA
OWNER: Pacific Bell Telephone Company

The northern California headquarters of Pacific Bell Telephone, built in the early 1960s, has extensive landscaped parking lots and ground-level gardens; it also has a ½-acre (0.2-hectare) roof garden. The entire building was raised one story to permit the provision of an extensive garage. The private roof garden is an atrium in the center of the building, atop the roof of the first floor, which houses the main billing computers for service in northern California. Accessed via doorways at opposite ends of the atrium, it is used by employees during coffee and lunch breaks. A cafeteria in the building provides easily available foodservice.

The roof was carefully waterproofed with asphaltic bitumen to protect the computers below. Although load restrictions were not a serious problem in this structure, weight was limited nonetheless because of the potential of catastrophic damage to the computer room below should any element of the garden system fail.

A very simple but strong design pattern is visible from the two floors above the garden.

At garden level, the open paved areas are softened by the trees' shade.

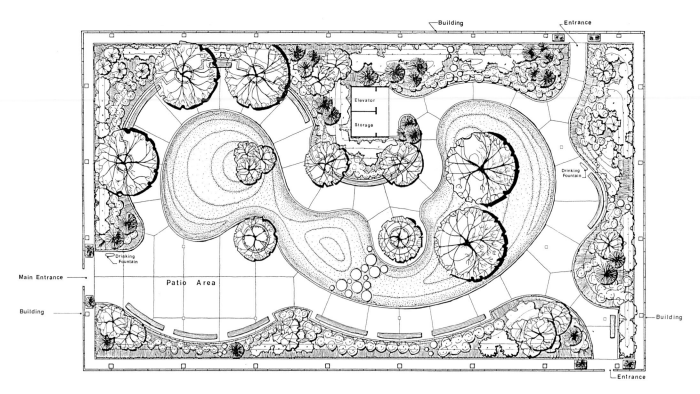

Plan, roof garden of
Pacific Bell

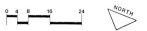

0 4 8   16   24   NORTH

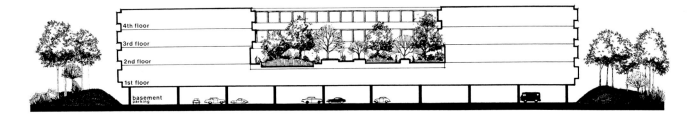

Section, Pacific Bell

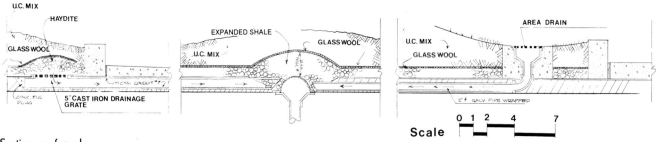

Section, roof-garden
drainage of Pacific Bell

Hence, the paving, drainage system, soil, benches, raised planters, and other elements were chosen and located to minimize their weight on the roof. All lawn areas have a maximum soil depth of 6 inches (15 cm), except for a crown that permits drainage, and all planted areas are automatically irrigated by overhead spray. Fruitless mulberry trees were planted directly over load-bearing columns on the first floor but were selectively placed in the design so as not to appear to be on a grid.

Right: Taken during construction, this photo shows the finished concrete curbs and raised beds before the placement of irrigation lines, final paving, and soil. Exposed built-up roofing is in the lawn bed at right.

Below: The garden is very accessible for a break or lunch. Two additional entrances are at the far end of the garden. Built-in seating is provided, but movable furniture—chairs and tables with umbrellas—would greatly improve the garden's usefulness and appearance.

Above: The paths are in sweeping curves, an integral and important part of the design.

Above: The designed effect has been only partly realized with the new planting. As the small, multitextured ground covers spread and the grasses grow in height, the continuity and contrast within the garden will increase. (Courtesy Dixi Carrillo; EDAW)

HARRISON MEMORIAL HOSPITAL

BREMERTON, WASHINGTON

LANDSCAPE ARCHITECT: EDAW, with Robert Shrosbree ASLA, project design
ARCHITECT: NBBJ
CLIENT: Harrison Memorial Hospital

When Harrison Memorial Hospital expanded its Bremerton campus in 1995, one of the features included in the addition was a unique roof garden. More than just ornamental, this garden, with its tranquil design evoking the shoreline of nearby Puget Sound, has a therapeutic function, providing a space for meditation and healing.

Although the design intent here was to echo the waterfront, the only water feature in the garden is a central fountain constructed of polished and naturally finished stone. The remainder of the "water" actually consists of river rock, beach stone, and gravel, carefully selected for size and placed in flowing curves to create the impression of beach, waves, and water. Large columnar stones provide a sense of depth and spatial definition. A wooden deck resembling a boardwalk, with movable tables and chairs, serves as the transition space between the hospital's interior and the garden. To complete the waterfront metaphor, natural found objects, such as shells and stones, from shore areas have been incorporated into the paving, seating, and walls of the space. Interestingly, the garden highlights the healing nature of its setting by containing only plants reputed to have medicinal qualities.

Because many of the garden's visitors would be hospital patients, the garden's design had to accommodate their special needs. Access from the adjacent waiting rooms and exam areas is accomplished with minimal grade change, and ramps ease the transition. Visitors' safety is ensured with the strategic placement of gates, walls, and lighting; the garden can also be monitored through the windows of adjacent hospital rooms.

Left: The plantings, stones, vertical rocks, and wooden decking give the impression of being on the edge of moving water. (Courtesy Dixi Carrillo; EDAW)

Concrete Relief "Beach Walk"

Memorial Garden Gate

Decking /"Board Walk"

Container Planting

Ornamental Grasses and Ground Covers

Focal Point / Water Spring

Stone Wall

Mechanical Court

Gravel "Beach" and Feature Stones

Resting atop the new surgical wing and waiting areas, this 12,000–square foot (1,115–square meter) garden of course had to meet careful structural criteria to make it a success. Loads were a particular concern, with 85,000 pounds (38,555 kg) of columnar stone and boulders an integral part of the design. These heavy loads were placed over structurally reinforced zones of the roof deck. The remainder of the space uses lighter-weight materials: plantings are limited to shallow-rooted specimens, grown in lightweight soil that does not exceed 18 inches (45.7 cm) in depth, and the paved "beach" area is a lightweight concrete. Low-volume sprinklers and drip tubing both automatically irrigate the space, and the drainage system was designed as an integral part of the roof and mechanical systems below.

Plan, roof garden of Harrison Memorial Hospital. (Courtesy EDAW)

FREEWAY PARK

SEATTLE, WASHINGTON

LANDSCAPE ARCHITECT: Lawrence Halprin and Associates

CLIENT: King County, Washington

In the early 1970s, Seattle was faced with the problem of extending Interstate 5, which was designed to pass through and sever its downtown from a heavily populated area uphill from it. After considering alternatives, the city decided to

bridge the freeway with a major public park of 5½ acres (2.2 hectares). Such a space would maintain physical access and visual connections to the downtown area.

In addition to supporting the park, the bridge had to connect to the existing infrastructure of the city. These connections were designed to meet surrounding street grades wherever possible; access from the city's newly built convention center to the park was also included. In one area, where an important connection could not be made at grade, a concrete ramp known as Piggott Walk, with switchbacks, fountains, waterfalls, and seating, was constructed.

A major walkway that meanders from the convention center off site to the upper extremity of the park includes a number of branches that connect to city sidewalks. Along this walk are benches, fountains, pools, and waterfalls, in a setting of large evergreens and deciduous trees. Twenty-odd years after its completion in 1976, the park today resembles a natural wood with walks easing through it.

Above: One of two small concrete water features, located near the convention center entrance.

Right: Mature trees and lawns strewn with bright autumn leaves belie the presence of the interstate below.

Above left: A variety of falling-water effects contribute to the great interest of this feature. Built against a steep slope, its steps and walks nonetheless allow visitors to experience the gushing waters up close.

Above right: The principal water feature, small but spectacular, is in perfect scale with the mature trees that surround it.

Left: Plan, Freeway Park

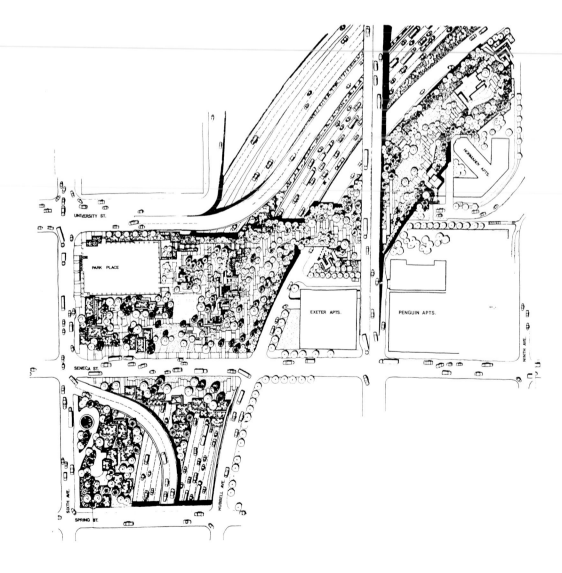

CHAPTER TWO

ROOF GARDENS THROUGH HISTORY

There is something fascinating about being up high, above people on the ground, looking farther and seeing more and feeling the different air of high places. And to be in a garden on a roof is the ultimate experience of being up high, for here a garden is not supposed to be. Even the ancients knew this, and although many of the buildings that supported them have crumbled into dust, roof gardens have existed since almost the beginning of recorded time. From the Hanging Gardens of Babylon to the roof gardens atop multistory buildings today, the pleasure of being in a garden above the ground has been possible wherever the opportunity, skills, and funds have permitted it.

ANCIENT ROOF GARDENS

Because of the fleeting nature of ancient gardens, and especially roof gardens, little tangible evidence of their existence remains. They are, however, mentioned often enough in classical literature to make assumptions of their existence a reasonable conclusion.

The Ziggurats of Ancient Mesopotamia

The first known historical references to man-made gardens above grade appear to be the ziggurats of ancient Mesopotamia, built from the fourth millennium until about 600 B.C. Located in the courtyards of temples in major cities, the ziggurats were great stepped pyramid towers of stone, built in stages. They were accessible via stairways spiraling upward on their outer edges. Evidence found by the British archeologist Sir Leonard Woolley indicated that, at landings on these stepped towers, plantings of trees and shrubs on flat terraces softened the climb and offered relief from the blazing heat of the Baby-

lonian plain. These are the first known instances of a serious attempt to build gardens on man-made space high above the ground. The most famous of the ziggurats, Etemenanki in Babylon, the tower of the Babylonian god Marduk, was built in the square of the city's great temple, Esagila. Etemenanki, believed by some to be the biblical Tower of Babel, was 300 feet (100 m) tall, with a base of 100 yards (100 m) on each side. It had seven stages, the topmost made of blue-glazed stone, a temple to Marduk. Built during the neo-Babylonian reign of Nebuchadrezzar II (605–562 B.C.), it was destroyed in revolts against the Persian king Xerxes I in 482 B.C.

The best preserved of the ancient ziggurats is the ziggurat of Nanna, in the ancient city of Ur (fig. 2-1). It was built by Ur-Nammu, the first king of the third dynasty of Ur, who reigned from 2113–2095 B.C., and by his son Shulgi, who reigned from 2095–2047 B.C. It was completely remodeled by the last neo-Babylonian king, Nabonidus, who reigned from 556–539 B.C., in an effort to surpass the splendor of Etemenanki in Babylon.

The Hanging Gardens of Babylon

Probably the most famous roof gardens of all time, the fabled Hanging Gardens of Babylon were one of the Seven Wonders of the World (fig. 2-2). The gardens, probably constructed during the rebuilding of Babylon by Nebuchadrezzar II, were purportedly built by that king to console his wife, Amytis, who missed the greenery of her homeland, Media. No contemporary accounts of their construction or existence have been found.

The first mention of the gardens are found in the writings of Berossus, a priest who lived around 290 B.C., some two hundred years after the probable destruction of the gardens. His

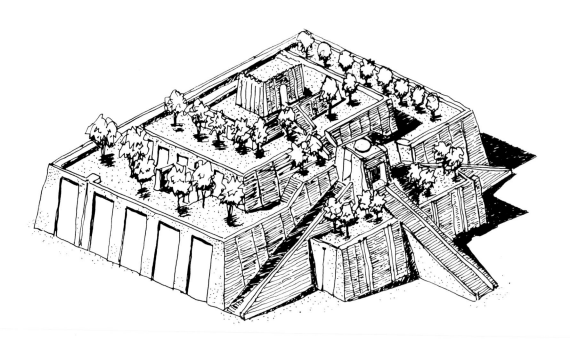

2-1. The ziggurat of Nanna in the ancient city of Ur (now Muqaiyir in southern Iraq) still stands today. Built during the third dynasty of Ur, beginning in 2113 B.C., it is the best preserved of the ancient ziggurats. The mud core and facing brick made a structure 68 feet (21m) high; the shrine at the top was accessible by stairs. (Drawing © The British Museum)

work, *Babyloniaka,* itself no longer exists except as quoted by later historians. The historian Josephus, in *Contra Apionen,* attributes the following description of the gardens to Berossus:

> Within this palace he [Nebuchadrezzar II] erected lofty stone terraces, in which he closely reproduced mountain scenery, completing the resemblance by planting them with all manner of trees and constructing the so-called Hanging Gardens because his wife, having been brought up in Media, had a passion for mountain surroundings (cited by Finkel, 1988, 42–43).

Fragments of later works, including those of the writer Antipater of Sidon (2nd century B.C.), the mathematician Philon of Byzantium (2nd century B.C.), the Greek geographer Strabo (20 B.C.), and the Roman historian Quintus Curtius Rufus (1st century A.D.) also mention the gardens, with Antipater being the first to list them among the Seven Wonders of the World. Typical of the detailed description of the gardens is that of Diodorus Siculus, a Greek historian who lived during the first century A.D.:

> The garden was 100 feet long by 100 feet wide and built up in tiers so that it resembled a theater. Vaults had been constructed under the ascending terraces which carried the entire weight of the planted garden.

2-2. This section drawing of the Hanging Gardens of Babylon, circa 500 B.C., is based on the archeologist Robert Koldewey's descriptions.

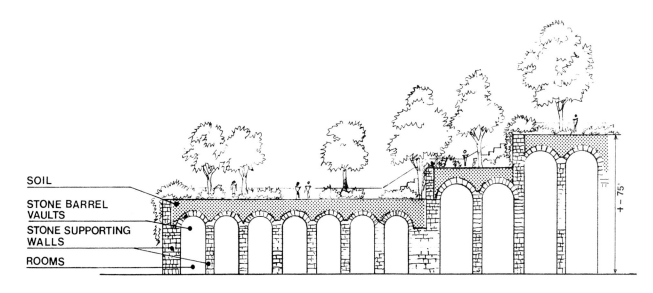

SOIL

STONE BARREL VAULTS

STONE SUPPORTING WALLS

ROOMS

± 75'

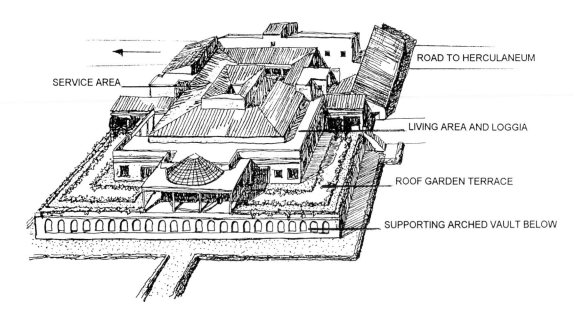

2-3. The Villa of the Mysteries, outside the Herculaneum gate, survived through the centuries because it was encased in Vesuvian ash after the catastrophic volcanic eruption in A.D. 79. The formal entrance of the structure is on the far side of the building.

SERVICE AREA

ROAD TO HERCULANEUM

LIVING AREA AND LOGGIA

ROOF GARDEN TERRACE

SUPPORTING ARCHED VAULT BELOW

The uppermost vault, which was seventy feet high, was the highest part of the garden, which, at this point, was on the same level as the city walls. The roofs of the vaults which supported the garden were constructed of stone beams some sixteen feet long and over these were laid first a layer of reed set in thick tar, then two courses of baked clay brick bonded by cement, and finally a covering of lead to prevent the moisture in the soil penetrating the roof. On top of this roof enough topsoil was heaped to allow the biggest trees to take root. The earth was leveled off and thickly planted with every kind of tree. And since the galleries projected one beyond the other, where they were sunlit, they contained many royal lodges. The highest gallery contained conduits for the water which was raised by pumps in great abundance from the river, though no one could see it being done (Finkel, 1988, 43–44).

The gardens, like the nearby temple Esagila and ziggurat Etemenanki, were probably razed by Xerxes I in 482 B.C. in the midst of a local revolt against Persian rule.

Although classical writings (presumably based upon oral histories passed along prior to any written record) described the gardens, no defini-

tive proof of their existence has ever been found. In 1899 the German archeologist Robert Koldewey began an extensive excavation of the site of Babylon in southern Iraq, which lasted eighteen years. Among many other finds, Koldewey discovered an unusual series of stone foundation chambers and vaults with a remarkably engineered well. He speculated that the structure could have been the site of the Hanging Gardens. Later archeologists have challenged the theory, believing the structure was too far from both the palace and the Euphrates River. Whether the gardens did exist is still open to question, but they nonetheless remain perhaps the most famous gardens in history.

Villa of the Mysteries, Pompeii

Little is known of individual roof gardens during the reign of the Roman emperors, although roofs were commonly used as outdoor living space throughout the Mediterranean world. However, the eruption of Mount Vesuvius in A.D. 79, which encased the nearby town of Pompeii in at least 13 feet (4 m) of volcanic ash, preserved almost perfectly a building with terraces that fits within the parameters of our definition of roof gardens.

A short distance outside the northwest gate of Pompeii, on the road leading to Herculaneum, the remains of three luxurious villas have been excavated. One, the very large Villa of the Mysteries (named for paintings of Dionysian rites on its

walls) has a **U**-shaped terrace along the northern, western, and southern perimeters of the building, where plants were grown directly in soil (fig. 2-3). This terrace is supported by an arched stone colonnade on all three sides, which was used in hot weather to escape the heat (figs. 2-4 and 2-5). During the eruption of Vesuvius, this colonnade became the tomb of people desperately trying to escape the falling ash.

Careful excavations, along with restoration techniques that involve pouring plaster into the empty spaces in soil where roots had been, have led to the discovery of the types of plants used in the garden. Efforts have been made to restore the plants, as has been done in other gardens inside Pompeii's walls.

GARDENS OF THE MIDDLE AGES AND THE RENAISSANCE

Mont-Saint-Michel, France

This cone-shaped granite islet in the Gulf of Saint-Malo just off the coast of northwestern France is home to a remarkable Benedictine abbey with many buildings dating from the thirteenth century. To meet the demands of Chris-

2-5. The stone arches of this elongated chamber support the roof garden above. (Courtesy of Soprintendenza Archeologica de Pompei)

tian ecclesiastical architecture of the time, the cloister had to be enclosed, with its center open to the sky. The ever-narrowing dimensions of each succeeding floor level required the cloister, with its garden, to be located on the roof of chambers below it, atop a stone building, to provide access to sunlight (figs. 2-6 and 2-7). The builders of the abbey sought every possible opportunity for a roof garden.

Piccolomini, that contains the roof garden (fig. 2-8).

Because Pienza is built on a ridge, its terrain drops away on both sides. Hence, the outer buildings were built along the slope of the ridge, with lower floors downhill, below grade, and the main floors at street level. For his own residence the pope chose a site next to the cathedral; the rear of the building looks beyond the valley of the river Orcia to Monte Amiata in the distance. After passing through the courtyard on the main floor, beneath the handsome open arches that support the second floor above, one reaches the garden at the rear of the building, which also seems to be at ground level (fig. 2-9). It is, however, built mostly on the roof of a structure resting more than a full story below the main floor of the palace. This structure is constructed of massive stone and contains four rectangular rooms perpendicular to the rear wall of the palace. These windowless chambers, with 10- to 12-foot (3- to 3.7-m) vaulted ceilings approximately 9 feet wide by 18 feet deep (2.7 by 5.5 m), are used for artisans' shops and storage today (fig. 2-10). About two-thirds of the formal garden above rest on this masonry edifice. During the reign of Pius II, the garden was the scene of much activity, as the pope greatly enjoyed holding audiences there. Today the garden, with its well-tended boxwood parterres and central fountain, is seen only by tour groups under the watchful eye of a guide.

Tower of the Guinigis, Lucca, Italy

The first view of this fortified Renaissance tower is startling, for unlike any other in Italy, it has a small garden of four 15-foot (4.5-m) live oaks on its roof 120 feet (36.5 m) above the street! The tower, formerly known as the Benettoni Tower, was incorporated into the magnificent house built by the wealthy Guinigi family of silk merchants around 1384 (fig. 2-11). The tower is open to the public, and access to the tiny garden can be easily gained via recently installed interior stairways. There is a sweeping view of Lucca and the surrounding landscape from the roof garden. The live oaks grow in raised brick beds about 2 feet (61 cm) high and are watered by an underground sprinkler system (fig. 2-12). Although the

2-6 (top). The cloister garden at Mont-Saint-Michel, on the highest level of the monastery, rests on a chamber below.

2-7 (bottom). Gardens were installed at Mont-Saint-Michel wherever space was available. This small garden overlooks the gulf.

Palazzo Piccolomini, Pienza, Italy

The creation of one of the first and best-preserved roof gardens of the Italian Renaissance can be credited to Pope Pius II, who reigned as pope from 1458–64. An early humanist and a prolific writer, Pius II was a patron of learning and the arts. During his papacy, he endeavored to establish a summer papal center in his native village of Corsignano, fifty miles (80.5 km) south of Florence. He renamed the town Pienza and hired the noted Florentine architect Bernardo Rossellino to create a new plan for the town, as well as to design its buildings. Within three years a complete ecclesiastical center had been built. Today Pienza is almost exactly as it was in the mid-fifteenth century, with a town square surrounded by a fine cathedral, palaces for cardinals, and a campanile. It is the pope's own palace, Palazzo

date of the original installation of the tiny roof garden cannot be established, the garden does appear in a drawing of the city of Lucca dated 1660.

Medici Roof Garden, Careggi, Italy

Little is known about this Renaissance garden, built in the early fifteenth century by Cosimo de' Medici. It has fallen into ruin and is not visited by large numbers of tourists today; the villa is used as a medical facility. Its supporting structure was built into the side of a hill; the roof of that building was loaded with soil and heavily planted with imported plant materials. That the garden was built on a roof and possessed so many exotic horticultural varieties became a source of Medici pride during a time when plants were being widely imported from foreign lands to delight both gardeners and their wealthy and powerful patrons.

Tenochtitlán

Although none of the roof gardens of the great Aztec city of Tenochtitlán survived its razing by the Spanish conqueror Hernán Cortés in 1521, evidence of their existence can be found in the writings of the Spanish invaders. Indeed, references to many roof gardens in the city, which today is the site of Mexico City, can be found in the correspondence of Cortés himself. In a letter to King Charles I of Spain in 1519, he described the great island city: ". . . there are many rich citizens who also possess very fine houses. All these houses, in addition to having very fine and large dwelling rooms, have very exquisite flower gardens both on the upper apartments as well as

2-8 (top). This aerial sketch of the Palazzo Piccolomini in Pienza, Italy, illustrates how the roof garden was built atop a structure that steps down the slope of a ridge.

2-9 (middle). The roof garden of the papal palace in Pienza looks out over the valley of the river Orcia, with Monte Amiata in the distance.

2-10 (bottom). Massive stone walls on the lower level support the gardens above. Doorways provide access into the chambers below, now used as artisans' workshops.

down below. The principal houses were of two stories, but the greater number of houses were of one story only."

The nineteenth-century historian William H. Prescott, in *The History of the Conquest of Mexico* (1843), described the principal ceremonial way, with its buildings and their gardens, along which Cortés's military retinue marched to meet the Aztec emperor, Montezuma II, for the first time:

> The great avenue through which they [Cortés and his army] were now marching was lined with houses of the nobles, who were encouraged by the emperor to make the capital their residence. They were built of red porous stone drawn from quarries in the neighborhood and, though they rarely rose to a second story, often covered a large space of ground. The flat roofs, *azoteas,* were protected by stone parapets, so that every house was a platform for trees. Sometimes these roofs resembled parterres of flowers, so thickly were they covered with them, but more frequently these were cultivated in broad terraced gardens, laid out between the edifices.

The city consisted mostly of man-made islands in Lake Texcoco, limiting the availability of ground-level space for gardening. The use of sunny residential roofs was necessary because so little other land could be used. Unfortunately, when Cortés destroyed the city, nothing remained of these glorious gardens. One can only imagine how beautiful they must have been.

ROOF GARDENS FROM 1600 TO 1875

Passau, Germany

The German cardinal Johann van Lamberg constructed a parterre garden on the roof of his residence in Passau at the turn of the seventeenth century. The walls of the building on three sides were decorated with trompe l'œil paintings, with the fourth side open to the view. Grottoes were constructed with planted terraces above.

The Kremlin, Moscow, Russia

In czarist Russia, roof gardens were regarded as a great luxury by the nobility. In the seventeenth century, an extensive two-level hanging garden was installed on the roof of a Kremlin palace. The upper garden of 10 acres (4 hectares) was built on the same level as the rooms of the mansion, with two additional terraces descending almost to the

2-11 (below left). The tiny garden atop the Guinigi Tower in Lucca, Italy, is clearly visible from the street below. The garden is accessible via a stairway inside the building.

2-12 (below right). The Guinigi Tower roof garden features oaks growing in 2-foot-high (61-cm) raised brick planting beds. The rail in the foreground is part of the access stairway.

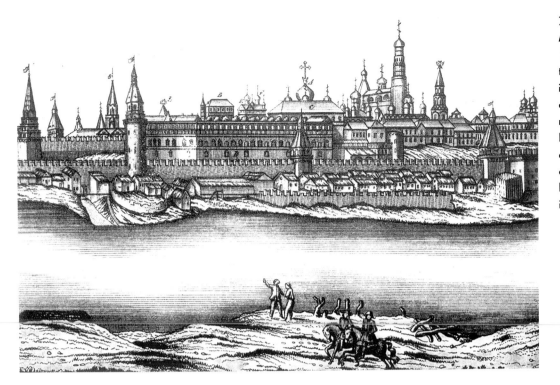

2-13. This drawing of the Moscow Kremlin, dated 1843, purportedly shows the fortress as it appeared in the late seventeenth century. The trees in the roof garden, built there by Patriarch Ioakim, can be clearly seen just below and to the left of the large building with the cross on its roof.

edge of the Moscow River. These upper and lower gardens were built on the vaults of the building. The upper garden, surrounded by a stone wall with embrasures, featured a large pond of 1,000 square feet (93 square meters) that included fountains. The pond was supplied by water lifted from the Moscow River by a device installed in the still-existing Vodovzvodnaya Tower of the Kremlin (figs. 2-13 and 2-14). The lower garden was built in 1681 on the roof of the stone building closest to the Moscow River. This 6-acre (2.4-hectare) garden also had a large pond with its own water-lifting tower and a lead-lined reservoir. As a child, the future czar of Russia Peter the

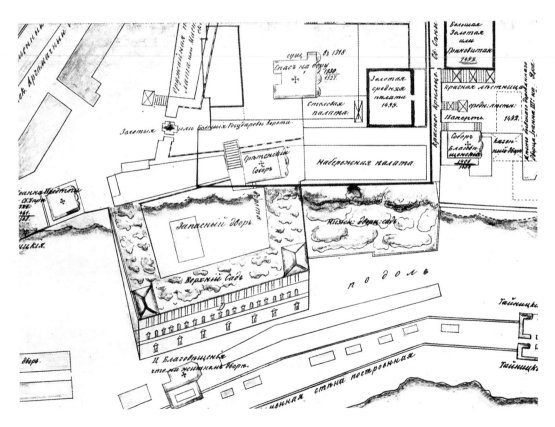

2-14. This plan of the Kremlin grounds and buildings shows the location of the garden on the roof of the palace. The Moscow River is at the bottom of the plan.

2-15 (top). The Hermitage roof garden was designed by the Russian czarina Catherine II's Italian architect, Bartolomeo Francesco Rastrelli. This view is from the opposite end of the parterre.

2-16 (bottom). From the Pavilion Hall gallery at the Hermitage, one can look out onto the fountain area of the formal parterre, which runs the full length of the garden.

Great used these ponds to keep a large fleet of toy ships. It is believed that it was here that Peter developed his love for sailing and ships.

These roof gardens used welded lead sheets as waterproofing. The upper garden, which was 400 feet long (122 m), required 10.24 tons of lead. Plants were in boxes or tubs, with a special emphasis on fruit trees, shrubs, and vines. Paintings on the interiors of the stone walls enclosing the lower garden gave the illusion of visually expanding the space. Their heavy weight required considerable reinforcing in the rooms below; props and heavy beams were used to carry the load. The original palace and its gardens were razed in 1773 to make way for a new Kremlin palace.

The Hermitage, Saint Petersburg, Russia

Catherine II of Russia (1729–96) commissioned some of the finest architects and landscape architects to design her palaces, gardens, and public buildings. The Italian architect Bartolomeo Francesco Rastrelli designed the Winter Palace in Saint Petersburg for Catherine's predecessor, the empress Elizabeth; Catherine retained Rastrelli to design the adjoining Hermitage to house her art collection when she became empress in 1764. It was on the roof of the stables of the Winter Palace, now part of the Hermitage, one of the world's great art museums, that Catherine commissioned Rastrelli to build a roof garden. The garden is in a long rectangular court surrounded by the palace walls. There are excellent views into this court from the magnificent Pavilion Hall gallery at one end and another hall gallery at the other. The garden is formal in plan, with a broad flagstone walk and an allée of small lilac trees and lawn connecting the stone paved courts at each end (fig. 2-15). All parts are embellished with statuary of classical figures. The main court, which can be entered through French doors from the Pavilion Hall gallery, is designed as a square formal parterre with four identical flower beds separated by flagstone walks. A pool and fountain serve as an axial feature for the entire garden (fig. 2-16). Four small white statues, equally spaced in each quadrant, emphasize the formal design.

No construction details or record of the garden's maintenance are available. The garden's lengthy life span, however, amply demonstrates that the system chosen and its care have been superbly successful.

Rabbitz Roof Garden, Berlin, Germany

In the late nineteenth century, Karl Rabbitz built a roof garden on a typical middle-class residence in Berlin. This was highly unusual for northern Germany, where the climate is notable for cold winters and rain year-round. Realizing the nature of roof garden problems, Rabbitz, a builder himself, used a vulcanized cement of his own patented design to seal the roof. A scale model of the design, recognized as a breakthrough in waterproofing, was exhibited at the Paris World Exposition of 1867.

The Roof Garden of King Ludwig II, Munich, Germany

King Ludwig II of Bavaria, an eccentric ruler famous for his extravagant building programs, including the famous Schloss Neuschwanstein, built a large glass-covered garden, or conservatory, on the roof of a building in Munich. It was noted for its luxuriant plantings and large pool. His builders attempted to waterproof the floor by using copper plates on stone arcading. Unfortunately, it leaked so badly that the gardens and their protective glass covering had to be demolished in 1897.

Sod Roofs

To withstand their long, cold winters, Norwegians devised methods for living under extreme conditions centuries ago. One of these methods was the sod roof, a roof covered with soil for insulation that was planted with grasses and other plants to stabilize the soil (fig. 2-17). It was necessary to devise a roof section to hold the soil in place properly and to allow good drainage to prevent the roof from rotting. With modern heating systems, this practice has practically disappeared in much of the country today, but a number of these sod roofs remain in the rural regions of Norway.

This technique was also used by the early settlers of the Great Plains in the mid- to late 1800s to great effect. With the shortage of timber on the open plains, structures were constructed of bricks of soil heavily grown with buffalo grass (often called "plains marble"). The grass provided some stability to the bricks during handling and while they settled into place. The roof slightly overhung the walls to protect them from erosion by rain. The roofs were made of growing sod, which provided insulation (fig. 2-18). The settlers, of course, did not intend these roofs to be ornamental, but some wrote to friends and relatives requesting flower seeds to plant on their

2-17 (top). Both farm buildings and homes in Norway have been roofed with sod for centuries, and the custom persists still today. Even a tree has taken root in the roof of this Norwegian house. (Photo by Gordon Osmundson)

2-18 (bottom). Sod houses like this exact reproduction in Gothenberg, Nebraska, were used by early settlers in the Dakotas and Nebraska in the middle nineteenth century. Buffalo-grass sod, called "prairie marble," was the basic building material. The roof was formed by covering a layer of saplings with overlapping shingles of sod. The plow was used to cut and lift the sod, which was then cut into 12- by 18-inch (30.5- by 45.7-cm) bricks for easier stacking.

2-19. The first theater specifically designed to use its roof for performances within a garden setting was Rudolph Aronson's Casino Theater, built in 1880. In 1882 seating and a full-size stage were added to its open-air flat roof, thus extending the theatrical season through the summer months. (Photo courtesy of the Museum of the City of New York, 29.100,885; The J. Clarence Davies Collection)

roofs. Throughout the frontier West, even some log or timber buildings, including Pony Express stations, schoolhouses, barns, and stores, had sod atop the roof. Because they served their transitory purpose dubiously well (these roofs leaked miserably when it rained), most of these structures were abandoned and replaced with the arrival of better building materials via the transcontinental railroad.

ROOF GARDENS FROM THE TURN OF THE CENTURY UNTIL WORLD WAR II

Theater Roof Gardens

Almost forgotten today is the highly successful use of rooftops for summer entertainment in major cities throughout the United States around the turn of the century. Yet the term *roof gardens* was originally coined around 1893 precisely for these spaces, and a number of theaters today recall that era in the names they still use: the Winter Garden and Madison Square Garden theaters in New York City are two such examples.

Rudolph Aronson, a New York conductor, musician, and impresario, had dreamed of a the-

ater within a garden in the heart of New York, much like those he had visited in Europe. On a visit to Paris, he concluded that the only way to overcome the high land costs of the inner city was to design the roof of a new winter theater to accommodate a summer outdoor garden theater. In 1880, after obtaining financing from wealthy patrons in New York, Aronson built the Casino Theater (named for a successful garden theater on Long Island) at Broadway and 39th Street, catercorner to the old Metropolitan Opera House (fig. 2-19). The roof garden theater was added in 1882. The Casino was the first theater designed specifically to include a stage on its roof to complement the interior theater during the summer months, thus extending the theater season to a year-round program. Aronson could now present operettas, musicals, concerts, and other entertainments in the busiest part of the theater district during the summer, rather than moving to outlying areas, where ground-level garden theaters had already been introduced. These suburban garden theaters had gradually changed to covered buildings similar to winter theaters and were a considerable distance from the city.

Like those that followed, the Casino Theater's

roof garden was used throughout the summer. It had a partial sliding-glass roof to protect the performers and the audience from rain. Aronson's year-round theater, designed in the Moorish style, was an instant success. Until 1890 the Casino Theater and its roof garden was the leading center for operetta in New York.

Aronson's successful Casino Theater was followed eight years after its opening by the original Madison Square Garden. Designed in the Italian Renaissance style by the prominent architectural firm of McKim, Mead and White, it covered an entire block between Madison and Fourth Avenues and 26th and 27th Streets. Like Aronson's theater, it had been financed by some of the city's wealthiest citizens, including the Vanderbilts and the Morgans. Its roof garden theater featured music-hall variety acts. Viewing the surrounding city was such an attraction that a renaissance-style bell tower was built at one corner of the roof garden. The 300-foot (91.5-m) observation tower was the tallest structure in New York at the time. The garden gained a dubious fame as the site of the murder of its architect, Stanford White, who was shot there by the jealous husband of one of White's lovers, Evelyn Nesbitt.

From 14th Street north past 34th Street, Broadway was the place to go on summer evenings during the 1890s. Tables for light refreshment lined the gaslit sidewalks in front of the hotels, bars, and restaurants. The theaters offered brightly lit stage entertainment, from the disreputable variety shows presented at Kostier and Bial's Music Hall, a block off Broadway, to operettas at the Casino Theater. At the peak of their popularity, nine roof garden theaters entertained audiences during the summer. Five were open to the sky, while four were predominantly glass structures, with or without sliding roofs, to allow use of the facility during rainstorms. The plantings—palms, ivy, and others in containers—were carefully positioned on the roof for maximum effect, as well as to provide plenty of room for seating and tables for the audience (fig. 2-20).

The most imaginative of these garden theaters was Oscar Hammerstein's Olympia Music Hall, built in 1895 (fig. 2-21). The roof garden was 200 feet long by 100 feet wide (30.5 m), running the full length of the block, and was completely enclosed in glass, with a 65-foot-high (19.8-m) ceiling shining with three thousand electric lights. A constant stream of water was pumped from the basement to the outer edge of the entire roof, ostensibly to cool the theater in summer, as well as to mask city noise. The interior itself featured pocket grottoes, arbors, and 10-foot-high (3-m) mountain crags. The left of the stage was designed to look like a bit of rocky mountainside, with a stream of water flowing into a simulated lake 40 feet long by 3 feet deep (12 by 1 m); live swans glided along the lake's surface. To the right of the stage was a wall painted with a mountain scene, with imitation rocks, a wooden bridge, and another pond that had ducks swimming in it. At night, under low artificial lighting, the setting seemed almost real, completely divorced from the dusty city below. On the theater's 42-foot-wide (12.8-m) stage, Hammerstein could mount the entire show from the main theater below.

After Hammerstein lost control of the Olympia, he acquired two adjacent theaters, the Victoria Music Hall (1899) and the Republic Theater (1900) at 42nd Street and Broadway. Although the Olympia had an enclosed roof garden, the Republic's adjoining roof garden was more elaborate (fig. 2-22). Its setting was

2-20. This roof garden atop the American Theater is typical of the eight that came into existence in New York City following the success of Aronson's Casino Theater. (Photo courtesy of the Museum of the City of New York, 93.1.1.10847, The Byron Collection)

designed as a Dutch farm, with a windmill, a miller's cottage with a stork's nest on one of its chimneys, a duck pond with a rustic bridge, and even two live cows!

After 1900, the Broadway scene gradually changed, and the roof garden variety shows, cabarets, and reviews no longer drew crowds. Changing times, the introduction of air conditioning, and the changing tastes of the theater-going public, especially with the introduction of motion pictures, eventually brought about the final demise of the roof garden theater in the 1920s. They eventually closed, one by one, and their buildings were demolished. Although relatively short in duration, the popularity of roof garden theaters very likely inspired the development of future roof gardens.

Residential and Hotel Roof Gardens

The theater roof garden boom in New York left some strong impressions on both entrepreneurs and residents of that city. Hotels and restaurants adopted the trend and proceeded to outdo the theaters. The Waldorf-Astoria, the Astor, and the restaurant Delmonico's, along with many lesser establishments, boasted of their dining, dancing, and refreshments atop elaborately designed roofs

featuring gardens, potted plants, formal fountains, vine-covered pergolas, tubbed palms, topiary trees, and brick or flagstone paving. As Robert H. Montgomery rhapsodized in one of the magazines of the period:

New hotels flower out in astonishing utilizations of their roofs. The restaurant al fresco, the roof café and substellar promenade spring into notoriety in exotic beauty and diversity. Italian pergolas, Venetian arbors, wisteria groves, and flowering alleys make mazes on the mansards of great hostelries. From early June until late September nightfall brings to birth a new and fairy city on hotel tops, a city of pleasure, of suave shaded lights, of tinkling fountains, of gay music, song and dancing, of luxurious food and wine.

The roof garden atop the Hotel Astor was one of the most outstanding of its time, from the early 1920s to just after World War II. The hotel, a massive pile of nine stories, with five hundred rooms, occupied a full block on the west side of Broadway, between 44th and 45th Streets. Its roof garden featured a thousand-foot-long (305-m)

2-22. The Paradise Roof on Hammerstein's Republic Theater featured a Dutch windmill, a rustic stream with a bridge, ducks, and a live cow. It was Hammerstein's third such theater. (Photo courtesy of the Museum of the City of New York, The Byron Collection)

tree-lined promenade, which was lit on summer evenings with thousands of starlike electric lights. During the 1940s, after the decline of Madison Square Garden, it featured such bands as Tommy Dorsey with Frank Sinatra and Harry James.

Wealthy New Yorkers pushed the concept even further, onto the roofs of expensive new apartment houses bordering Central Park and its environs. The best landscape architects in the city, such as Vitale & Geifert and Annette Hoyt Flanders, were engaged to design these elevated gardens. As new high-rise apartment buildings proliferated during the 1920s, penthouses with roof gardens became a status symbol for those with the means to afford them. One of these, atop a seventeen-story building built by Fred F. French and Company in 1924, is described in detail in the portfolio of historical gardens at the end of this chapter.

Frank Lloyd Wright and Le Corbusier

Although their architectural philosophies were radically different, two of the most influential architects of the twentieth century, Frank Lloyd Wright and Le Corbusier, both designed buildings that incorporated rooftops as functional space. Wright included roof areas as extensions of the interior function; his designs were not true gardens, although minimal planting was incidentally included. His Midway Gardens, built in Chicago in 1914, made use of the roof as an outdoor sitting terrace for summer use. Unfortunately, the Midway Gardens, which opened to wide acceptance and acclaim, met with financial difficulty because of Prohibition in 1918 and was closed and demolished in 1923. Wright's Larkin Building (built in 1904, demolished in 1950) in Buffalo, New York, included a terrace on the roof intended as an extension of the lunchroom adjacent to it. His Imperial Hotel in Tokyo (completed in 1922, demolished in 1967) also included roof terraces as garden areas.

Charles-Edouard Jeanneret, known as Le Corbusier, the Swiss architect and design philosopher, strongly embraced the use of roofs as living areas. Indeed, he included roof terraces as one of the elements of his five tenets of modern architecture. Although his focus on the roof was an integral part of his architectural philosophy, he did not go so far as to recommend that the roof deck be planted as a garden; rather, he considered the roof to be an exterior room, a place to be within and to look without. The roof of his famous Villa Savoye (1928–31), just outside of Paris in Poussy, France, is a space surrounded by the sky, with views of the countryside and, through the glazed windows, of the spaces within as well. Sigfried Giedion, in his book *Space, Time and Architecture* (1941) described the intent of this space: "The city dweller for whom it was designed wanted to look out over the countryside rather than be set down among the trees and shrubbery. He wanted to enjoy the view, the breezes, and the sun—to experience that unhurried natural freedom which his work deprived him of." An examination of the roof deck of Villa Savoye reveals built-in raised planters for permanent greenery on the roof.

Other buildings that demonstrate Corbusier's use of roofs include the Domino houses (1914–15), the Pessac workers' housing estate (1926), the Unité d'Habitation apartments in Marseilles (1946–52), and his government buildings for Chandigarh, in Punjab, India (1952–56). However, he never took the types or arrangement of plant materials very seriously.

While Le Corbusier was acting as a consultant to Lúcio Costa in the design of International-style structures in Brazil in the 1930s, the landscape architect Roberto Burle Marx was engaged to design two roof gardens for Costa's Ministry of Education building in Rio de Janeiro in 1938 and the Brazilian Press Association building in 1940, along with others.

PIONEERING ROOF GARDENS OF THE PRE-WAR ERA

Two gardens built before World War II have inspired numerous roof garden designers over the years and continue to do so today. The Derry and Toms garden in the Kensington section of London and the gardens atop the roofs of Rockefeller Center in New York were both built in the 1930s; the portfolio of historical gardens at the end of this chapter tells their stories.

A third garden, actually completed while the war was being fought, has been equally influential. Union Square in San Francisco was originally created in 1850 during the Gold Rush, when John Geary, the city's first mayor, donated land for the square to the city, for a public park. It

remained undeveloped for a time, a place of wind-swept sand dunes, used for dumping, and sandlot baseball and frequented by prostitutes and squatters. During the Civil War, it served as a rallying place for pro-Union groups and acquired the name Union Square in the process. It remained largely undeveloped, gradually acquiring lawn, palms, Norfolk Island pines, and other exotic plant material by the 1870s. At the turn of the century, it boasted several churches around its perimeter, including the Calvary Presbyterian Church, which would be shortly replaced by the Saint Francis Hotel. In 1903 President Theodore Roosevelt visited the city to dedicate the 97-foot-high (30-m) Dewey Monument in the center of the square, which commemorates the defeat of the Spanish fleet in Manila Bay during the Spanish-American War. The monument still stands today.

The present square, designed by Timothy Pflueger, is a park atop a 1,700-space parking garage. Completed in 1942, it was the world's first roof garden atop an underground garage. The surrounding buildings came to house San Francisco's upscale shopping district, making the square the center of the city's successful downtown (see fig. 1-6).

In recent years, after receiving complaints about the square's rundown appearance, the city government, civic planning organizations, and neighboring building owners unified to sponsor an international competition to redesign Union Square. The competition drew over two hundred entries. The winners, the design team of April Philips ASLA and Michael Fotheringham ASLA, have begun working drawings for the new plaza (fig. 2-23). Construction of the new design is expected to begin in the year 2000.

ROOF GARDENS AFTER WORLD WAR II

Although the roof gardens of the pre-war period had a large impact at the time, the Depression of the 1930s followed by the Second World War, which lasted until 1945, virtually halted large-scale public building construction until the 1950s. By this time, a relatively small and new generation of architects and landscape architects

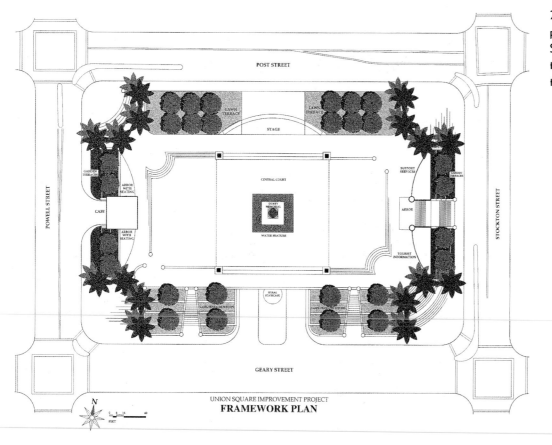

were coming up who were not only unconscious of the possibilities and advantages of roof gardens but were turning their attention to the design and development of new housing and small-scale commercial structures. Not until the late 1950s and early 1960s were new large-scale public and private roof gardens designed and built. This period saw the construction of the roof gardens at Kaiser Center and at the Oakland Museum in Oakland, at Saint Mary's Square and at Portsmouth Square in San Francisco, at Mellon Square and at Equitable Plaza in Pittsburgh, at Constitution Plaza in Hartford, and at Harvey's Department Store in Guildford, Surrey, England, by Sir Geoffrey Jellicoe.

This period has continued into the present. Many fine and extensive roof gardens have been built, though their number is relatively small if one considers the number of buildings that could accommodate them. The move to landscaped campus-style office complexes in the suburbs may have diverted interest from the downtown areas. Office buildings in the business cores of our cities, where access to the greatest conveniences and cultural facilities already exist, could have been designed to include outdoor roof gardens with amenities for employees. Apparently, such development has not been considered a viable option by many developers or corporate owners, and planted rooftops are still a rarity in the central downtown areas of our cities. That must change, or our cities will continue to become more crowded, sterile, and unattractive places to live and work.

A WALK THROUGH THE PAST
A PORTFOLIO OF HISTORICAL ROOF GARDENS

DERRY AND TOMS ROOF GARDEN
LONDON, GREAT BRITAIN

LANDSCAPE ARCHITECT: Ralph Hancock
ARCHITECT: B. George
CLIENT: Derry and Toms Department Store

The Derry and Toms garden, sometimes called simply the "Derry Garden," is located in London at the intersection of Kensington High Street and Derry Street, 100 feet (30.5 m) above the street on the roof of a six-story former department store. It is accessible by elevator from Derry Street. One of the most famous roof gardens of modern times, the Derry and Toms garden opened in 1938. After its opening to the public, each spring, when the garden was in perfect condition to receive guests, it became the setting for very social events, including charitable functions hosted by nobility and royalty. In 1978 the department store went out of business, and the garden went into decline. The building now has new occupants, and the garden has been successfully restored by the owners of the restaurant and night club on the roof.

In the original garden, more than five hundred different varieties of trees and shrubs were planted, including apple, ash, cherry, fig, horse chestnut, maple, mulberry, palm, poplar, sycamore, walnut, willow, and yew. Age, drought, and poor maintenance have taken their toll, so that the garden has far fewer plantings today and the planting has been simplified, though it does not seem underplanted. When the building was renovated, most of the dead or diseased trees were replaced with new specimens raised to the roof by crane. The remaining original trees, after sixty years, are mature, and much of the shrub planting is large and well tended, giving the garden the appearance of being in natural soil at ground level.

The 1-acre (0.4-hectare) garden is divided into three principal areas: the English Woodland Garden, on the upper side of the T-shaped main building on the roof; the Tudor Garden, occupy-

The Moorish pool and fountain in the Spanish Garden.

ing the right side of the T, and the Spanish Garden, on the left side of the T. In the original design, the English Woodland Garden was at the roof level, slightly below a large south-facing paved terrace. Comparison of the original plan with the present one indicates that this garden has been greatly changed to make room for additional elevators and an extension of the building into the terrace area.

A load-bearing capacity of 250 pounds per square foot (psf), or 1,220 kilograms per square meter, increasing to 500 psf (2,441 kg per square meter) in the deeper areas, was designed as part of the roof's structure by the architect, who knew it would have to support the roof garden. At the time of construction, contemporary horticultural standards called for deep soil to support trees and shrubs on a roof. Although it is now known

The Tudor Garden is a quiet space enclosed by fences and large shrubs and trees.

A view into the Tudor Garden from its entrance. The fountain was added more recently.

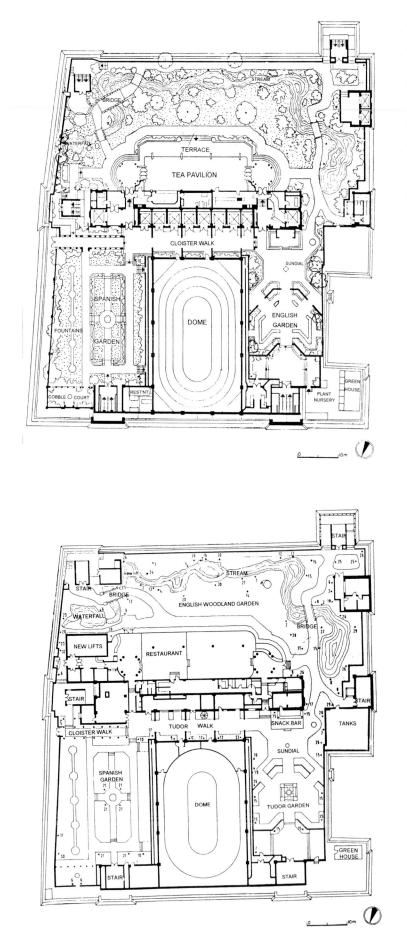

that plants can be successfully grown in far less soil, it is obvious that, if the roof is designed to carry the load, such a depth is close to ideal. Such depth not only provides better anchorage and a better growing medium for trees, but it also avoids problems that result when large roots are grown in more shallow soils.

The technical aspects of the garden also differ considerably from modern-day practice. Starting at the waterproofing level, the cross section consists of a layer of bricks spaced 1 inch (2.5 cm) apart, a 6-inch (15-cm) layer of clinkers for drainage, and 3 inches (7.5 cm) of breeze (the residue from the making of coke or charcoal), used as a filter layer to prevent the soil from silting into and blocking the drainage layer. Atop this drainage layer is 20 inches (50 cm) of topsoil, to which no humus was added, and then 2 to 3 feet (61 to 91 cm) of topsoil enriched with peat and manure. The total depth from the waterproofing at the bottom to the top of the planting medium is 4½ to 5½ feet (1.4 to 1.7 m), although some areas are as thin as 2½ feet (76 cm). Recent investigations have revealed that, although the breeze has mixed thoroughly with the clinkers, the drainage layer and mastic asphalt waterproofing still function and are in good condition after sixty years. Roots have not penetrated the drainage layer.

Although the garden has been restored and is now in use once again, permanent maintenance has been discontinued and the grounds are being tended by contract labor. Their services generally consist of watering by hand (unfortunately, an irrigation system was not included in the renovations), lawn mowing, weeding, and general cleanup. No longer performed is root pruning, which was once done every three to eight years, to restrict growth and prevent damage from root penetration beneath walls, walks, steps, drainlines, and other elements. In addition, the large numbers of bedding plants that were once planted each spring for the annual reopening of the

Top: Plan of the original Derry and Toms garden (Courtesy *The Architects' Journal*)

Bottom: Plan of the restored Derry and Toms garden (Courtesy *The Architects' Journal*)

garden to the public have been replaced by less costly lawns. Restoration of lost planting medium, due to the decay of humus in the soil and resultant seepage into the drainage system, has also been discontinued. Neglect of this task will likely result in a much poorer soil and in slumping from the elevations originally intended, which will be particularly noticeable near such structures as walks and walls.

Nonetheless, during renovation of the roof, repairs to the flashing were successfully made around the roof's periphery, and much of the garden has been restored to its original condition. Fortunately, this historic roof garden, the first of such size in modern times, can still give pleasure to visitors and will do so for many years to come.

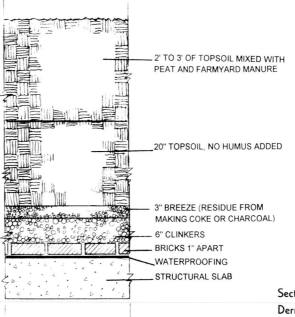

2' TO 3' OF TOPSOIL MIXED WITH PEAT AND FARMYARD MANURE

20" TOPSOIL, NO HUMUS ADDED

3" BREEZE (RESIDUE FROM MAKING COKE OR CHARCOAL)
6" CLINKERS
BRICKS 1" APART
WATERPROOFING
STRUCTURAL SLAB

Section through the Derry and Toms garden (Courtesy *The Architects' Journal*)

The English Woodland Garden has been encroached upon by the addition of a restaurant and night club, which replaced the original tea pavilion on the south side.

ROCKEFELLER CENTER

NEW YORK, NEW YORK

LANDSCAPE ARCHITECT: Ralph Hancock and A. M. Vanden Hock
ARCHITECT: Reinhardt and Hofmeister; Corbett, Harrison and MacMurray;
Hood and Fouilhoux
CLIENT: Rockefeller Center

The first major and certainly the most famous rooftop gardens in the United States were the five installed on the roofs of Rockefeller Center in New York City between 1933 and 1936. The initial concept for these gardens, which were unique at the time, came from Raymond Hood, one of the most forward-looking architects for the new office center. Appalled at the ugliness and disorder of the hundreds of neighboring roofs that would be visible from the center's office windows, he determined that higher rent could be charged for views of gardens and proposed that the lower roofs be designed and planted as foreground "viewscapes." He envisioned a series of gardens connected by aerial bridges across streets, but his death in 1934 and the deep economic depression at the time cut short the fulfill-

ment of his vision. Nevertheless, the idea of gardens prevailed, and four gardens atop four buildings along Fifth Avenue and another on the RCA Building were completed by 1936.

The first two gardens, for the Maison Française and the British Empire Building, were designed by Ralph Hancock, a fellow of the Royal Horticultural Society and designer of the Derry and Toms roof garden in London. They feature central parterres of lawn framed by trimmed hedges of privet, along with fountains in 6- by 12-foot (1.8- by 3.7-m) ponds. These ponds are only 2 inches (5.1 cm) deep. The first gardens were completed on March 31, 1934.

The more elaborate gardens of the other two towers along Fifth Avenue, on the seventh-floor roofs of the Palazzo d'Italia and the Internation-

The four restored roof gardens along Fifth Avenue, looking west, with the spires of Saint Patrick's Cathedral on the left. From right to left: the International Building North, the Palazzo d'Italia, the British Empire Building, and La Maison Française. (Courtesy David Murbach)

al Building North, were designed in 1936 by A. M. Vanden Hock, chief horticulturist for the Rockefeller Center. These Mediterranean-style gardens, each 229 feet long by 52 feet wide (70 by 15.8 m), originally had long central areas of lawn framed by undulating trimmed hedges and accented by sheared shrubs in large terra-cotta pots. At one end of the Palazzo d'Italia garden are two sculptures of mythical beings by Paul Manship, the sculptor of the famous golden figure of Prometheus in the plaza below.

A fifth roof, atop the tenth floor of the RCA Building, contained a collection of gardens illustrating different garden-design styles. Designed by Ralph Hancock and built in 1934, this group, called the Gardens of the Nations, featured gardens with Spanish, Japanese, Dutch, French, and Italian themes, a vegetable garden, and a modern garden. This last had a central area with zigzagged raised beds for flowers. The gardens on the RCA Building, open to visitors for a fee, were no longer profitable by 1938 and were removed. All that remains today on this roof is a general garden area of about ¾ acre (0.3 hectare).

The designers of these roof gardens faced the same challenges that roof garden designers confront today, including problems with drainage, irrigation, shelter from wind and sun, city soot, and snow. The drainage system consists of 4-inch (10-cm) agricultural tile, laid 20 feet (6.1 m) apart on the roofs, connected to 8-inch (20-cm)

Close-up views of the gardens of La Maison Française (above) and the Palazzo d'Italia (left). (Courtesy David Murbach)

Left: This early rendering by the architects clearly indicates the intention to cover all roofs, including those protecting underground facilities. Notice the proposed bridges, connecting the buildings' roofs. (Illustration © The Rockefeller Group 1996)

Right: This early perspective rendering of the entire project illustrates how ambitious the original design was. Much of the roof development shown here was never installed. Four of the final five gardens are in the foreground, along Fifth Avenue. (Illustration © The Rockefeller Group 1996)

roof drain outlets. The drainpipes were covered with a 4-inch (10-cm) layer of coarse cinders to provide a continuous drainage layer between the pipes. A 4-inch (10-cm) layer of crushed stones and pebbles was placed above the cinders to prevent the silting and loss of any of the 1 foot (30 cm) or more of rich surface topsoil through the drainage cinders and drainpipes. Although different in detail, the cross section of the soil and drainage system is similar in purpose to that used in present-day roof gardens.

The construction and planting of the five gardens required the lifting of hundreds of tons of cinders, over a mile of drain tile, and 3,000 tons of topsoil in the service elevators. Brick windbreak walls 6 to 10 feet (1.8 to 3 m) high and garden walks required 100,000 bricks and 500 tons of concrete and mortar. Most of the material had to be transferred from trucks to wheelbarrows, placed in the building's service elevators, and raised to the roof, where it was again transferred to wheelbarrows, trundled by hand out onto the roof, and dumped by hand. Two thousand trees

and shrubs were placed on the roof in the same way. Fifty-foot (15.2-m) Scotch pines weighing 3 tons each would not fit into the elevators and had to be hoisted by triple block-and-tackle 140 feet (43 m) to the roofs, where they were taken over the parapets to their final locations.

Over time, most of the construction and plant material deteriorated: lawns were replaced by ground covers; stone, concrete, and brick walls and walks loosened, settled, or tumbled because of heaving during winter freeze/thaw cycles; pools cracked; and plants long past their prime were not replaced. All this conveyed a general feeling of neglect throughout. Management in recent years has taken a much greater interest in the gardens and has made an admirable effort to restore them in a slow but systematic way. With so much neglect, restoration has been a costly, long-term process. But the mere existence of these restored prestigious gardens will have a dynamic effect not only on Rockefeller Center but on future projects in the United States and around the world.

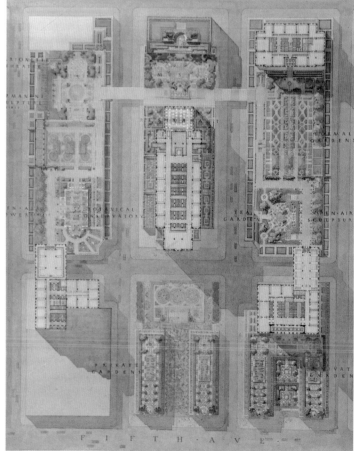

BARBARA HUBSHMAN ROOF GARDEN

NEW YORK, NEW YORK

LANDSCAPE ARCHITECT: Theodore Osmundson and Associates
ARCHITECT: Fred F. French Company
CLIENT: Barbara Hubshman

A penthouse garden has existed on this aerial site since the apartment building was built in 1924. Situated on Fifth Avenue directly across the street from the Metropolitan Museum of Art, the roof has a fine 180-degree view of Central Park to the west. The French family, which owned the firm that designed and built the building, resided in the penthouse soon after the building was constructed. The architect's wife, Cordelia W. French, in the November 1927 company publication *The Voice*, wrote:

> It was our privilege to fall heir to the ready-made variety [of roof garden]. Along with our apartment . . . , we rented a garden, one hundred thirty-five feet above the sidewalk. The garden soil, being nearly three feet deep, comes up to the sills of the living-room windows while stone steps lead up from the living-room door to the gar-

den walk rather than down in the usual way. From both door and windows one may gaze upon a suburban scene, grass lawns, flowers, shrubs, trees and a sprinkling of butterflies.

Above: The area of the garden path on the Central Park side before the garden was replaced.

Left: After restoration, the former garden path on the park side of the L can now accommodate a larger garden party or more outdoor lounge furniture.

Mrs. French described her family's use of the garden for children's play (including the building of snowmen in winter), gardening, and her husband's handball games. She also touched upon the concerns of others regarding the presumed danger of the weight of the soil collapsing the roof structure:

Nearly forty tons of steel were added to the skeleton of the building at the time of construction to avert . . . catastrophe. Copper flashings protect the outside wall of the roof apartment from the dampness of the garden earth. A drainage system of copper leaders and endless iron pipes, conducts the excess rain and melted snow down between other peoples' living-rooms, bedrooms, and closets to the distant sewer.

In addition, a concrete slab was poured over the waterproofing to protect it from damage. Moreover, both sides of the garden were enclosed by glass windscreens 10 feet (3 m) high. Obviously the designers of the building and garden knew a great deal about roof garden construction and design.

The building is now a cooperative apartment house, and the penthouse and garden are owned by an avid gardener. Although a great deal of care was given to the garden, leaks appeared in the ceiling of one of the apartments on the far side of the building in the late 1970s, and the garden was completely removed by court order in 1983–84. After lengthy examinations of the structure, roofing, and drainage by engineers during the course of litigation, it was decided that the roof garden could be restored following extensive repairs. Restoration of the garden was to include sealing of the building's parapets and windows, along

Above: The garden area, looking toward the park, after the former roof garden was removed.

Right: After restoration, looking toward the entrance to the living room.

Although the layout and design of the Hubshman garden underwent minimal changes when the garden was restored, more important alterations were made in unseen parts of the space. With allowable dead-load limits of 400 pounds per square foot or 1,953 kilograms per square meter (very high for a residential building, thanks to the French Company's foresight), loading was nonetheless kept to under 120 pounds per square foot (586 kg per square meter) . This small load is attributable to the use of a light but structurally sound soil mix, a hollow plastic drainage layer (Grass-Cel), and a varying subfill depth of expanded plastic sheets (Geotech), as outlined below in two of the most important sections.

Weight of Deepest Section, 18 Inches (45.7 cm) of Soil Mix	psf	Weight of Soil and Drainage Section for Main Patio	psf
Saturated soil mix, 18" deep @ 76.42 psf	114.63	Brick, 2⅜"	11.66
		Sand leveling course, ½" to 1"	10.00
Geotech drainage layer, 2" thick	0.33	Planting soil, 5" to 6"	38.21
Grass-Cel drainage layer	2.00	Grass-Cel, 2"	1.00
Protection board, ¼"	1.80	Geotech filler, 1' x 1' x 1'	1.00
Total Weight	**118.76**	Protection board, ¼"	1.80
		Total Weight	**63.67**

These weights, exceptionally low for a roof capable of carrying 400 pounds per square foot of dead load, were formulated to provide extra proof to the court that the restored roof garden would not cause any future excess weight problems. With the roof's wide safety factor of 281.24 pounds (1,367 kg)—71 percent of its load limit—the court had to agree that excess weight would not be a problem.

with the installation of a new elastomeric water-proofing membrane and flashing for further insurance against leaks. Also, the garden had to be restored in accordance with the plans and details of the landscape architect. All of this was done in 1987. The court did not rule that the garden had caused the leaks.

Following the desires of the owner, the design is similar in overall effect to the one that had existed before the garden's removal, with a few notable exceptions. First, the level of the main patio or terrace was lowered to the living-room doorsill level, thus eliminating the necessity of stepping over a high sill from the living room and walking up three risers on the outside to reach the terrace. Two risers were added inside the living room to reach the terrace level. Second, two additional sitting areas were added, one at the corner of the garden overlooking Central Park and the other along the Fifth Avenue side of the penthouse, also overlooking the park. Finally, a 4-foot-high (1.2-m) glass windbreak was added to

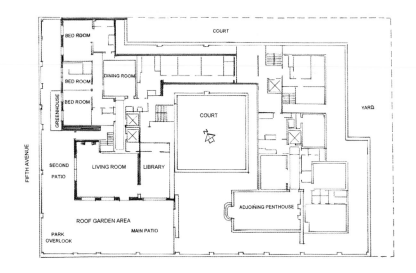

the top of the brick parapet walls to provide protection from wind while maintaining views. All planting has been restored, and an automatic irrigation system was installed. The restored garden now has over ten years of growth and excellent maintenance. It is a very enjoyable space to experience in the heart of New York City.

Plan of the original seventeenth floor of the building on Fifth Avenue by the Fred F. French Company.

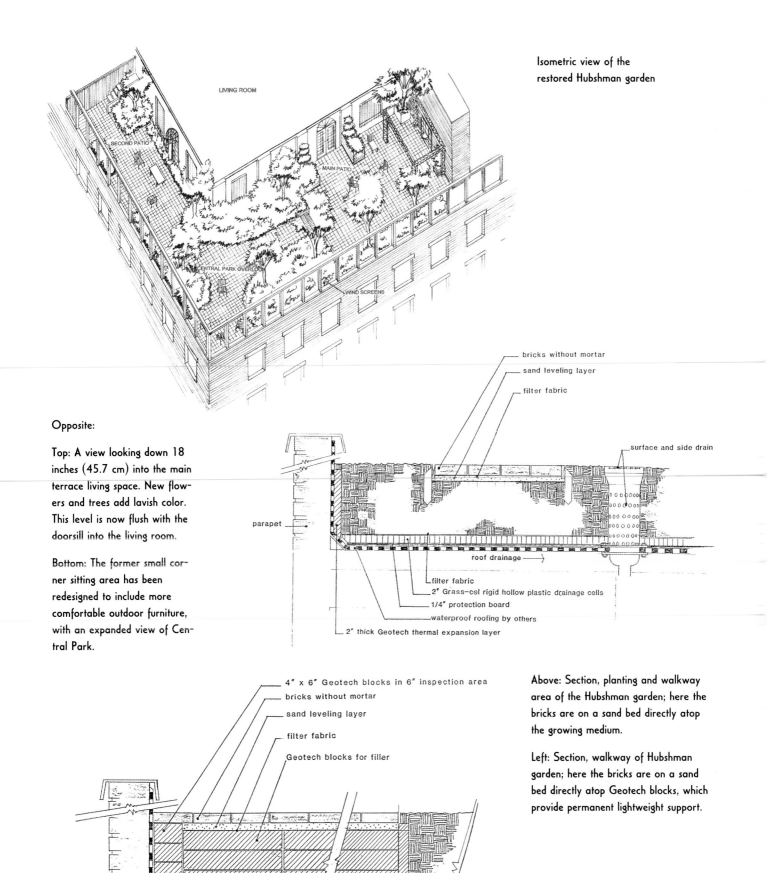

Isometric view of the restored Hubshman garden

LIVING ROOM

SECOND PATIO

MAIN PATIO

CENTRAL PARK OVERLOOK

WIND SCREENS

Opposite:

Top: A view looking down 18 inches (45.7 cm) into the main terrace living space. New flowers and trees add lavish color. This level is now flush with the doorsill into the living room.

Bottom: The former small corner sitting area has been redesigned to include more comfortable outdoor furniture, with an expanded view of Central Park.

bricks without mortar
sand leveling layer
filter fabric
surface and side drain
parapet
roof drainage →
filter fabric
2″ Grass-cel rigid hollow plastic drainage cells
1/4″ protection board
waterproof roofing by others
2″ thick Geotech thermal expansion layer

4″ x 6″ Geotech blocks in 6″ inspection area
bricks without mortar
sand leveling layer
filter fabric
Geotech blocks for filler

Above: Section, planting and walkway area of the Hubshman garden; here the bricks are on a sand bed directly atop the growing medium.

Left: Section, walkway of Hubshman garden; here the bricks are on a sand bed directly atop Geotech blocks, which provide permanent lightweight support.

parapet
filter fabric
ss-cel rigid drainage layer
waterproof roofing

CHAPTER THREE

SITE CONSIDERATIONS

s with any architectural project, a roof
garden's site plays a key role in its success or failure. Siting considerations can
be complicated in landscape architecture,
because a project's users—people—are not the
same as its inhabitants—plants; and the needs of
both must be met for any landscape design to
function effectively. A good site will be inviting to
people and nurturing for plants, whereas a poor
site will discourage visitors, require increased
maintenance for plantings (if they can survive at
all), or both. Roof gardens complicate matters
further, for all the site requirements of landscape
design must be met in an environment that is not
natural for living plants.

Moreover, landscape architects working on
roof gardens have little control over the choice of
site. At best, the garden is included as part of a
new building, but its location may well have been
determined by the client and the architect before
the landscape architect has even been consulted.
Just as often, the garden must be retrofitted onto
an existing building, which may limit options
regarding loads, size, view, climate, access, and
other issues.

Fortunately, the site is only one component in
determining the quality of a roof garden. A skillful landscape architect can mitigate the flaws of a
less-than-optimal site by incorporating design
features that enhance the site's strong points and
minimize its weaknesses. Of course, to accomplish this feat, the designer must first recognize
the strengths and flaws of the site. This chapter
highlights the most common site considerations
a landscape architect confronts when designing a
roof garden.

THE GARDEN'S FUNCTIONS

Although the questions of who will use the garden and how it will be used affect design choices
more than site considerations, they nonetheless
play a role in determining how appropriate a site
is and how its features may be handled.

The first consideration is whether the garden
will be accessible to people or not. A garden that
is intended only for viewing from without—
through adjacent windows or from the heights of
neighboring buildings, for example—imposes
fewer restrictions on site and design because only
the welfare of the plantings requires consideration. Concerns about access, safety, loads, circulation, and climate are only important as they
affect the care and maintenance of the garden
itself. Such a garden is more easily adaptable to a
wide range of sites and lends itself to more heavily planted designs, as well as more delicate garden features, such as sand gardens and gravel
paving, which would require extraordinary
maintenance if access to the garden was not
restricted (figs. 3-1, 3-2, and 3-3).

Conversely, a site that is intended to be experienced directly by people must accommodate
the needs of those people, as well as the needs of
the landscape. The degree of use can vary,
depending on whether the garden is public or
private. The site of a public garden, open to all,
should be easily accessible, accommodating a
wide range of users, from children to the elderly,
including strollers and wheelchairs (fig. 3-4).
Extra safety features may be necessary to prevent
injury, particularly when the garden is not at
ground level. Protection from crime is another

3-1 (top left). This roof garden with bubble skylights over Kolomyagi Airport's ticket counters in Saint Petersburg, Russia, gains interest with granite sets, concrete borders, and plantings. In an enclosed court open to the sky, it can be viewed from a dining hall and adjacent offices but is not accessible except for maintenance.

3-2 (top right). This japanesque sand garden is part of the roof gardens at the Federal Reserve Bank in Boston. Unlike the remainder of the gardens, which are open to employees and visitors, this space can only be viewed from the adjacent walkway through the cafeteria windows at right. The coarse sand has been raked into a design recalling the rippling of water, echoing the view of Boston's harbor from the open area of the gardens.

3-3 (bottom left). Because of severe load limits, the roof gardens atop the Westin Saint Francis Hotel in San Francisco can be accessed only for maintenance. The garden nonetheless provides an attractive view from adjacent rooms, as shown here, far superior to the messy mechanical structures, vents, and pipes that once cluttered the space.

3-4 (bottom right). A model of public access, the Yerba Buena Gardens in San Francisco feature wide patterned walkways, a ramp leading to upper-level restaurants, and plenty of seating.

3-5. Early roof garden above an office building in San Francisco.

group, may require the same considerations as a public garden does or may have almost as many options as a closed garden, depending on the size of the group and the nature of the intended use. A roof garden that is to serve all the employees of a large corporation has much different needs than that of an apartment penthouse. Key to both, however, is access. A private roof garden must limit access to the public at large while at the same time encouraging visits by the targeted group of users. It is this type of garden that may be most ideally suited to the traditional notion of a roof garden as a "garden in the sky." Elevation naturally restricts access while allowing the building's occupants to use the space (fig. 3-5). Another consideration in such a space is separation of uses: a private garden is usually attached to a building whose primary purpose is not recreation. The garden should be located in such a way that it does not interfere with the main activities of the site, be they business-related, as in an office space, or rest, as in a hotel. Noise, in particular, should be considered.

CLIMATE AND MICROCLIMATE

Climate and exposure can be prime contributing factors in the success or failure of any outdoor space for human use and enjoyment. The climate in the United States is largely temperate, but regional variations are significant. The Northeast, with its cold winters and hot summers, contrasts sharply with the generally mild year-round climate of southern California, and both are unlike the rainy Northwest and the hot and dry Southwest. In short, widely different regional climates affect the design of usable landscapes, including roof gardens. In the contiguous United States, however, nowhere is there weather so consistently inclement as to make roof gardens unusable; all regions experience enough seasonally good weather to allow the enjoyment of roof gardens.

In addition to regional differences, each site has its own microclimate—climate conditions specific to that site, caused by its particular location—that the landscape architect must recognize. Examples abound in which unrestricted high winds, cold drafts, scorching sunshine, or

consideration in a public garden, where both visitors and the garden itself can be easy targets. A site that encourages heavy use and provides an open view of the entire space, with few hiding places behind which criminals could lurk, will help prevent both vandalism and crimes against others. To encourage frequent usage, the comfort level of the garden must be high. Care must be taken to reduce climate factors that discourage visitors. The space must be large enough to allow for easy circulation and seating. The structure on which it rests must be strong enough to carry the weight of large groups of visitors. Because heavy usage will lead to more maintenance, the site should allow easy access for equipment, including storage space if at all possible.

The site of a private garden, intended for the use of a specified group of people, be they employees, residents, hotel guests, or some other chilling shade have made outdoor areas so uncomfortable as to be virtually unusable. In elevated roof gardens, these effects are often greatly magnified because of the space's height above the ground. The conditions can be greatly mitigated by carefully placed plantings, windscreens, and other design elements. Of course, if the garden is to be built atop an as-yet undesigned new building, the more severe effects of microclimate can be ameliorated by the design and orientation of the building itself.

Sunlight

Although the heat and glare generated by the sun can make a roof garden quite uncomfortable, it is preferable to site a roof garden in the sun, using design features in the garden itself to mitigate the sun's effects. (Although little can be done to prevent adjacent buildings from being built close enough to existing roof gardens to block their sunlight and views, in the design of new buildings, it may be possible to design the roof garden at a higher elevation so that fewer existing or future adjacent buildings will be so high as to obstruct the sun.) Ideally, a roof deck should be located so that it is flooded with sunlight from the east, south, and west whenever possible. A northern exposure may be a relief on a very hot day, but it more often will be cold, damp, and gloomy, with its colors muted, and little can be done to improve the situation. In most latitudes in the temperate zones, the sun shines on the northern side of buildings only during the longest days of the year at the beginning of summer, and even then for only a few hours. Except for the hottest areas of the Southeast and Southwest, where glare and heat from day-long solar exposure is especially forbidding, the north side of the building is the least desirable. Even in such hot climates, orientation toward the east is still usually the best exposure for a roof garden, allowing the roof to receive sunlight as late as the noon hour, with cooling shade from the south and west in the afternoon and evening.

Except for the confirmed sun worshiper or suntan enthusiast, few people prefer to be in the sun on a hot day for more than a few minutes. An extreme example of the adverse effects of a relentlessly open exposure could be seen at Con-

vention Center Plaza in Phoenix, Arizona. Built at ground level on the roof of an underground parking structure, it received very little shade at any time of the day from trees or shade structures. The entire area was exceedingly uncomfortable because of heat and glare. Fortunately, the plaza was recently redesigned. Although this is an extreme case, it points to the need for a very careful evaluation of the effects of sun and shade on proposed roof gardens.

Shady relief, usually found under trees, may be at a premium where trees do not spread widely and provide a canopy or at least an umbrella of dappled shade (fig. 3-6). Trees should be located where they will cast shade across sitting areas during high-use periods of the day. To supplement shade from trees, pergolas planted with vines can be constructed; shade structures of various designs are another option (fig. 3-7). Still another solution is to provide outdoor furniture with umbrellas for shade. These are now available in durable colorfast plastic and require little care other than lowering and tying the canopy to the pole in high winds. (See chapter 5 for more about shading options.)

Glare can be a problem even in spaces where heat is almost never an issue. Glare is usually a

3-6. Welcome relief from the sun's heat and glare is provided by shade from zelkova trees in this plaza atop the underground portion of the Shinjuku Nomura Building in Tokyo.

3-7. A shade structure like this one at the East Bay Municipal Utility District office building in Oakland, California, can shield people from the sun, provide additional seating, and serve as the focal point in the design of a roof garden.

concomitant of sunlight, and it is often a concern in spaces containing or adjoining reflective materials: the skins of neighboring buildings can be major culprits, as can snow cover. Glare is not relieved by immediate shade in the area of the user, and rooftops are seldom planted so closely with trees as to eliminate glare. Glare reduction can, however, be achieved by using lawns, ground covers, and shrubs, as well as dark, light-absorbing paving materials, such as brick, flagstone, or dark-colored concrete. These common garden elements absorb sunlight and so can counteract the effects of nearby reflective surfaces.

Wind

Wind can also be a source of discomfort on a roof. While mild breezes can greatly increase the comfort of outdoor areas in the warm months, a battering wind can be as annoying and uncomfortable as too much heat or cold. Most sites, even elevated sites, have enough intermittent windless periods to make roof gardens feasible, but some seem never to be without a blast of moving air. Those spaces that do have some periods of calm are well worth the extra analysis and design necessary to construct protected areas

where the roof garden can be enjoyed even on occasional days when wind seems to be uncontrollable. In a space subject to constant high winds, however, the problem is often impossible to solve, and such areas should be abandoned as useful outdoor space for people. Such areas can, however, be designed as gardens to be enjoyed from inside a building, from other points outside of the roof, or from adjacent buildings.

Even roof gardens with restricted access, however, require attention to windy conditions, because winds can also have a damaging effect on plantings. Research into wind-resistant plants is necessary for blustery sites; local nursery people can be very useful sources of wind-resistant plants and should be consulted before a planting plan is prepared. In addition to plantings, attention must be paid to lightweight objects, such as tables, chairs, umbrellas, and awnings, which can be blown about and cause significant damage. Elevated gardens, which are often above the level of protective windbreaks, are even more vulnerable to this danger than gardens at ground level are. In spaces subject to continuously windy conditions, the best protection is to avoid the inclusion of any nonstationary features. In gardens subject only occasionally to high winds, constant vigilance is the best solution. Potential missiles should be moved out of harm's way temporarily until the wind abates.

Although some areas, such as seacoasts and mountains, are naturally subject to constant strong winds, in urban areas, man-made structures often exaggerate the slightest breeze. The volume and velocity of a prevailing wind blowing against the flat side of a high-rise buildings can increase at the building's ends to gale force (fig. 3-8). Landscape architects must recognize the potential of this situation occurring at the roof garden level and include measures to alleviate it in their designs.

Strong winds can be mitigated to some degree in roof gardens just as they can be in ground-level gardens. Windscreens and windbreaks are commonly used to divert or obstruct winds. These can take a variety of forms, depending on the materials used. For example, the roof garden on the New England Merchants National Bank in Boston has a 7-foot-high (2.1-m) frame-and-glass screen anchored just inside the existing parapet (fig. 3-9). By using glass, the garden's designers preserved the outstanding views of downtown Boston from nearby sitting areas. The windscreens also have the advantage of preventing vertigo and help to prevent children from climbing over the typical railing of standard height. The garden's designers recall that their client originally did not want to build the windbreak, but when told that it would prevent potentially suicidal persons from jumping over the edge, the bank officials approved the construction of the glass screen.

Attention should be given to the type of material used for the windscreen, especially when glass is chosen. The pressure from heavy winds could shatter the windbreak, unless shatter-proof glass or acrylic is specified. In areas subject to hurricanes or typhoons, the windbreak's composition should be specified by a structural engineer. In spaces where views are not a concern, solid walls, fences, dense plantings, and perforated screens can be used as windbreaks (fig. 3-10).

It should also be noted that the ends of the protecting building generate strong swirling winds that batter plants and people in these

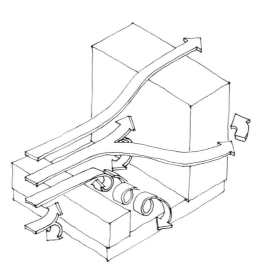

3-8. When wind strikes a tall building, it breaks up into many swirls and eddies, the strongest of which are shown here. These areas require shelter on a roof. (Reprinted, with permission, from Pierre Teasdale, *Roof Decks Design Guidelines*. Ottawa: Canada Mortgage and Housing Corporation, 1979)

areas. This problem can be alleviated somewhat at roof level by building windscreens parallel to the ends of the building and roof garden.

Windscreen structures installed in interior spaces of the garden can be freestanding or be a part of an overhead structure designed to provide shade. They can also be oriented to create separate areas for meditation, study, or privacy. Properly designed as an integral part of the entire scheme, they can be strong, multipurpose, three-dimensional design elements.

Winter Cold

The effects of winter cold on roof gardens are especially severe in the northern tier of the United States and Canada. (The western coast of

3-9. Plate-glass panels function as a windbreak while preserving the view from the roof garden at the New England Merchants National Bank in Boston. They also provide a greater sense of security than parapets alone can.

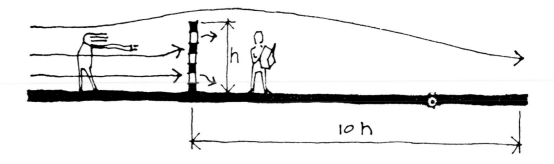

3-10. Perforated screens will prevent eddying of winds. They are most effective when they are two-thirds solid and one-third void. Such screens provide protection on the leeward side from direct winds for a distance of five times the height of the screen, and a sheltering effect for a distance ten times that height. (Reprinted, with permission, from Pierre Teasdale, *Roof Decks Design Guidelines*. Ottawa: Canada Mortgage and Housing Corporation, 1979)

British Columbia and the state of Washington are exceptions because of the warming effects of the Japan Current.) Yet, as examples throughout this book demonstrate, a roof garden can survive even the harsh winters of New England and Québec. Keys to their success are choosing plants that can survive the cold temperatures of the region and adapting site conditions to enhance survival.

In preparing for winter cold, special attention should be given to long-term freezing of plant roots. Dr. Francis Gouin, a horticulturist at the University of Maryland, has studied the effects of numerous factors on container plants (all roof garden plants are in containers of some kind) and has found that intense cold kills a plant's fine fibrous roots first, the intermediate-sized roots next, and finally the main roots. Fibrous roots are usually replaced in the spring, and plants will recover satisfactorily if the intermediate roots have not been killed back too extensively. The loss of all intermediate roots usually results in the death of the plant, as the main roots are not able to generate enough smaller roots in time to prevent loss of the upper story of the plant. The degree of cold a plant can withstand depends in part on its innate hardiness: different species can endure different temperatures. Appendix A includes a list of some of the more commonly used landscape plants and the winter temperatures they can survive.

In the northern United States and southern Canada, it is not unusual for the upper 30 inches (76.2 cm) of earth to freeze solid for long periods in open country such as farmlands. The species of trees and other plants growing in these areas have adapted over the millennia to regional temperature extremes and other severe climatic conditions, as well as the soil and subsoil conditions. It should be noted that much of the upper ground surface of these regions was scarified by the polar ice cap as it moved southward during the Ice Age, which often scraped the topsoil away, until little remained except rock substrate. Much of this topsoil clung to the moving ice and was later deposited in the middle tier of states as the ice melted. The base rock remaining gradually eroded, replenishing the soils of the northern regions and slowly permitting the return of the tree cover we see today. Thus, northern forests are not standing in deep, fertile topsoil, such as is found farther south, but in relatively shallow soils. Why, then, do roots survive even though they are in a layer of frozen earth to a depth of 30 inches (76.2 cm) or more? If they can survive in nature under such conditions, can they thrive in a similar depth of soil on a roof?

It should be noted that trees, in their natural environment, rarely have more than 30 inches (76.2 cm) of good fertile soil in which to grow. In Norway the soil is very shallow, in some places only 1 foot (30.5 cm) deep, with solid granite below. Yet dense stands of birch forest grow profusely in this shallow upper layer, surviving sub-zero winters. Similarly, in the United States, the lower strata can be clay, hard pan, or even rock; the tree draws almost all of its sustenance from the upper soil layer. Indeed, because of the lack of air at lower depths of even good soils, roots will not penetrate more deeply except under unusual circumstances. The tree is supported by the flangelike spread of its roots around it and the frictional resistance of these roots against their soil cover. (In dense forests trees also protect each other against windthrow.) This thin layer of life-supporting soil permits the warmth of summer to reach the subsoil, where it is stored until winter. The warmth of the strata below moves upward as the temperature of the upper layer drops, thus moderating the temperature of the upper layer of soil, which contains the roots. Snow and, in forests, the debris on the forest floor (leaf drop and the like) contribute to this moderating effect by protecting the upper stratum from cold temperatures, essentially functioning as insulation.

To mediate the effects of cold temperatures in roof gardens, these natural conditions must be duplicated as closely as possible in the construction of the roof and the growing medium for the plants. Such efforts, combined with the use of native plants that have the hardiness necessary to survive cold, can allow for successful planting of roof gardens in cold climates.

Such natural conditions can be re-created in roof gardens; the method to do so depends on the type of structure on which the garden rests. Sites that are heated but have no or little insulation in their roofs will leak heat into roof garden planters. This leakage will protect the lower part of the soil from freezing but may, if heat loss is excessive, also fool deciduous plants into sensing the arrival of spring during a pleasant spell of warm weather in the winter months. Such plants would begin to send out new growth, only to be frost-killed with a sudden drop in temperature. Such problems can be avoided by insulating the bottom of the plant container or bed. Modern office buildings have insulation in their roofs that should prevent such heat loss from occurring.

The roofs of elevated parking structures usually have no insulation for the simple reason that parked cars do not require heating. If a roof garden is to be built atop the garage, however, planting areas must be protected from the cold in the garage below. Freezing ambient temperatures above the soil as well as below will cause the soil to freeze solid, and the plants may be damaged or die. Adding a layer of insulation between the plant containers and the garage below or a layer of Styrofoam to all inside surfaces of the container will help protect the soil from the cold below (see also the discussion of roof insulation later in this chapter). In addition, the surface of the soil should be top-dressed or mulched with a 3-inch (7.6-cm) layer of ⅛- to ½-inch (3.2- to 12.7-mm) pine or redwood chips, to prevent heat loss to the cold air, when there is no snow cover.

Further protection can be provided by installing electric heating coils or radiant heating in copper tubing inside or below the container to maintain the soil temperature. Dr. Gouin describes this heating technique:

> Vinyl jacketed heating cables should be spaced 8" to 10" apart on top of the fibre soil separator and along the insulated walls of the container. The temperature sensor for the thermostat should be placed along the inside north wall of the container midway between the top and bottom of the growing media area. . . . Thermostats for each container should be set to maintain the growing media temperature 4 to 5 degrees F above the minimum root killing temperature of the plants. Relatively little electrical energy will be needed to accomplish this task providing the containers are well insulated, the root balls are thoroughly watered in late fall or early winter and periodically during the winter months, and the surface growing media is properly mulched.

Installation, operation, and maintenance costs are much higher in gardens requiring these methods than they are in heated buildings where supplemental heat is not needed. If a roof garden is to be built, a qualified mechanical engineer, an arborist, and a knowledgeable local nurseryman should be engaged to advise on appropriate protection from cold.

Of course, cold weather affects more than plants. People avoid outdoor activities when the temperatures drop, and outdoor spaces are often deserted; roof gardens are no exception. Many do participate in winter sports, however, and one in particular, ice skating, can be enjoyed in a roof garden, where a temporary rink can be set up. The rink at Rockefeller Center, which is atop the below-grade complex, is a major attraction during the winter months. Even the Kaiser Center in sunny Oakland, California, has featured ice skating in winters past. Obviously, few people enjoy lounging in a freezing place, but activities such as skating, combined with the pleasure of the garden in the warmer months, can make roof gardens vital even in northern climes.

Snow removal, a regular maintenance chore at ground level in cold climates, must also be done in roof gardens if they are to remain open during the winter. This task is particularly important if the space serves to ease circulation and provide access to nearby buildings. A number of northern gardens have been constructed with radiant heating systems below their surface for snow melting; Constitution Plaza and Mellon Square are two. Such systems ease maintenance during snowy weather and keep pathways open.

BUILDING CODES, HEIGHT ORDINANCES, AND SAFETY RESTRICTIONS

Safety requirements in the building codes of cities apply just as strictly to roof gardens as they do to the balance of the building. When a roof is to be used for gardens, the codes almost universally require that there be two separate means of egress (figs. 3-11 and 3-12). Moreover, for any elevated structure, the space must be bounded by railings, parapets, or other blockades that are at least 42 inches (106.7 cm) high, with vertical surfaces that are impenetrable to small children (fig. 3-13, 3-14, 3-15, 3-16, 3-17, and 3-18). As is true for the rest of the building, no wood con-

3-11 (top left). San Francisco's planning department required pedestrian access from the street for the Crocker Terrace roof garden. This structure houses the roof-level entrance to the elevator, which descends to the street.

3-12 (top right). At Crocker Terrace, the second exit required by building codes is a stairway leading to the adjacent Galleria shopping mall.

3-13 (left). A 42-inch-high (106.7-cm) wall that is 24 inches thick (61 cm) is an effective edge barrier at the Federal Reserve Bank roof garden in Boston.

struction is permitted. Most municipalities have adopted one of the existing model building codes, such as the Basic Building Code, National Building Code, Uniform Building Code, or Standard Building Code, and adapted it to meet any local concerns (such as hurricanes or earthquakes, for example). The owner and his design team should check the local code carefully to determine what regulations apply to roof gardens. An awareness of code requirements before planning begins will allow the basic design of the building to be modified as needed to accommodate code requirements; bringing a building up

3-14 (top left). An ornamental railing also acts as a safety barrier atop the roof garden at the Casa de la Raza housing development in San Francisco; HKIT, architects.

3-15 (top right). Steel railings shield the edges of an open atrium that provides light to the underground rooms at the Bechtel Engineering Center at the University of California at Berkeley.

3-16 (bottom left). Safety at the edge of a roof garden is a primary concern. Most building codes require an edge barrier with a minimum height of 42 inches (106.7 cm). Shatterproof glass in a metal frame, like this barrier at Constitution Plaza in Hartford, Connecticut, is one way of meeting code requirements.

3-17 (bottom right). Edge barriers can be incorporated into a garden design in various ways. At the East Bay Municipal Utility District building in Oakland, California, a concrete planter topped with pipe railing does double duty as an edge barrier.

3-18. Various 42-inch-high (106.7-cm) edge-barrier configurations: (a) railing set well back from the edge, with planting between edge and barrier; (b) railing attached to inside face of parapet; (c) railing attached to top of parapet, with planter separating path from parapet; (d) center: railing attached to paving, with space between railing and parapet. (Reprinted, with permission, from Pierre Teasdale, *Roof Decks Design Guidelines.* Ottawa: Canada Mortgage and Housing Corporation, 1979)

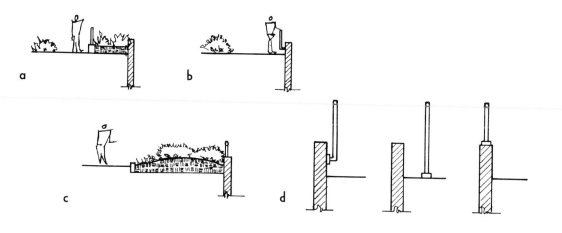

to code after it has been built, though feasible, is far more costly.

It should be noted that, in some municipalities that include height restrictions among their planning or zoning ordinances, a roof garden is considered a floor of the building. Hence, the builder would lose a floor of rental space if a garden is included in a building of maximum height. There is some difference of opinion as to whether a roof garden should be so designated. The garden has no walls or ceilings, is not con-

nected to the building's HVAC system, and requires no separate access. Nonetheless, in some places, the space is considered a separate floor. Developers should research local ordinances to determine if such designations apply to their facility.

ACCESS

As noted earlier in this chapter, evaluating the access to a roof garden depends in part on the

3-19. Convenient access can affect the amount of use a roof garden will receive. The most convenient is to walk directly through the doors from the interior of the building into a roof garden on the same level. The roof garden at the Crown Life building in Vancouver is directly accessible from the eighteenth-floor offices of Kaiser Resources.

garden's intended users. Access may be public, limited, or prohibited entirely except for maintenance. Regardless of the degree of access required, however, entry for targeted users must be easy if the garden is to be well used. Ideally, it should be located off a heavily used indoor gathering place, such as a common dining room, game room, or entrance lobby. Visitors' ability to see the garden from such a space is key to its use. Even visibility from an elevator door in a hallway helps to make the garden inviting and seem easily accessible (figs. 3-19, 3-20, and 3-21). On the other hand, an entrance through a solid fire door at the end of a poorly lighted and little-used corridor contributes little to the usage of even the

3-20 (top left). Direct access from the building's interior increases the garden's visibility, inviting more frequent use. This entrance to the roof garden at Pacific Bell's northern California headquarters in Sacramento exemplifies how easy access can encourage use of the space.

3-21 (top right). When interior space is not at the same level as the roof garden, adjustments can be made to facilitate access. At the Kaiser Center roof garden in Oakland, California, a generous transition from the roof garden to the floor of the adjacent building eases the change in grade.

3-22 (bottom left). Access via the grand staircase at right, known as the Bunker Hill Steps, to the roof gardens at 444 South Flower in Los Angeles, is complemented by escalators.

3-23 (bottom right). The roof garden at Crocker Terrace in San Francisco is reached by exterior elevators from street level and by escalators and stairs inside the Galleria mall next door. Notice the clearly marked entrance to the roof garden, included as part of the storefront signage, at the upper left.

best of gardens. Easy ramps or outside paving as close as possible to the inside floor elevation are required by law for use by the disabled.

Elevator or escalator access should be provided to roof gardens that are beyond ground level (figs. 3-22, 3-23, and 3-24). Stairways beyond an elevator stop at the last floor, as well as exterior steps, should be avoided (fig. 3-25). When stairs are necessary to gain access to the roof, a lift attached to the stairway railing or other suitable device should be provided for the disabled (fig. 3-26).

Access for garden maintenance equipment should also be available, although it need not be via a separate entrance. Ideally, storage space for commonly used tools should be provided in the garden, to avoid carrying equipment up through the building in the tenants' elevators.

SECURITY

As in city parks and other open spaces, high use is one of the best guarantees against crime. Private gardens that are open to the public should and usually do have security guards as well. A weatherproof shelter is necessary for the guard during inclement weather, unless the garden is closed at such times.

In addition, the elements of the garden should be arranged to allow easy surveillance. Choosing and designing an open, visible space can reduce or eliminate hiding places favored by would-be criminals. Site access can also affect security: a space with many routes for entrance and escape is less secure than that with limited access.

3-24 (top). The three-level roof garden atop the Pacific Gateway Plaza building in San Francisco is isolated between two freeway ramps (now removed). To enter the buildings and gardens, an escalator from street level leads to a bridge over traffic. The bridge ends at the entrance to the building and the gardens. The gardens themselves are connected by stairways.

3-25 (bottom left). The bridge connecting the Ordway Building and the Kaiser Center garage in Oakland, California, provides protection from the elements and ready access to parking, but it is less convenient to users of the roof garden atop the garage. An open-air walkway atop the roof of the bridge, leading directly into the garden, would have greatly improved access.

3-26 (bottom right). A simple but efficient means of providing access for the disabled is this chair on a rail. It is especially useful for access to roof gardens to which building elevators do not extend. The seat can be folded vertically when not in use.

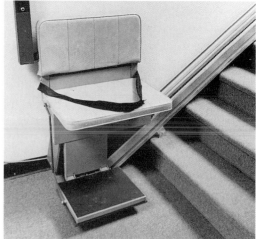

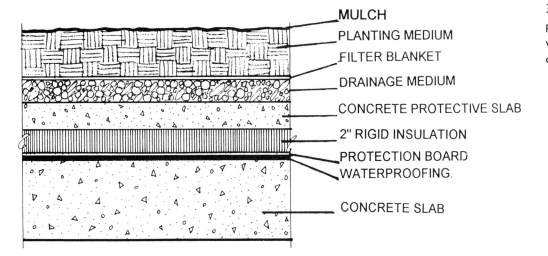

MULCH
PLANTING MEDIUM
FILTER BLANKET
DRAINAGE MEDIUM
CONCRETE PROTECTIVE SLAB
2" RIGID INSULATION
PROTECTION BOARD
WATERPROOFING.
CONCRETE SLAB

3-27. The layers of a protected-membrane roof, with the garden above also shown.

THE STRUCTURE BELOW

Just as the strength of a building depends to a large degree on its foundation, so too does the success of a roof garden depend to a great extent on its compatibility with the roof structure upon which it rests. Special attention must be given to the materials and design of the added construction to ensure that the integrity of the roof structure and its waterproofing is not compromised. The landscape architect needs to have a basic understanding of the roof structure that will support the garden and, in the case of a building that has not yet been constructed, must strive to create a close and sympathetic collaboration with the building's architect, structural engineer, and roofing contractor. In no other landscape is the relationship among design, construction detailing, drainage, and long-term maintenance so interdependent. Not only is each strongly affected by the other, but all are wholly dependent on the building's ability to support the garden's additional weight, the location and size of the roof drains, the integrity of the waterproofing, and the availability of ready access to bring the necessary construction materials to the site.

In addition, bulky maintenance and garden-rebuilding materials may be necessary years after the construction is complete. The site must be able to accommodate these needs, for although some roof gardens atop modern buildings have been in place for fifty to sixty years without requiring major repairs or replacement of waterproofing, soil, or plantings, there is always the possibility that these and other roof garden elements may need to be replaced. Despite the availability of modern cranes and service elevators, accomplishing such work after the building has been occupied can be an expensive undertaking and is to be avoided if at all possible. Although most of the experience with roof gardens dates from the post–World War II era, a relatively short time span, many have demonstrated no problems thus far, indicating that essentially permanent roof gardens can be built if properly constructed and maintained.

The roof upon which a garden rests typically consists of several levels or layers of materials. The responsibility for their selection and method of installation usually belongs to the building's architect, in consultation with the structural engineer, landscape architect, roofing contractor, and client. The sequence of the layers occasionally varies, depending on the architecture of the building. The so-called protected-membrane roof is the best arrangement for roof gardens; it is illustrated in figure 3-27. However, particularly when constructing a garden atop an already existing building, landscape architects should be aware that other arrangements are possible; notably, insulation may be below the roof slab or between the slab and membrane, and in other cases the concrete protective slab above the insulation is omitted. The layers of a protected-membrane roof are listed below, starting from the bottom and working up; a more detailed discussion of each follows.

1. The *roof slab* is the structural surface that supports the roof. It may be plywood over wood joists, solid wood decking over heavy timber framing, corrugated steel decking, wood-fiber panels bonded with portland cement, poured gypsum over foamboard, site-cast concrete, or precast concrete. Because the weight of a roof garden requires a structure strong enough to support it, site-cast or precast concrete is most prevalent. The slab's design is usually determined by the building's architect and structural engineer. Other than providing an approximation of the loads that the deck must ultimately support and a general plan to minimize roof penetrations, the landscape architect has little input into its design.

2. Immediately above the slab is the *waterproof membrane*, selected by the architect in consultation with the roofing consultant and landscape architect. The membrane may be a layer of asphalt-impregnated felt embedded in hot tar, a single-ply elastomeric sheet, or a fluid that is painted or sprayed onto the deck.

3. *Protection board* is placed directly above the waterproofing to protect it during construction.

4. *Insulation* is placed on top of the protection board to prevent heat transfer. Rigid polystyrene foam board (such as Styrofoam), 2 inches (5.1 cm) thick, is often used.

5. Finally, a 2½- to 4-inch-thick (6.4- to 10.2-cm) *concrete slab* is placed above the insulation. Its upper surface is sloped to allow water to flow into roof drains. This smooth concrete slab is often the finished surface of the roof, regardless of whether or not additional construction is planned. It is, however, an ideal base for roof garden construction, as it protects lower layers from rapid changes in temperature, mechanical damage from tools and other equipment, and ultraviolet rays, and it allows for perfect drainage.

Loads on the Roof Slab

Without an engineering background, calculating the load-bearing capacity of a roof can be very difficult. Although most roof garden designers are not structural engineers, they should be aware of the load limitations of a roof and the consequences of overloading. A roof garden designer should have at least a basic understanding of the structure and know how to determine

the additional loads being proposed for the roof. Most engineers will answer the question, "How much load can be put on a roof?" with the question, "How much do you want to put on the roof?" That simply means you should work together to come up with a reasonable answer.

The first question concerning loads centers on whether the building is being newly built or whether it already exists. In new construction, if the desired weight of the garden is determined beforehand, the roof's structural system can be strengthened as necessary and columns can be added to accommodate the additional load while the building is under design with relatively little extra cost. In the case of existing buildings, where load-bearing capacity has already been established, it may be possible to obtain copies of the original structural calculations and drawings from the engineer who prepared them or the architect for whom he or she consulted. If the original structural engineer is not available, the drawings can be reviewed by another engineer who can then advise on the parameters that will guide the design of the roof garden. If the original drawings cannot be obtained from the designing architects or engineers, it is often possible to review a file copy at the building department of the municipality or county in which the building is located. This review, of course, should also be done by a structural engineer.

Structural engineers divide the loads delivered to a roof structure into two major categories: dead loads and live loads. The *dead load* is generally the weight of the roof structure itself and any *permanent* functional elements that are part of the roof structure. This would include the weight of the roof components themselves, including waterproofing and insulation, as well as snow load (in cold climates) and any permanent utility structures or mechanical equipment, such as ventilation pumps or fans and air-conditioning equipment. The dead loads in excess of these standard static loads are the concern of the roof garden designer. Every permanent material used in the roof garden is an additional dead load.

The *live load* is much as the name implies and includes human occupants, furnishings, temporary maintenance equipment such as movable window-washing equipment, and other items of a transient nature. This loading is usually much smaller than the dead load but is still very important, especially if the roof may be used to accommodate a large number of people or a public assembly.

Whether the building exists or is under design, the roof garden designer must receive from the structural engineer the following information: (1) the allowable dead load beyond that of the roof structure and its appurtenances; (2) the allowable live load. In addition, the differences in allowable loads at the center of roof bays between columns and beams and those directly at the tops or columns and beams should be given. (Points located above the internal supporting columns and beams can carry a far greater load than spans between them.) The engineer should state the allowable load at a given point on the roof (called a *concentrated load*). This data may all seem very complex, but the need for these calculations is well known to structural engineers. They should be computed before the roof garden is designed, to serve as criteria in the design of the garden and the choice of materials used in it. These figures can also be used to limit the number of people allowed on the roof at a given time.

An existing steel-and-concrete building can usually accept the loads imposed by a roof garden if the garden's designer is knowledgeable, resourceful, and imaginative. Load limitations of 250 to 300 psf (pounds per square foot) (1,220 to 1,465 kg per square meter) can usually easily accommodate almost any reasonable garden design, its furnishings, and a substantial number of people. However, structures with far more severe load limitations can still provide the base for very useful and attractive roof gardens. As an extreme example, the garden at the Westin Saint Francis Hotel in San Francisco had a total load restriction of 25 psf, but by limiting development to varicolored gravel paving patterns, using only container-grown plants, restricting public access, and watering by drip irrigation, an attractive roof garden was developed (fig. 3-28; see also the portfolio of American gardens for more information about this roof garden).

Although the arrangement of supporting columns in the building below is almost always

rectilinear, so that trees placed directly above them can appear static in arrangement, such is not always the case. A fluid planting pattern is still possible with skillful design, for example, by omitting tree placement at various points on the grid. A good example is the Kaiser Center roof garden in Oakland, California (fig. 3-29). A careful study reveals that these trees are indeed on the grid of the supporting columns.

Wood-frame multifamily buildings have considerably less structural strength than steel-frame and/or concrete buildings do, and this limitation is directly reflected in the weight that can be placed on their roofs. Generally speaking, roof gardens on wood-frame buildings are limited to boxed or potted plants, wood decking, safety railings, and trellises. Even with these limitations, remarkably fine roof gardens have been built on these roofs. Most municipalities have code restrictions covering the design and construction

3-28. When load limits are severe, roof patterns alone can provide pleasant viewing from adjacent windows. In San Francisco, the unsightly roof of the dining rooms between the old Westin Saint Francis Hotel and its new tower had an additional load limit of 25 pounds per square foot (122 kg per square meter). To improve the view from exterior elevators and adjacent guest rooms, a pattern of several colors of gravel, 1½ inches thick (3.8 cm), was used along with a minimum number of plants in containers. Public access to this space is prohibited.

Select an area of the roof garden plan that contains the heaviest construction and that is farthest from structural beams and columns. Draw a 1-foot square on the plan at the point of the heaviest proposed construction. Identify all the materials used in that square foot of space, regardless of their weight or depth.

Choose one material from those in the sample space. Calculate in cubic feet the volume that material occupies within the sample by multiplying height by width by depth in feet within that space. Look up the weight of 1 cubic foot of the material (see Appendix A, or contact the manufacturer). Multiply the weight of 1 cubic foot by the volume of the sample material. Do this for every material in the sample square, and total the weights.

For example, if one of the materials in the sample is a 3-inch-deep layer of expanded shale in the drainage layer, the volume of that material is .25 x 1 x 1 (.25 foot depth, 1 foot width, 1 foot length), or .25 cubic feet. The weight of expanded shale is 45 pounds per cubic foot, so the weight of the sample is .25 x 45, or 11.25 pounds. Note this figure in a column for addition, and proceed to the next material.

Assume that the next material in the sample area is brick for a wall that is 2 feet high by 8 inches wide by 1 foot long (the length is equal to the length of the sample square). The volume of this part of the sample is thus 2 x .666 x 1, or 1.333 cubic feet. Multiply 1.333 by the weight of 1 cubic foot of brickwork, which is 115 pounds, to find the weight of the brickwork in the sample, which is 153.18 pounds. Add this number to the addition column beneath that for expanded shale, and proceed to the next material.

Finally, assume that the last material is a Plexiglas pond that holds 4 inches of water, adjacent to the brick wall. The pond extends only 4 inches into the sample square. Plexiglas is so light that its weight can be ignored. To find the volume of the water, multiply .333 foot (depth) by .333 foot (width) by 1 foot (length), or .1109 cubic feet. Multiply that number by the weight of 1 cubic foot of water, 62.4 pounds, to learn that the sample area of water weighs 6.920 pounds. Add this figure to the addition column, which now looks like this:

3-29. The flowing curves of this garden's design and the selective placement of trees disguise the fact that all the trees in the Kaiser Center roof garden in Oakland are located on support columns arranged on a rectilinear grid.

of roof gardens on wood-frame, as well as steel and concrete, structures. Check with the local building department before proceeding with design and installation.

Calculating the Weight of a Roof Garden. While the expertise of a structural engineer is necessary to calculate and verify the loads of a roof garden, the landscape architect can use the following simple method to arrive at a close approximation of the load the roof garden will impose. This data will give you an idea about whether the weight limits set by the structural engineer are being exceeded. You may also use these calculations as a guide in basing a request for a practical load limit on the roof of new construction. The structural engineer may then design the roof structure in considerable excess of your calculations as a safety factor. After completing the calculations, consult with a structural engineer for verification.

The purpose of this technique is to calculate the weights of every material in a sample square foot of the plan and then total them to determine the weight of that square foot of space.

Expanded shale	11.25
Brick work	153.18
Water in pond	6.92
Total weight of sample area	**171.35 pounds**

Your final calculation gives you an approximate concentrated load. However, if adjacent areas are considerably lighter, that heavier weight will be spread over a larger area than 1 square foot and so the load will actually be much less than the average load that you calculated.

Loads can be estimated in a similar manner for any square foot within the plan. Calculate several heavy and light squares to get a sense of the weights being planned for the roof.

Waterproof Membranes

The membrane used on the surface of the roof must have as its primary characteristic the ability to prevent water from entering the building from the outside. Under a roof garden, it must also be capable of resisting mechanical damage from gardening tools, repairs, and the like, as well as the penetration of plant roots. Finally, it must be durable, capable of lasting without repair or replacement for the life of the building. Clearly, the industry-standard fifteen- to twenty-year roof is not acceptable if the roof garden must be completely removed to replace the membrane.

The selection of a suitable waterproof membrane is the responsibility of the architect or designer of the building, simply because the roof must be waterproof whether or not it has a roof garden. The architect therefore should take special care both in the design of the membrane and in its installation. (Although the architect is responsible for specifying the roof's waterproofing, in the world of torts, all persons involved are usually named in litigation if it fails.) The roof garden designer must develop garden design and construction solutions that will not damage the waterproofing and that will contribute to the longest life possible for the membrane. The best practice therefore requires the closest cooperation between the architect and landscape architect to install a permanent waterproof surface that will also meet the stringent requirements of successful roof garden design.

Understanding the nature of the various products and methods used by architects and engineers to protect their structures from water is a very necessary part of the roof garden designer's knowledge. Proper selection of materials and assurance of the highest quality of workmanship possible in the current state of the art are of utmost importance. After the roof garden has been installed, it is very difficult to find the exact location of a leak unless the membrane adheres tightly to the roof to prevent water migration; hence, the entire garden may have to be removed to repair the membrane. Because the roofing cannot be repaired or replaced without great expense after the roof garden has been installed, it is imperative that the membrane adheres completely, that it meets the highest standards with regard to both material and installation, and that the membrane is protected during other phases of construction. Anything less could be a great source of trouble and expense in the future for all concerned (fig. 3-30).

The design and protection of roof membranes is a complex subject that cannot be covered completely herein. This discussion will be limited to a brief overview of the various types of waterproofing and their relevance to roof garden design and construction. More detailed information may be found in membrane manufacturers' literature, texts on roofing and waterproofing, and reports by various testing organizations. (The National Roofing Contractors Association's waterproofing manual is an excellent source.) Many architects maintain personal libraries that include these, and the landscape architect would do well to consult them. It should be remem-

3-30. An owner's and a roof garden designer's nightmare: replacing the waterproof membrane beneath high-quality paving and structures in a roof garden. Here, workers prepare the roof for a new built-up membrane after removing the paving at Constitution Plaza in Hartford, Connecticut, in 1988, almost twenty-five years after its installation.

bered, however, that little of the information in these sources relates directly to roof gardens. Moreover, American manufacturers have generally ignored the specialized needs of roof gardens and so tend to recommend products they already manufacture, rather than those designed just for roof gardens. To find information particularly about membranes beneath roof gardens, one must review the research of German manufacturers and organizations, but the language barrier is formidable.

The methods and materials currently in use for waterproofing flat or relatively flat roofs fall into three categories: the built-up roof, the single-ply membrane, and the fluid-applied membrane.

Built-up Roofs. The *built-up roof,* used on residential, commercial, and industrial buildings, has been the standard method of waterproofing roofs for many years and is still the most commonly used. Simply stated, it essentially consists of sandwiching slightly overlapping sheets of asphalt-impregnated felt between two layers of hot asphaltic bitumen. Although the felt was originally made of cellulose fibers, it is now more usually made of glass fiber (fiberglass), which is more resistant to deterioration. In this system the asphalt or bitumen is the primary waterproofing material, while the felt is a strengthening and stabilizing medium.

Sixty-year-old roof gardens constructed atop built-up roofs, such as Derry and Toms in London (1938), Rockefeller Center in New York (1934–36), and Union Square in San Francisco (1942), have had no problems with leaks or other membrane failures. However, others of more recent construction have failed. It is difficult to determine why these earlier gardens have succeeded while later ones on built-up roofs have not. During these years coal-tar bitumens were commonly used; they are much more resistant to moisture degradation and decay than the asphaltic bitumens used today. Differences in the construction of the roof gardens themselves may also account for it. The Derry and Toms and Rockefeller Center gardens have sections quite different from those installed following World War II. For example, the Derry and Toms garden

has a very deep (by modern standards) 3- to 5-foot (1- to 1.5-m) layer of soil and positive drainage through the use of a layer of clinkers (hard pieces of burned bricks), with a layer of spaced bricks directly on top of the membrane. The Rockefeller Center gardens have a similar section, without the layer of brick. In both, the built-up waterproofing seems to have remained intact, with no decomposition or damage from roots.

Although built-up roof membranes have a mixed record of success, they have inherent weaknesses in that bitumen is an organic material subject to decomposition from standing water, exposure to sun, temperature changes, and air pollutants. Ultraviolet rays and changes in atmospheric temperature and humidity can dry out and cause shrinkage, cracking, and leaks in these materials. The common application of a layer of broken gravel over the roof's surface, to shade and modify temperatures, greatly prolongs the useful life of such roofs. They are, however, rarely guaranteed by manufacturers or installers for more than fifteen or twenty years, regardless of whether they are covered by garden materials or are completely exposed to sun and atmospheric conditions. This fact alone would not necessarily rule out the use of this type of membrane beneath roof gardens. Indeed, the presence of insulation, drainage material, and soil above the membrane reduces exposure to the sun and extends the life of the membrane.

Another characteristic of built-up roofs, however, can cause serious problems especially beneath a roof garden. Because asphaltic bitumen is an organic material, the roots of some plants have the propensity to feed upon and penetrate this material, thus causing leaks in the waterproofing. This problem has been little noted and seldom considered in roof gardens in the United States, although it is well known in Europe, especially in Germany.

Built-up roof membranes, can, however, be protected somewhat from root penetration. The practice of pouring a concrete protection layer above the built-up roof can add many years of life to such roofs. The concrete topping protects the roof from the intrusion of roots as well as from damage by hand tools, and if sloped to drains (as it should be), it provides a positive subsoil drainage surface that will not hold water and thus attract root growth. (Note, however, that layers of impenetrable materials that are loosely placed on the surface of waterproofing to protect it from wear and damage during construction have too many openings at junction points to provide long-term protection against root intrusion. Such a material's greatest value is during the construction process.) A layer of root-proof material can also be added to the top of the membrane, so long as it is compatible with the built-up roof. One root-proof material available in the United States is Hydroplex RB, produced by American Hydrotech (see Appendix B for more information). Built-up waterproofing membranes should be used in conjunction with roof gardens only when a concrete protection layer or slab or other root barrier is also specified.

Single-ply Roof Membranes. Introduced after World War II, elastomeric materials, including such synthetic substances as artificial rubber or neoprene, have become common waterproofing materials. Single-ply membranes are rolled sheets of inorganic plastic or synthetic rubber material, usually overlapped at joints and sealed with heat or adhesive. Like most nontraditional materials, their acceptance has been resisted considerably by installers accustomed to working with built-up roof membranes. Traditional materials and methods, even with serious shortcomings or higher cost, are often preferred over newer ones whose characteristics have not been proven by long practice. The introduction of, resistance to, and final acceptance of plastic pipe and plasterboard are cases in point. Elastomeric roofs have undergone such a trial period.

Modern elastomeric roofing products, if properly applied, have not only proved their worth in comparison with traditional built-up roofs but indeed have more advantages than do built-up roofs. Because they are synthetic rather than organically based, they are less subject to root penetration. Hence, not only will the membrane be more durable, but, assuming that the roof has been sloped to drain (at least ¼ inch per foot), a concrete protective slab is not necessary. Moreover, because single-ply roofing is applied in one operation, its workmanship can be more easily checked. Built-up membranes, applied in three or more layers, are impossible to check below the topmost layer. Finally, because some elastomeric materials resist deterioration by ultraviolet rays, they are easier to flash at their edges. Asphaltic bitumel-based roofs are not resistant to ultraviolet rays

The waterproof membrane's greatest potential for leaks and future failure is at joints between sheets and with other materials. The waterproofing should be completely protected from contact with ultraviolet rays, rapid freezing and thawing, and excessive drying. The points of greatest exposure to such hazards include seals around roof drains, adjoining sheets of membrane, exposure of the membrane at flashings, and the area between the flashing and the top of the surface of the roof garden such as soil or paving. Also, in all horizontal areas, there should be complete coverage of the membrane with permanent garden materials. This means that the uncovered membrane between the top of the soil and where it is attached to the vertical face of walls or parapets should be flashed (covered) with sheet metal, stainless steel, or copper, which permanently shades and protects this otherwise exposed area of membrane. In addition, the membrane should be protected from mechanical damage, such as that from gardening tools, as well as from compromise caused inadvertently when other systems are repaired.

Elastomeric sheet is manufactured from many different formulas, yielding materials with different characteristics under field conditions. Roof gardens require sheet that: resists root penetration, ultraviolet rays, and severe changes in temperature and atmospheric conditions; is flexible to meet building movement at construction joints and intersections with vertical elements; resists surface wear during construction; can withstand attack by insects and microorganisms, subsoil animals, and soil chemicals; can stay in place over an indefinite life span without deterioration; and of course, prevents water penetration. The German waterproofing product Sarnafil, which meets these requirements, particularly those regarding root penetration, is now available in the United States (see Appendix B for further information).

Elastomeric material is available in types that are not resistant to ultraviolet rays and in types that are. The former are less expensive than the latter. Because, in a roof garden, most of the membrane will be covered by soil and other materials, ultraviolet rays present no problem except where the material meets the atmosphere, at the upper edges of vertical surfaces of built-in plant beds or vertical wall surfaces. This situation can be resolved by covering the membrane at this edge with a strip of metal flashing wherever it will be exposed to the sun. The roof garden designer should be very careful to see that these critical tasks are included in the specifications and they are implemented on the roof before the addition of the garden materials.

Fluid-applied Membranes. In addition to single-ply sheets, many elastomeric membranes are available in a hot or cold liquid form that is sprayed or painted onto or applied with a squeegee to the roof. This method eliminates the problem of joints, a site for potential failure in sheet elastomers. It also can be easier to apply to vertical structures and corners, such as those on raised planter beds, and thus is less likely to fail at these critical points. The top edge of the fluid-applied sheet also adheres well to a vertical planter wall, though metal counter-flashing is still required.

This comparison of built-up waterproof membranes and sheet or fluid-applied elastomeric membranes suggests very strongly that an elastomeric membrane is more permanent and less likely to be compromised by the elements that deteriorate waterproofing. The selection of the membrane is, however, only half of the battle. Poor workmanship and construction damage can undo the best of specifications. Constant inspection by a well-trained, knowledgeable roofing consultant and by a representative of the membrane's manufacturer is of the greatest importance.

No matter which type of membrane is used, before any additional materials are added to the roof, all drains should be plugged and the roof should be flooded to 2 inches (5.1 cm) above the highest point of the membrane for a period of at least forty-eight hours, to check for leaks. No further work on the roof should proceed until the membrane has been proven waterproof. At that point, the remaining parts of the roof can be installed.

Roof Penetrations. To protect the integrity of the roof's waterproofing, the roof and its membrane should be penetrated in as few places as possible: every penetration is a potential leak. Penetrations are almost impossible to eliminate, so other means must be used to minimize their effects. The simplest means, if possible, is to carry the piping, conduits, vents, and the like to a single point on the roof and to take them up together into a small, inconspicuous, well-waterproofed structure. If a leak occurs at this inconspicuous point, it will be easier to locate and more accessible for repair. The location of such mechanical structures should be coordinated with the design of the roof garden. Obviously, pipes should not emerge from a paved patio or any other highly visible spot. If they can be located within a planting bed, plants can be used to obscure the small structure, as in figure 3-31.

Parking structures, which have the fewest systems to be carried to the roof, are the easiest buildings in which to install ceiling piping and vents and are the most accessible for repairs. The most difficult spaces are offices, hotels, apartment buildings, and other occupied areas, where

3-31. Planting is used to conceal skylights and other roof penetrations in the roof garden atop the Munich Hospital in Germany; Klaus Wittke, landscape architect.

pipes and vents from toilets, air conditioning, exhaust systems, and water connection must all reach the roof. What seems to be an orderly system on the interior resembles a random and vexing agglomeration of mechanical equipment at roof garden level (fig. 3-32). The only way to deal with this problem is to try to group these necessary outlets in a single, well-designed structure on the roof, leaving the balance of the roof space for the garden (fig. 3-33).

Protection Board

To protect the waterproofing from damage during construction, as well as from damage caused by garden tools, repair equipment, and the like later, a layer of protective material should be installed directly on top of the membrane. This material should be hard, strong, and durable. Until its manufacture was discontinued because of health concerns, a ¼-inch-thick (6.4-mm) sheet of asbestos, usually 4 by 8 feet (1.2 to 2.5 m), was used. Today other materials are available, such as Hardipanel, which is often used during construction, though it has never been tested under planting media (see Appendix B for source of supply). In Europe 8-millimeter polyurethane film has proven effective as well.

The protection board should be placed loose (not fastened) above the membrane and should be left in place throughout construction, covered by the insulation and the protective concrete slab that tops the roof. The protection board is a permanent component of the roof. If weight constraints forbid the installation of the concrete slab at the top of the roof, then expanded polystyrene insulation should be placed directly on the waterproofing, followed by the protection board. The garden components are then installed above the protection board.

Insulation

Public awareness of the need to conserve energy has resulted in many national and local legislative measures requiring the insulation of all new construction and the installation of insulation in existing buildings. Roofs are a primary location for heat transfer. Heat energy always moves from warm to cold areas (that is, cold never enters a structure; heat merely leaves it). Insulation

3-32 (top). A rooftop community garden atop an apartment building does not require the same aesthetic considerations as an ornamental roof garden does. Nonetheless, roof penetrations such as vents, pipes, and inappropriate floor drains can prove to be hazardous obstacles, as this garden atop Woolf House in San Francisco illustrates.

3-33 (bottom). In San Francisco, the West Side sewage pump station was designed to serve as an ocean outlook deck as well. Vent stacks were shaped and placed to form sculptural elements on the upper platform. Theodore Osmundson and Associates, landscape architects.

restricts the transfer of heat energy by creating a barrier between spaces of different temperatures. In an insulated structure, heat is less able to leave a building during winter and less able to enter it in summer; thus, the amount of energy (such as gas, oil, or electricity) required to operate heating and air-conditioning systems is reduced. The most common means of reducing heat transfer in the roofs of buildings is the installation of a 2-inch (5.1-cm) layer of rigid extruded polystyrene foam (such as Styrofoam) above the board protecting the waterproofing (fig. 3-34). In some cases, as when the vertical dimensions of the roof garden section cannot be accommodated between the roof's surface and the adjacent floor level, insulation is installed beneath the roof deck. (Such an installation is quite different from that used for the protected-membrane roof discussed here. The significant ramifications of it are the province of the building's architect.)

Styrofoam has an R-value of 5.0 per inch at 75°F, the minimum required by law for roofs. (R-value is the measure of thermal resistance of a particular material at a particular thickness.) Note that the depth of soil and other materials in the roof garden above have little consistent measurable insulation effect, as their R-values vary constantly because of the differing amounts of moisture they can contain. This variability, combined with the different types of cover across the roof (from soil to paving to concrete, for example), makes the garden's R-value very difficult to calculate; therefore, it is almost never considered in meeting local and state insulation requirements. The garden does, however, convey a positive insulating effect, even if it cannot be measured accurately. One need only look to the experience of the Newton Vineyard in Napa Valley, California, for ample proof of the efficacy of 4 feet (1.2 m) of soil on the roof of their barrel-storage chamber. This concrete structure is kept at a constant low temperature without additional insulation or mechanical air conditioning. (See the portfolio of American gardens for more information about Newton Vineyard.)

Rigid extruded polystyrene foam board is light in weight, comes in 4- by 8-foot (1.2- to 2.5-m) rigid boards, is easy to cut to size and handle, is moisture resistant, and is strong enough to resist light traffic on its surface. Although it has almost no bending strength, its flat surface can withstand surprisingly heavy weights if they are applied evenly over its surface.

Often shown in the cross section of roof garden construction, insulation is an integral part of the architect's initial responsibility in conserving energy and meeting building codes and is seldom a part of the roof garden design.

Concrete Protection Slab

It is common practice to pour a smooth-surfaced 2½- to 4-inch-thick (6.4- to 10.2-cm) layer of concrete above the waterproofing, protection board, and insulation to protect the roof from the elements. The slab also provides a drainage surface sloped at approximately ¼ inch to 1 foot to drains. This concrete surface is typically provided regardless of whether a roof garden will be constructed above it. In cold climates, however, it is often omitted because of its tendency to spall and crack during the freeze/thaw cycle of cold winters. This problem does not occur when a roof garden is constructed above the concrete slab, because the additional layers above protect the slab from temperature fluctuations. The protective slab beneath a roof garden provides an ideal surface to receive and dispose of water seeping downward from the planting medium and drainage material above it.

CHAPTER FOUR

ROOF GARDEN CONSTRUCTION

L ike the roof on which it is to be built, a roof garden is constructed in layers (fig. 4-1). And like the roof, which is intimately connected to the building below it, the garden is in turn intimately connected to that roof. Just as failure in the roof components can cause significant damage to the building it shelters, so too a failure in the garden's components can cause significant—and costly—damage to the roof that supports it and, consequently, to the building below. Perhaps needless to say, it is therefore imperative that care be taken in choosing and installing materials of the highest quality possible. This chapter examines some of the many options available for roof garden construction, including some of the more innovative European systems available.

Any roof garden should include four essential layers (other components, such as plantings, paving, and the like, are particular to individual gardens and are discussed in chapter 5, "Design Elements"). These components, beginning with that closest to the concrete slab protecting the roof, are the drainage system, filter fabric or blanket, the planting medium, and a top dressing of mulch. Like the roofing components, all four of these layers must be provided, but a number of options for materials in each layer is available.

1. The *drainage layer,* directly above the concrete protective slab, should be very porous to permit water to pass easily through it. It must be permanent, continuous over the entire roof surface, and strong enough to support the weight of the garden materials above it. This layer must be kept free of any material that could block the free flow of water through it to the drains.

2. To prevent the planting medium from going into solution and being lost in or clogging the drainage layer and roof drains, *filter fabric,* a water-permeable barrier, is needed. It must be resistant to rot, easy to transport and install, inexpensive, strong, and permanent. The material most commonly used today, which meets all of these requirements, is a thin fabric very similar to felt but made of polypropylene fiber.

3. The *planting medium* is placed on top of the filter fabric to depths as needed. This layer can range from carefully selected topsoil to mixes that contain no topsoil at all.

4. To retain moisture in the planting medium, to cool the soil, to prevent weed growth, and to provide a continuous supply of decaying humus, the surface of the planting medium should be top-dressed with a 1-inch (2.5-cm) layer of *mulch,* preferably ¼- to ½-inch (6.4- to 12.7-mm) pine, redwood, or fir nuggets.

In addition, many roof gardens, particularly those of some size, include some type of automatic irrigation system. Although the operation of these systems is a maintenance function and is described in chapter 6, they are typically installed

4-1. A typical section of a roof garden in the United States.

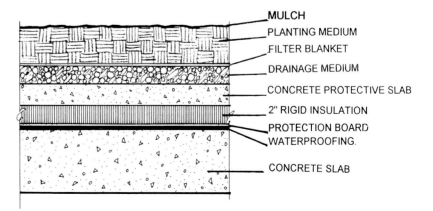

MULCH
PLANTING MEDIUM
FILTER BLANKET
DRAINAGE MEDIUM
CONCRETE PROTECTIVE SLAB
2" RIGID INSULATION
PROTECTION BOARD
WATERPROOFING
CONCRETE SLAB

with the other garden components. Thus, a variety of available systems is discussed in this chapter.

DRAINAGE

Good drainage is a crucial requirement of roof garden design. Any blockage of the drainage system can cause the loss of plants as well as the penetration of water into surrounding structures, with expensive repair and cleanup work as a result. A well-designed drainage system will provide the clean and reliable roof surface necessary for the maintenance and enjoyment of the roof garden.

The drainage system consists of two closely related elements. The first is a layer of drainage material that rests atop the concrete protective slab of the roof; the second is the system of drains and pipes that lead directly to the roof's downspouts and from there to municipal storm sewers. In addition, successful drainage depends in part on the layers above the drainage system; the type of planting medium and the inclusion of filter fabric directly influence the effectiveness of the drainage system. Although such considerations are examined later in this chapter, they should be kept in mind when considering the drainage system's makeup.

The Drainage Medium
The drainage layer consists of rot-proof material through which water flows to the building's roof drains. A variety of alternative materials can be used for it, some traditional and some of which are more recently developed products.

The first drainage material used in modern times consisted of pebbles, broken rock, and clinkers (pieces of burned brick). These were used in two of the earliest large-scale modern gardens, Derry and Toms in London and Rockefeller Center in New York (fig. 4-2). Because both are from the same period, the 1930s, and by the same designer, Ralph Hancock of London, it is not surprising that they have identical drainage materials. Perhaps these materials were not considered to be the most effective for draining a roof garden or perhaps the method was not well known to later designers. Whatever the reason, these materials were not used in post–World War II gardens. Although they have proven effective over time, they do have shortcomings (such as weight), and it is just as well that new thinking was applied to the problem.

In the late 1950s and early 1960s, the drainage medium used was simply a 3- to 4-inch (7.6- to 10.2-cm) layer of 1- to 2-inch (2.5- to 5.1-cm) broken drain rock, with no filter material above. This material worked well, but it is heavy, where weight is a critical factor, and is labor intensive in both delivery and application. The lack of filter material above permitted the topsoil layer to wash down into its open spaces, where it clogged them, or to enter the building's roof drains and be washed away completely. In the mid-1960s, filter fabric was added on top of the rock, permitting the passage of water without loss of soil. However, the other faults of drain rock remained.

As time went on, garden designers found success adapting products originally intended for other purposes. In the late 1970s, for example, a

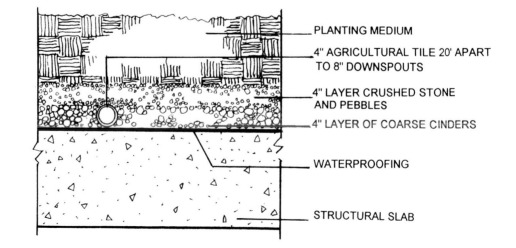

4-2. A section of the drainage system of the Rockefeller Center roof gardens, designed in the 1930s.

PLANTING MEDIUM

4" AGRICULTURAL TILE 20' APART TO 8" DOWNSPOUTS

4" LAYER CRUSHED STONE AND PEBBLES

4" LAYER OF COARSE CINDERS

WATERPROOFING

STRUCTURAL SLAB

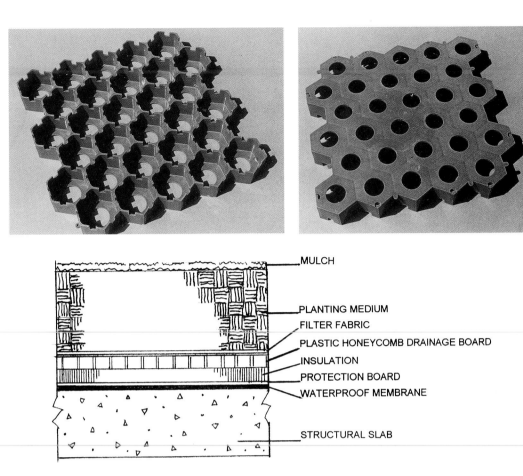

MULCH
PLANTING MEDIUM
FILTER FABRIC
PLASTIC HONEYCOMB DRAINAGE BOARD
INSULATION
PROTECTION BOARD
WATERPROOF MEMBRANE
STRUCTURAL SLAB

4-3 (top left). This 1-foot (30.5-cm) square of Grass-Cel is oriented to be used for its original function, to hold soil for turf used under vehicles.

4-4 (top right). This square of Grass-Cel, placed with the open side down, permits water to penetrate the holes in the cells. Drain holes in the sides of each cell allow excess water to travel across the concrete protection layer to building drains. Filter fabric is placed on the flat side.

4-5 (left). A planter bed with Grass-Cel as a positive drainage layer.

product designed for growing grass on areas of light vehicular use was introduced. Called Grass-Cel, it is made of high-impact plastic formed into a honeycomb-like structure of hollow notched hexagons, sold in roughly 1-foot (30.5-cm) interlocking squares that are approximately 2 inches (5.1 cm) thick (fig. 4-3). By turning the squares upside down (the opposite of their intended position beneath automobiles), designers found an almost perfect drainage layer for roof gardens and planters of all kinds (fig. 4-4). Covered with a layer of plastic filter fabric, Grass-Cel made a strong, easily handled and cut, very lightweight drainage layer between the surface of the roof and the planting medium above. Below grade, protected from ultraviolet light, it is a permanent and highly efficient drainage medium. Figure 4-5 shows a section drawing of it in use.

Products developed in other countries and introduced to the United States were also adapted for roof gardens. Two such products, Enkadrain and Geotech, were originally produced for the German market for drainage behind retaining walls, where heavy and difficult-

to-handle drain rock had been used before. When laid flat on the roof's surface and covered with filter fabric, these products provide a permanent free-flowing lightweight drainage layer below the planting medium. Both are made from plastic but, once buried, are safe from the damaging ultraviolet rays of the sun. Enkadrain is made of coarse, strong plastic threads in a loose but uniform thickness (fig. 4-6). It is delivered to the job site in 100-foot (30.5-m) rolls. Geotech, in section, resembles caramel corn but actually consists of expanded polystyrene beads held together with asphaltic adhesive (fig. 4-7). It is sold in 4-by 4-foot (1.2- by 1.2-m) sheets in various thicknesses. Both materials can be supplied with polypropylene filter fabric attached to one face.

These products have been followed by others (figs. 4-8 and 4-9). All are made of long-lasting plastic and will give satisfactory service if protected from long periods of direct exposure to the sun. They are easy to handle and install by unskilled labor and require no additional work once they have been rolled out and trimmed to fit.

4-6 (top left). Enkadrain, a product originally designed to drain the backs of concrete retaining walls, consists of strong plastic wires pressed into a porous sheet, with filter fabric attached to one side.

4-7 (top right). Geotech, with filter fabric attached to the upper surface, provides drainage below the planting medium.

4-8 and 4-9 (bottom). A variety of plastic materials can be used as drainage materials. The shape can vary, as shown in these two examples.

The system for carrying away water beneath the surface of the growing medium can also consist of materials that do not cover the entire roof surface. Such a system is Multi-Flow, which works on the same principle as agricultural tile used to drain farmland but is of more sophisticated material. It consists of lengths of perforated 1-inch (2.5-cm) tubing made from high-density polyethylene; the tubes are joined horizontally and wrapped permanently with polypropylene filter fabric. Commonly used to drain athletic fields, it drains the area via capillary action: water flows across the horizontal surface of the roof to the drainage tubing, which leads to the roof's drains. Laid out flat on the roof's surface like the spokes of a wheel, with the fixed roof drain in the center, the tubing covers the roof with a system of independent drainage areas. Taken together over the entire roof, it forms an overall system comprising independent parts. At the central location of the roof drain, the ends of the Multi-Flow tubing should be covered with loose gravel and a layer of filter fabric to prevent soil from entering the fixed roof drain.

Multi-Flow is made in three lengths, 6 inch, 12

inch, and 18 inch (15 cm, 30.5 cm, and 45.7 cm). End caps, side outlets, in-line couplings, end outlets—all of which snap together easily—and over two dozen specialty connector options are available. This product shows promise as an alternate drainage medium for roof gardens, but it should be noted that it has not been tested either through controlled field testing or actual installation in roof gardens. (See Appendix B for source of supply.)

Drains

The second element of roof drainage, and an equally important part of the drainage system, consists of the drains that collect water. They are plastic or metal, usually brass or cast iron. Several types are available, each designed for specific purposes.

The first is the *round drain,* also called a *deck drain,* which has a grille on the top horizontal surface and perforated sides beneath the surface (figs. 4-10, 4-11, and 4-12). Such drains are usually available with additional sections, to increase or decrease the depth of the drain. Their design permits water to flow into the top at ground-sur-

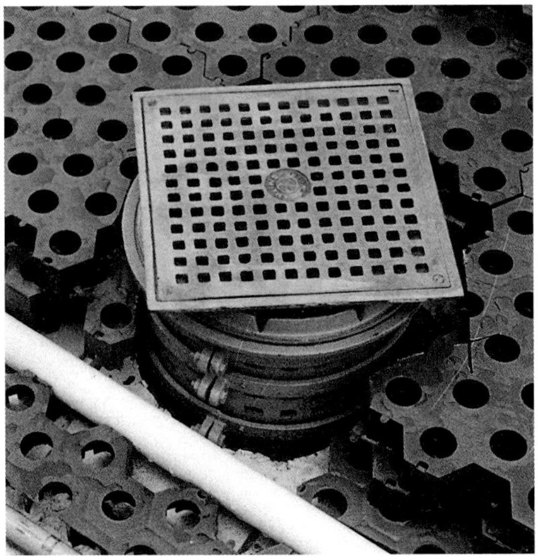

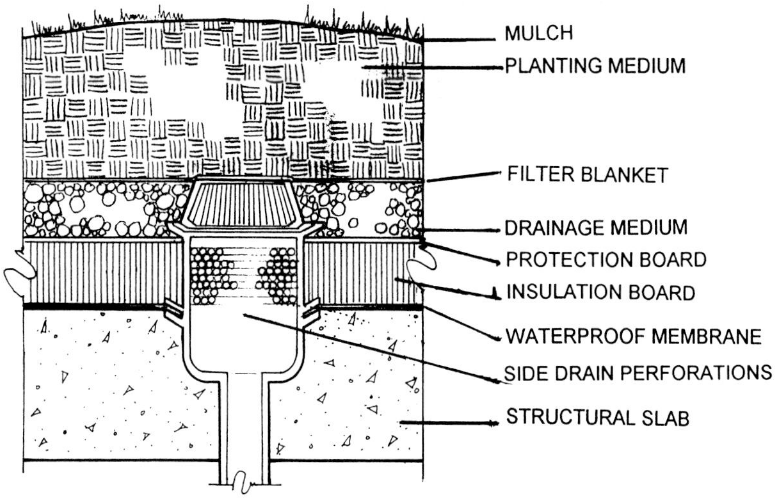
MULCH
PLANTING MEDIUM
FILTER BLANKET
DRAINAGE MEDIUM
PROTECTION BOARD
INSULATION BOARD
WATERPROOF MEMBRANE
SIDE DRAIN PERFORATIONS
STRUCTURAL SLAB

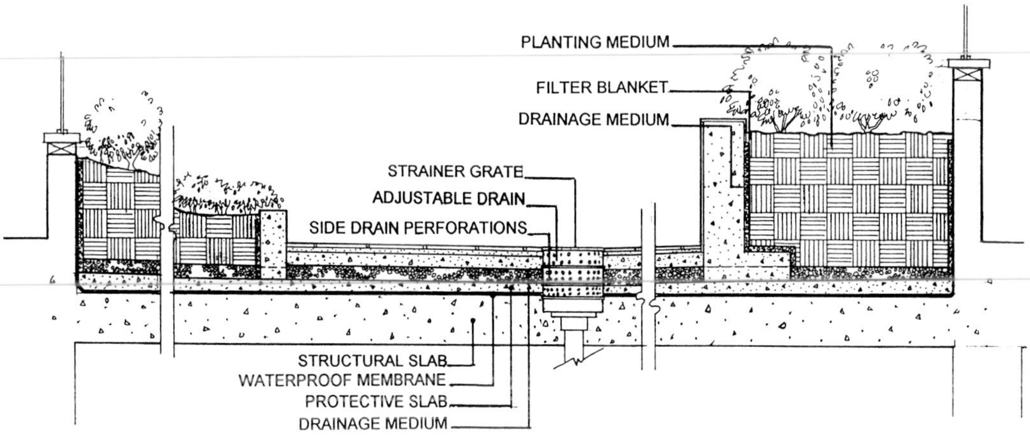
PLANTING MEDIUM
FILTER BLANKET
DRAINAGE MEDIUM
STRAINER GRATE
ADJUSTABLE DRAIN
SIDE DRAIN PERFORATIONS
STRUCTURAL SLAB
WATERPROOF MEMBRANE
PROTECTIVE SLAB
DRAINAGE MEDIUM

4-10 (top left). This deck drain, with top and side perforations, is a very good combination drain for surface and subsurface drainage. The lower half of the unit is set into the roof slab, waterproofing is placed tightly around its perimeter, and the drain is caulked. The upper half of the unit is attached to the lower half with screws. A perforated stainless-steel extension allows the drain to be used at different depths. The flat-top grille is supplied for use with paved surfaces.

4-11 (top right). A round, or deck, drain in place in a roof garden section.

4-12 (bottom). A deck drain can be used to drain both paved areas and adjacent planting spaces.

face level as well as through the sides of the drain below the surface, allowing for water runoff from the garden's surface and the subsurface drainage layer.

The round drain is useful whenever a drain in a paved area that is near a planting area is needed. The paving may be poured on the drainage layer; however, filter fabric should be installed on the surface of the drainage layer first to prevent the wet concrete from leaking into the drainage layer. Water falling onto the sloped paved surface can enter the top of the drain, while water from the planting medium can move down into the drainage medium below, through the perforations in the side of the drain, and into the drain itself.

The second type of drain, the *dome drain,* has a dome-shaped perforated surface, which can be used above grade to permit water to enter even if the lower perforations are blocked by leaves or other debris. This type of drain is not recommended for walking surfaces above grade. It is sometimes used under the drainage medium in roof gardens. In the latter installation, it is usually covered with filter fabric to prevent soil from entering. Figures 4-13 and 4-14 show dome drains in use.

The third drain type, the *flat-topped drain,* is installed flush with the surrounding ground surface. Such drains are usually used in paved areas, where they present no obstacle to walking, but can also be satisfactory for underground drainage with a drainage medium and filter blanket.

The fourth type of drain is the *lateral, channel,* or *strip drain.* This drain works well in concrete or other hard surfaces, where "sheet" drainage against a wall or other permanent vertical surface is needed and sloping surface drainage to a catch basin is not desirable or possible. These drains are manufactured in cast iron, galvanized steel, or

4-13 (top left). In this community garden, a dome drain protrudes from the pavement. Although this type of drain is effective for drainage, for safety, a flat-topped drain would have been a better choice.

4-14 (top right). At Pacific Bell's headquarters in Sacramento, outside drainage is carried in lateral oval pipes to a single dome drain. Shallow lawn areas will be planted here. Filter fabric will be added to protect the dome drain from silting. (The piping is for electrical fixtures.)

4-15 (bottom left). In a strip drain, used for paved surfaces, the perforated top can be removed for cleaning. These drains are made of high-impact plastic that is UV-resistant.

4-16 (bottom right). This concrete strip drain with a metal grille functions as the primary drain in this area of Portsmouth Square in San Francisco.

high-impact plastic, in a choice of colors, and are resistant to ultraviolet rays (fig. 4-15). The grille on the top surface is flush with the paving (fig. 4-16); it can be removed to permit cleaning of the drain. These drains are usually used for short runs and do not have a sloping bottom. If long runs are needed, a sloping pipe is installed in the ceiling of the floor below, directly below and parallel to the strip drain. Short down-pipes between the strip drain and sloping pipe carry water off more rapidly.

Another drain, popular in Europe, is a combination of a sloping concrete trough or gutter in the concrete protective slab covered by a continuous half-section of perforated plastic pipe covered with filter fabric (fig. 4-17). It is installed in planting beds above the insulation and roof deck. Water entering the drainage medium drains across the protective slab and into the gutter.

Lateral or secondary drain lines are sometimes necessary when surface contour grading prevents the use of the primary drain. A smaller drain may be installed in this isolated area, with its pipe leading under the soil to the main drain.

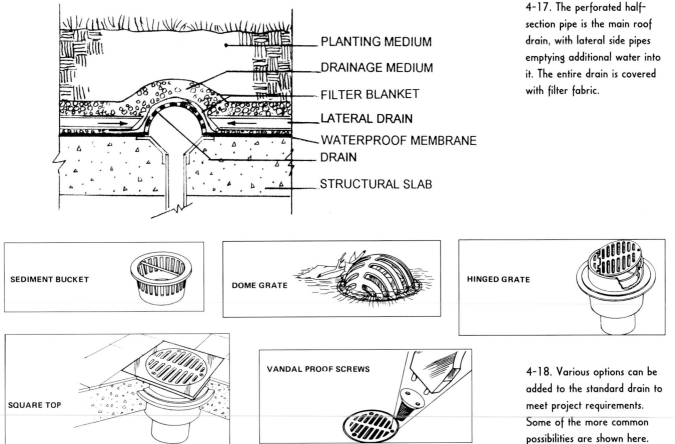

PLANTING MEDIUM
DRAINAGE MEDIUM
FILTER BLANKET
LATERAL DRAIN
WATERPROOF MEMBRANE
DRAIN
STRUCTURAL SLAB

SEDIMENT BUCKET

DOME GRATE

HINGED GRATE

SQUARE TOP

VANDAL PROOF SCREWS

4-18. Various options can be added to the standard drain to meet project requirements. Some of the more common possibilities are shown here.

At this junction point, the lateral is brought to the side of the main drain. The drainage medium here should be thickened and covered with an additional layer of filter fabric to prevent seepage of the planting medium into it.

Regardless of the type of drain used, all drains should be equipped, wherever possible, with debris-collection basins to prevent the system's pipes from clogging. Assorted other options are also available, as shown in figure 4-18. With imagination, the five drain types just described can meet almost all drainage requirements of roof gardens.

The pipes to which the drains lead are part of the building's drainage system, designed by the architect, and are not a concern of the landscape architect.

FILTER FABRIC

Water passing through the planting medium to the drainage system can carry with it bits of soil, mulch, and plant debris. If this water is not fil-tered, not only is valuable planting medium lost to the building's drainage system, but the drains themselves can become clogged or blocked. Providing effective drainage of the planting medium while simultaneously holding the soil in place has been a challenge throughout the history of roof gardens, but only in the last thirty years has that challenge been met. Once the need for a filtering system was recognized, a material that was lightweight, rot-proof, inexpensive, easy-to-install, and permanent had to be found. In the 1960s, a product developed as insulation, fiberglass batting, was the first material used as filter fabric. Although it performed satisfactorily, it was bulky and not easy to install. Soon thereafter, another material, developed to cover graded slopes to prevent erosion, was adapted for roof gardens. This filter fabric, made of polypropylene fibers, resembles felt, comes in several thicknesses, and meets all the requirements of a roof garden. It has become a standard material in the roof garden cross section (figs. 4-19 and 4-20).

4-19 (left). Filter fabric made from nonwoven polypropylene fibers should be placed atop the drainage layer. Adjoining pieces should overlap 8 inches (20 cm).

4-20 (right). Fiberglass insulation batting, used as filter fabric before the advent of polypropylene blankets, here is placed atop gravel drain rock at Pacific Bell's headquarters in Sacramento.

PLANTING MEDIA

The soil used for roof gardens is the least understood element of the roof garden cross section, and it is the area in which the least research has been conducted. Most landscape architects are not soil experts, and the special conditions of the roof garden, which requires a strong, light, well-drained, moist (but not wet), long-lasting, stable, and inexpensive soil, can be confusing to the designer. To make matters more difficult, soil scientists know little about the demands on roof garden soils as compared to soils for surface gardens.

One of the dictionary definitions of *soil* is "a medium in which plants take hold and develop." This definition is especially appropriate for the growing medium for roof gardens, for some of the substances and mixes used are a far cry from the growing media normally found on the surface of the earth. Indeed, some of the substances supporting plant growth on roofs both in the United States and in Europe contain no topsoil.

Certain processes that commonly occur in roof gardens make their planting media requirements quite different from those of ground-level gardens. First, roof gardens require good drainage. To prevent loss of soil through the drainage medium, a root-proof filter fabric must separate the growing medium from the drainage layer. The growing medium must be free of silt to prevent blockage of the filter fabric, which would cause excess water to be held in the soil, resulting in the rotting of plant roots and an additional live load on the roof. An example of this problem

occurred at a high-rise condominium in Boca Raton, Florida, where a silty soil was used for raised beds, contrary to the specifications. Frederick Stresau, Jr., a landscape architect, has studied these beds and determined the silt clogged the filter fabric, causing failure of the drainage system. Soggy soil was the result.

Even a filter fabric cannot prevent the loss of organic material from the soil. These substances, necessary for the nourishment of plants, decompose into matter so small that they can easily go into solution in water, pass through the filter and drainage layer, and be lost to the system. Only compacted sterile sand or other inorganic material eventually remains as the primary, and sometimes the only, soil component.

Once the organic materials are lost, few are replaced. Indeed, it is very difficult to replace the organic material in deep soil with plants growing in place. Replacement of humus in natural soils at ground level is a long-term process in which organic materials such as dead leaves, twigs, and other parts of living plants decay and mix with existing soil and dust to form new layers of fertile, open topsoil above the original layer. This process is much too slow to keep pace with the rapid decomposition of organic additives in a formulated roof garden soil. Simply put, an artificial soil mixture of sand and organic materials will lose its amendment long before it can be replaced from above by natural processes. Consequently, in a short period of time, perhaps three to five years, organic amendments will rot, go into solution, pass through the sand and into the drainage layer, and be carried away in the storm-water system. Although this process has not been documented by available research, it seems reasonable to assume. Certainly, a visual study of numerous roof gardens over time indicates that such is the case in old roof gardens.

The loss of organic material poses two problems. The first, loss of nutrients for the plantings, can be resolved to some extent by adding fertilizer and other amendments. The second, a decrease in the medium's original volume, is not so easily solved. Shrinkage, or slumping, deprives plants of space needed for root growth and encourages compaction of the remaining medium, which prevents aeration of the root zone.

Clearly, the growing medium for roof gardens cannot be the same as that for ground-level gardens. Can it be the same as that used for pot- and container-grown plants? After all, isn't a roof garden simply a giant container? Such was the thinking of roof garden designers some thirty years ago (and, indeed, of some roof garden designers even today). What they failed to consider were the ramifications of size and time. The consequences of such thinking are illustrated in a comparison of two roof gardens built in the 1960s, at the Kaiser Center and the Oakland Museum, both in Oakland, California.

Before examining these two gardens, it is worth noting that the development of suitable soils, drainage, filter fabrics, waterproofing, root-proofing, protection layers, and fertilizers and the appropriate combination of these elements into a workable section has proceeded with a remarkable lack of coordination, solid research, and communication between the professionals who design roof gardens and those who study them. The lack of readily available information on state-of-the-art technology in the United States has resulted in the failures of some of the most important roof gardens in this country. The goal of achieving a set of conditions on the roof that will result in a nearly permanent roof garden, requiring only the replacement of occasional plants as they age and die, apparently has not been an important factor in the design of cross sections and the soil mixes for the gardens. Such shortsightedness has been the rule rather than the exception, and there is no wish here to find

unusual fault with any particular person, garden, or set of circumstances. Anyone who designs an unusual project works with what is perceived to be the state of the art at the time. Roof gardens even today can be considered unusual, and thirty years ago they were practically unheard of. State of the art was primitive at best. The following examples illustrate the point.

The Kaiser Center

The garden atop the Kaiser Center in Oakland, California, completed in 1960, was the first major private roof garden constructed after World War II. Literature on the subject was scarce and difficult to find, and it was necessary to solve every problem as if it were new. The success the garden has enjoyed has been the result of good luck as much as understanding and perception (fig. 4-21).

The first challenge was to meet the load limitations imposed by the roof's structural slab. One

4-21. The Kaiser Center roof garden today, more than thirty-five years after its completion. Since its opening, the plants have become fuller and more mature, a few trees have been replaced, and the walks to the left of the ventilation building have required minor repair after the 1989 Loma Prieta earthquake. Otherwise, the garden's components are essentially the same as they were in 1960.

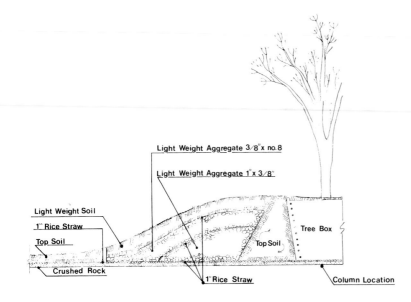

Light Weight Aggregate 3/8" x no.8

Light Weight Aggregate 1" x 3/8"

Light Weight Soil

1" Rice Straw

Top Soil

Crushed Rock

Tree Box

Top Soil

1" Rice Straw

Column Location

4-22. The fill used in the Kaiser Center roof garden. The lightweight aggregate is expanded shale.

of the then-new soil mixes developed by the University of California in the 1950s for growing nursery plants was chosen but was adapted to make it lighter. The formula chosen was similar to UC's Basic Mix B, which was composed of 75 percent fine sand and 25 percent peat moss, sawdust, or ground bark. This formula was modified by substituting expanded shale, from 1/16- to 3/32-inch (1.6- to 2.4-mm) particles up to 1/2-inch (1.3-cm) pieces, for the fine sand, to reduce the weight of the mix. A last-minute change, ordered by the company's vice president without the designer's knowledge, substituted crushed lava rock mixed with the expanded shale. Fortunately the lava rock had characteristics somewhat similar to that of the shale. Today, little remains of the original soil mix except the lava and expanded shale, and there has been considerable shrinkage of the mix because of the decay and loss of the organic matter. The lightweight substitute was, nevertheless, far better than the originally formulated sand and humus of the basic UC mix because expanded shale and lava retain air and water (with available nutrients in solution), whereas fine sand does not. Hence, the growing medium remains somewhat aerated (that is, it retains air spaces in its depth, a necessary condition for root growth) and can retain some moisture and nutrients; a mix that consisted of only sand would be sterile and compacted. Such a result was fortunate over the long term but was not foreseen at the time of design. The recommendation to use expanded shale was based on weight considerations only.

The successful drainage of this roof garden has also been a combination of luck and foresight. The architects designed the structural roof slab of the Kaiser Center without any advice from the landscape architect but fortunately provided an ideal platform for a roof garden. They designed the slab in 28-foot-square (8.5-m) panels, each sloping to a drain in the center at the location of a supporting column, where a vertical drainpipe to the city's storm system was located. After waterproofing the structural slab with a built-up tar membrane, the architects covered the roof with a 3- to 4-inch (7.6- to 10.2-cm) protective concrete slab sloped to the drains. This surface made an ideal base for the garden.

Unfortunately, the use of plastic filter fabric was completely unknown at the time, and no permanent filter material was used to prevent the soil from washing into the drainage layer of broken rock. The landscape architect was aware of the need for such a filter, however, and a layer of rice straw (a fibrous organic material commonly used at the time for erosion control on freeway embankments) was spread over the drainage layer (fig. 4-22). This material allowed water to drain but kept the soil above from entering the drain rock long enough to allow it to establish a structure that prevented it, temporarily, from going into solution and being lost via drainage. This method was not permanent, and obviously it would not be tried today. The garden now has areas of poor drainage, where the soil and rock below have become thoroughly mixed. Fortunately, these are in lawn areas in open sunlight, where poor drainage can be better tolerated.

The Oakland Museum

The Oakland Museum, built in the 1960s and designed by Kevin Roche, Dinkeloo and Associates of Connecticut, is one of the most well-known roof garden projects in the United States. Its design concept centers around dropping much of the building below grade and developing a green city park on much of its roof. This concept was so radically different in the 1960s that it was hailed as a breakthrough both in museum design and in maintaining a natural relationship between a site and its surroundings (fig. 4-23). Certainly no major example of urban

public architecture had been built before with such an admirable and overwhelming emphasis on landscape. Even today it is considered by most as a highly successful project, and so great is the mystique of its success that no one has thought to consider its shortcomings.

The technical foundation upon which any roof garden rests is the growing medium, irrigation system, drainage, and of course, waterproofing. The use of the term "state of the art" in conjunction with roof garden construction in the early 1960s is to stretch the point of the phrase. So few roof gardens had been built that there was little "art" of which landscape architects or architects could be aware. Even the suitability of waterproofing techniques for roof gardens was unknown. The built-up asphaltic membrane was the standard, and a useful life of fifteen years or so was all that could be guaranteed. The inclusion of a concrete protection layer, as well as ways to develop successful roof gardens on them, was not widely recognized as a requisite for a successful roof garden.

Although, only a few blocks away, the Kaiser Center roof garden had been completed in 1960, it was so new that its ultimate success or failure was not known. Other roof gardens built after World War II, such as Saint Mary's Square and Portsmouth Square in San Francisco, Mellon Square and Equitable Plaza in Pittsburgh, and the New England Merchants National Bank garden in Boston, were too new to have been published. When they were, little technical information was included, and each garden was designed without reference to the work of others. To put it simply, roof garden design and construction were "flying blind," a fact that became painfully evident at the Oakland Museum a few years later.

The Oakland Museum opened following a difficult planting season that included an extremely wet winter. The period of fascination with the UC soil mixes was much in evidence in California, and the enthusiasm for them carried the day at the Oakland Museum, where a planting medium formulated from UC Mix C was used. For one cubic yard (0.76 cubic meters), this standard mix consisted of:

60 percent fine redwood sawdust, up to ⅛ inch (3.2 mm)
40 percent fine sand, of particle sizes 0.05 to 0.55, with 85 percent passing a 30-mesh screen (must also pass a salinity test)
5 pounds blood meal or hoof-and-horn meal, 13 percent nitrogen
3 pounds single superphosphate, 0-20-0
8 ounces muriate of potash, 0-0-60
5 pounds calcium carbonate (ground oyster shell)
10 pounds dolomite lime
1 pound ferric or ferrous sulphate

One cubic yard (0.76 cubic meters) of a special mix formulated for acid-loving plants, such as ferns, azaleas, and the like, consisted of:

50 percent fine sphagnum peat moss
50 percent fine fir bark, up to ⅛ inch (3.2 mm)
4 pounds blood meal or hoof-and-horn meal
1 pound single superphosphate
4 pounds calcium carbonate
4 pounds dolomite lime

These mixes were devised to meet the needs of the nursery trade, which was growing rooted cuttings and seedlings of shrubs and trees in 1-gallon and 5-gallon containers for later sale. The mixes were highly successful for this purpose (though they have since been replaced by more effective formulations). They were easy to mix uniformly, drained well but retained sufficient moisture to promote growth, and had a built-in supply of soil nutrients that would last for a year or so in 1-gallon cans, when the established plants could either be sold to the public or moved to larger 5-gallon containers. If they were moved up, additional soil mix was added to accommodate the larger cans.

It was quite natural, in the absence of solid research on planting mixes designed for roof gardens, to assume that if one needed a uniform soil mix for any purpose, one of the UC mixes would work very well. Such was not the case. They were not designed for long-term use but only for growing young plants quickly in nurseries. They failed in fixed planters on roofs.

An examination of the above formulas explains why. The primary components of the standard mix were redwood sawdust and fine sand. Redwood sawdust, an organic material, is subject to decay, eventually going into solution and draining out of the plant containers along with most of the fertilizer additives in the normal process of drainage. After a few years, little remains in the planters except fine sand, and slumping of the soil mix is apparent. Fine sand alone will pack very hard, forming a dense, sterile growing medium that drains rapidly, with little ability to retain sufficient moisture and nutrients to support plants without extensive fertilization and irrigation. In addition, the loss of redwood sawdust will cause the original soil mix to shrink by 60 percent of its original volume. All of the foregoing would also apply to the special mix for azaleas and rhododendrons, except that theoretically the shrinkage would be 100 percent!

Here is where the ramification of size comes into play. While a roof garden may be nothing more than a giant container-grown planting, *giant* is the key. If the soil in a tub or pot shrinks significantly because of the loss of organic matter, the plant can be repotted. A roof garden cannot be "repotted," at least not without a great deal of work and expense.

Another problem at the Oakland Museum gardens is that the roofs, as well as the bottoms of the planters, lack a slope to drain. The concrete planters rely on the sand in the planting mix to permit drainage to the 4-inch (10.2-cm) perforated pipe at the bottom of the planter, the open end of which is pressed against a drainage opening in the lower inside wall at one end of the planting container. To keep sand out of the perforated pipe, the pipe was covered with ordinary burlap. This arrangement does not allow water to flow quickly away but requires the water to overflow out of the end of the perforated plastic pipe and into the drain opening in the wall of the planting container. Today the burlap covering the perforated pipe has long since rotted away, and drainage water enters the pipe directly through the sand, allowing some of the sand either to be carried away or to plug the perforations in the pipe and the drain lines embedded inside the poured roof slab. No sand-settlement basins were installed, and the drain lines are plugged. Because the drain pipes in the structure are made of plastic, rotary-blade pipe-clearing devices cannot be used to unplug them.

In 1988 the city of Oakland recognized the seriousness of the problems and invited proposals for studying both the roof and the roof garden. A landscape architect, Robert LaRocca and Associates, was selected to head a team to look into the entire roof condition, including plant failure, lack of drainage in the planting beds, shrinkage of soil, and loss of humus, as well as other serious roof deficiencies unrelated to the plantings, soils, and landscape drainage. These included many leaks in the roofs and melted tar

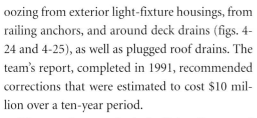

oozing from exterior light-fixture housings, from railing anchors, and around deck drains (figs. 4-24 and 4-25), as well as plugged roof drains. The team's report, completed in 1991, recommended corrections that were estimated to cost $10 million over a ten-year period.

The experiences at both the Kaiser Center and the Oakland Museum obviously demonstrate that a serious look at roof garden soils is long overdue. A comprehensive research project is needed to establish, once and for all, a database from which appropriate soil mixes can be specified.

Optimum Planting Media

In the absence of controlled research by soil scientists over a long-term period, it is impossible to declare that any given soil mix will meet all the requirements of a satisfactory and permanent planting medium for roof gardens. The best that can be done is to make assumptions based on experience and a process of deduction. The mix proposed herein may well be challenged. So be it, if a better rationale and conclusion can be devised. No attempt will be made to guarantee the success of the recommendation in all cases.

The optimal growing medium should meet the requirements of roof garden soils listed earlier in this chapter. That is, it cannot contain any silt that would clog the filter fabric, it must provide a permanent means of supplying internal aeration to prevent compaction of the mix, it must drain adequately, it must be able to supply or absorb water and nutrients for the plants to use over time, and it must retain much of its original volume.

Topsoil. Field topsoil, the natural growing medium of ground-level plants, usually contains fine particles of silt that must be removed before use. Field soils meeting the necessary specifications for granule size are difficult to obtain, and those not meeting the silt-free specification are expensive to process for removal of the silt. Moreover, Swiss and German research into field topsoil has uncovered a number of other shortcomings:

1. It is heavy when wet, a concern particularly when loads are limited.

2. It has a relatively low percentage of organic matter and so must be amended.

3. Its low porosity is often corrected by short-lived organic soil conditioners, which decay and must be regularly replaced.

4. It often lacks macropores, needed for root growth and water retention.

5. If high in clay content, it compresses and compacts from pedestrian contact. It also will retain too much moisture.

6. If high in sand content, it will drain too rapidly. It will also not be able to retain nutrients very well.

7. It may harbor weed seeds, pests, and diseases, unless sterilized.

8. Because of its high microbiological activity, organic substances rapidly decay and are leached out of the soil, resulting in shrinkage.

9. The components of field topsoil are often

4-26 (left). Workmen in Germany install sod over a layer of Leca, or expanded clay.

4-27 (right). A ball of Leca and a cross section of that ball.

inconsistent: one load may be high in sand, whereas another is high in clay, for example.

Hence, field soils are not a good choice for roof gardens.

Sand. Another option is sand. Sand can be sorted for granule size fairly easily, and because this grading is commonly done for many construction and industrial uses, graded sand is relatively inexpensive. Sand is also relatively easy to leach if harmful salts are present, because of its natural structural porosity. However, this last characteristic, high porosity, is a serious drawback to using sand alone. Sand is unable to retain available water and nutrients for plant use. A growing medium of only sand will require extensive watering and replacement of lost soil nutrients because of rapid leaching.

A growing medium of sand must therefore be amended with a permanent material that will retain water and nutrients, provide aeration of the root layer, and reduce or eliminate slumping of the medium.

Expanded Shale, Slate, or Clay. One such amendment for sand is expanded shale, slate, or clay. Often used alone as the growing medium in hydroponics, expanded shale or clay is sold under a variety of names in the United States; the German product Leca is one brand. Leca alone, without sand or other soil components, has been widely used as a growing medium in Germany for extensive roof landscapes that include turf, wildflowers, and/or ground covers (fig. 4-26).

Leca is produced by kiln-firing clay, shale, or slate to extremely high temperatures, in the range of 2,100°F (1,150°C) until the parts expand, forming round pellets (fig. 4-27). The air spaces formed by the expansion are capable of retaining liquid. The air spaces also significantly reduce the product's weight, which is 450 kilograms per cubic meter.

Leca has 50 percent broken parts, which gives it the unusual ability to absorb 35 percent of its volume in water and to retain 28 percent of its volume in water for slow release to the root environment. It can be watered by flooding the surface of the roof below (see the discussion of the Optima system later in this chapter) or by overhead irrigation. Leca absorbs excess water from the root area. Although a natural product, it is inorganic, so that it will not decay and is not sensitive to strong chemicals, such as those that may be found in fertilizer. Its almost neutral pH of 6.6 to 7.5 does not affect the acidity of the mix. Even after decades, Leca will not compact, providing ample aeration for the plants' root systems.

In addition to being used for hydroponics, expanded shale is also used in the United States to replace stone or rock aggregate in lightweight concrete. Hence, it can be ordered from suppliers of products in both these industries. It is relatively inexpensive and is generally available in bulk.

Because of expanded shale's light weight and low ability to adhere to itself, however, it alone cannot form a strong soil structure for general planting. While it can be the only medium for extensive planting, for larger plants, another inorganic soil material is necessary, such as silt-free sand, which will not clog the filter layer and which will give the soil mix some body or structure and additional weight. Taken together, a mixture of sand and graded sizes of expanded shale provide a planting mix that is permanent, stable, provides good drainage, retains water and nutrients, and is sturdy enough to support a full range of plant sizes with minimum danger from windthrow.

Humus. In addition to sand and expanded shale, a relatively small amount of organic humus can be added to provide additional water-holding capacity and the beginnings of a long-term humus component that will gradually be created from the decay of plant waste and mulch. Humus will also help in holding the mix together while it is being mixed, delivered, and placed, and it serves a cosmetic function as well, making the growing medium look more like ground-level soil.

The *optimum growing mix* for a roof garden would thus consist of 45 percent graded sand, with no fines; 45 percent expanded shale (equal parts of 2- to 4-mm, 4- to 8-mm, and 8- to 16-mm pellets), and 10 percent humus, preferably nitrolized pine bark (half ⅛-inch [3.2-mm] and half ¼-inch [6.4-mm] screen). The mix should be delivered to the site and placed while damp but not wet. A dry mix is susceptible to wind erosion before plants are in place; a wet mix will destroy the air spaces within the mix. A complete liquid or dry fertilizer should be added when it is placed. The mix should be crowned in the center of the bed, installed to the very top of the surrounding planter walls, and thoroughly watered for one week. The surface should then be topped off with additional media to the top of the surrounding bed walls and crowned 2 inches (5.1 cm) high in the center of the bed to allow for further settlement after planting. After this process is complete, planting may begin.

Other Amendments

Diatomaceous Earth. In recent years another product on the market in the United States has been explored as an alternative to organic humus. Like expanded shale, it can absorb and

4-28. Diatomaceous earth is processed into pellets that are used as a soil amendment.

retain water and nutrients for plants without decomposing. Again like expanded shale, it has been used extensively for other purposes but appears to be adaptable to roof gardens. Diatomaceous earth is commonly used as an abrasive, in the filtration systems of swimming pools, as an inert ingredient in explosives, and as insulation for boilers and steam pipes, but it recently has been identified as an important soil additive for golf courses and in growing nursery plants. Diatomaceous earth consists of the remains of ancient one-celled sea algae, diatoms, whose tiny silicate skeletons are found in deposits around the world. After processing, the result is a hard, lightweight, stonelike substance that is highly water-absorbent and does not compact. The product is offered in coarse, regular, and fine particles (fig. 4-28).

Researchers at the University of Florida have tested diatomaceous earth as a soil amendment for nursery-grown plants. Its ability to wick water containing nutrients upward in the soil profile increased the size of plants by as much as 40 percent as compared to control plants without diatomaceous earth. Under conditions of water stress, incorporating 10 percent diatomaceous earth in the soil mix still resulted in a significant growth increase of 25 percent in both top and root segments of the hibiscus plants tested.

The University of Ohio tested the value of diatomaceous earth in the root-zone-soil mixtures for golf greens. One process that improves the consistent supply of water to grass roots in the root cross section is the wicking of water from the bottom of the profile up to the roots closer to the surface. Previous research had indicated that in uniform sand mixes, which have a narrow pore-size distribution, wicking would fail: much of the perched water at the bottom of the section would be untapped while surface tensions exceeded 0.01 MPa. In other words, irrigation would still be required even though a large reservoir of water storage remained in the soil profile. In one test a mix of 70 percent graded fine sand, 20 percent peat, and 10 percent diatomaceous earth was compared with a mix of 80 percent sand and 20 percent peat; the percentage of available water was increased by about 74 percent in the mix containing diatomaceous earth.

What is the significance of these tests with regard to roof gardens? While promising, the results are inconclusive because the material has not been tested in a roof garden setting over time and in different climates. As the adoption and subsequent failure of the UC soil mixes in roof gardens has demonstrated, amendments that work well for nursery stock are not always appropriate for the more permanent requirements of roof gardens. Similarly, golf greens, with turf as their only plant component, are not necessarily analogous to roof gardens. Moreover, the inclusion of peat in the golf greens mix complicates the application of those results to roof gardens, for in roof gardens peat is temporary at best and almost impossible to add after it has decayed and been washed away. Perhaps replacing the peat with additional diatomaceous earth or with broken particles of expanded shale would produce an effective roof garden growing medium. (The supplier recommends that diatomaceous earth be 5 to 20 percent of the total soil mix by volume.) Once again, roof garden designers are left to experiment on their clients' projects. Although diatomaceous earth could be considered as a replacement for short-lived organic humus such as peat or nitrolized sawdusts in roof gardens, until controlled testing produces verifiable test results in roof gardens, the benefits of its inclusion in the growing medium remain unproved.

Isolite. Another amendment, produced and used in Japan for golf greens, is Isolite, a chemically inert, porous substance derived from sea plankton and algae. It is a natural mined product that has been in use in Japan for fifteen years in various landscaping projects. It is not degraded by freezing and thawing. Its purpose is to permanently aerate heavy soils and to retain water and fertilizer in suspension in the planting mix.

Although it has not been tested specifically for roof gardens, it would appear from tests on golf greens that mixing Isolite thoroughly with graded sand and a small amount of peat would produce a blend similar to the optimum growing mix recommended earlier in this chapter. Because the particles are much smaller than those of expanded shale or clay, the mix would require less space while maintaining the same balance of ingredients. Approximately 10 percent Isolite to 90 percent of sand by volume is the mix recommended by the American distributor. To include a bit of humus in the mix, 10 percent peat should also be included, mixed damp and homogeneously with the sand and Isolite to achieve best results. Isolite weighs 850 pounds per cubic yard or 32 pounds per cubic foot (512 kg per cubic meter).

Although this material seems to be a promising addition to the planting mix for roof gardens, it has not been field-tested or extensively used in the United States under controlled conditions. It has, however, been used for roof gardens in Japan. (See Appendix B for source of supply.)

Perlite and Vermiculite. Perlite and vermiculite are widely used in the soil mixes of small nursery growing containers, pots, and hanging baskets. Like expanded shale, they are natural inorganic materials that have been heated to expand and produce air pockets inside (perlite is expanded volcanic glass, and vermiculite is expanded mica). These two materials work well in the sheltered environment of the nursery, where they can retain water and nutrients within the soil and provide aeration as well. They are, however, both quite fragile, and their durability in a roof garden environment has never been tested. Dr. Francis Gouin of the University of Maryland states that they cannot withstand the freeze/thaw cycle of northern climates; rapid disintegration would result from such exposure.

Soil-less Media

The search for appropriate growing media for roof gardens has been far more sophisticated in Europe, and especially in Germany, where some radically different approaches have been adopted. These systems not only eliminate soil of any kind, but some also do not require gravel or other drainage material, nor filter fabric (because there is nothing to filter); moreover, they add substantially to the insulation of the roof. Organic material does not need to be replaced—plants grow in the planting medium without humus.

Technoflor. The Technoflor system includes all the elements necessary for a complete growing medium as well as for drainage and water retention, and it can support a great range of plants on roofs. It also can be and often is used as a substrate for a more typical soil mix on its surface.

The material used in Technoflor is a structurally stable elastic polyurethane foam compound of low density. The foam is bound in panels similar to plywood in the United States but resembles soft Styrofoam in texture and weight. Seed is embedded in the material. The pores of this material occupy 95 percent of its volume; its fine pores can retain 40 percent of their volume in available water, whereas excess water may pass through the larger pores, thus eliminating the need for a drainage layer. A square of Technoflor that is approximately 1 square yard and 4 inches thick (1 square meter by 10.2 cm) will hold almost 11 gallons (40 liters) of water, with the excess draining off in two hours. The rapid drainage of unusable water creates voids that increase the air space in the material to 15 percent of its volume, providing ample root aeration. The surface of this substrate, when exposed to the atmosphere, dries rapidly, thus reducing evaporation through the capillaries, as well as the growth of weeds on its surface.

Technoflor is remarkably low in weight. A thickness sufficient for small plantings such as lawns and ground covers—2⅓ inches (6 cm)—weighs less than 9 pounds per square yard (4 kg per square meter). Sheet thicknesses of 4 to 6 inches (10.2 to 15 cm) or more are also available from the manufacturer. Depths can be varied on the same roof. Planting is accomplished simply by cutting a plug from the foam panel and inserting the root ball of the plant. Sheets with grass or ground-cover seed embedded in the surface are also available. Irrigation is supplied by an overhead sprinkler system in combination with rainfall. Long-term fertilization is achieved by applying dry or liquid fertilizer to the surface or by including it in an overhead sprinkler irrigation system.

Technoflor also shields the roof membrane from ultraviolet radiation and contains no elements that can harm the membrane. In addition, it provides some thermal and sound insulation. The material has been thoroughly use-tested on roofs for more than thirty years.

Technoflor is currently not available in the United States, but additional information about it can be obtained from the manufacturer (see Appendix B).

Grodan Planting Medium. Grodan's medium, developed in Denmark, consists of sheets or blocks of a special form of basalt rockwool fiber, which is sometimes used for thermal insulation. Processed to hold water, it becomes a reservoir for plant growth but releases any excess water into the drainage layer below (fig. 4-29). Container-grown or bare-root plants can easily be inserted into the medium by removing sufficient material with a knife to accommodate the root ball or bare roots. The roots then grow into the damp Grodan.

When dry it is very lightweight and easy to handle and to cut to shape. A pack of shrub slabs weighs only a bit more than 25 pounds (11.5 kg) and will cover about 17 square feet (1.62 square meters). An equivalent area of topsoil for a shrub border would weigh more than 3,850 pounds (almost 1,750 kg). When laid in place and soaked with water, it provides a stable root zone for plants and is guaranteed to be free of pests, disease, and weed seeds. It is made in a range of dimensions and densities to be applicable to any planting needs. Grodan slabs are simply butted together on the top of the drainage layer and cut to fit with a sharp knife. Their stable structure prevents the major problem of settlement, often associated with topsoil roof gardens. The medium maintains its original form over time and can even occasionally be walked on for maintenance. Irrigation can be achieved using one of the standard methods of overhead watering, and liquid or dry fertilizers can be applied to the surface.

Grodan also offers a system for sloping roofs. All of their media are available in the United States. (See Appendix B for sources of supply.)

TOP DRESSING OR MULCH

The final, top layer of the roof garden section is mulch. Applied to the surface of the growing medium in a 1-inch (2.5-cm) layer, organic mulch can insulate the soil to prevent excess heating and, in northern climates, help protect plant roots from frost damage; it also helps to keep down weeds and slow the evaporation of moisture from the soil. Even more important, its gradual decay will replenish part of the volume of organic matter, keep the medium more friable, and increase its moisture retention.

The longest-lasting organic mulch is ¼- to ½-inch (6.4- to 12.7-mm) cedar, redwood, fir, or pine bark chips. Sawdust and shredded bark are more short-lived. Because decaying wood and bark use nitrogen as they decompose, the chips should be nitrolized with 15 percent nitrogen by volume to compensate for any loss from the growing medium below.

Permanent inorganic mulches, such as colored gravel or pebbles, should not be used, as they cannot replace organic matter in the planting medium that is lost through leaching.

4-29. Section of a roof garden that includes the Grodan planting medium.

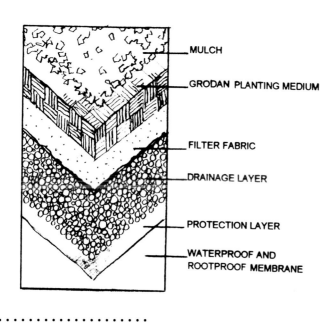

MULCH

GRODAN PLANTING MEDIUM

FILTER FABRIC

DRAINAGE LAYER

PROTECTION LAYER

WATERPROOF AND ROOTPROOF MEMBRANE

IRRIGATION SYSTEMS

Roof gardens demand an availability of water not found in ground-level plantings. Water falling on the ground penetrates the surface, and part of it is stored immediately below for short-term future use of plants. This condition is a benefit, depending on the nature of the plants. Woody plants and succulents can store water for use over a longer period of time than nonwoody plants such as most garden flowers, ground covers, and lawn. Most growth in nature has adapted itself to the average rainfall and soil retention of water found in different zones. The shallow soil, relatively quick drainage, and low water-storage capacity of the roof garden demands that a ready source of irrigation water for distribution over the entire planted surface is provided. This source can be provided by an underground irrigation system spraying water into the air above the planted areas or a selected drip system delivering water to each shrub, tree, or plant large enough to justify its cost. Where both lawns and plants are present, a combination of spray and drip irrigation may be practical.

There are advantages and disadvantages to each of these systems. The overhead system is difficult to control in its own area of irrigation, the water spray being blown about into planted areas where water on plants is not wanted. Many flowers, for example, mildew from too much water on leaves and stems. Also, the height of the plants block off the spray at the planters' outer edges, leaving the center of the planting areas relatively dry. Lawns, shrub, and flower areas have to be subdivided to receive different quantities of water from separate valves. Most of the problems can be reduced by careful selection of the component parts of the system. In addition, because of the shallow depth of the irrigation system, its supply lines can be frozen and will break in cold climates unless the lines are drained before winter begins. This ability should be built into the system.

Drip irrigation, the slow release of small quantities of water from emitters or small spray heads at the end of ¼-inch (6.4-mm) flexible plastic tubing above the roots of plants, also has its drawbacks in a roof garden. This system is based on emitters releasing a small quantity of water at a given point, which spreads in a widening pattern below the ground surface, shown in section as a pear shape. Again, the shallow roof garden soil does not permit the area to widen out as it penetrates, requiring a great many emitters to cover a wide area, such as one chosen for ground cover. Shrubs, trees, and flower beds require many emitters to provide a sufficiently wide irrigated area. Also, the slightly buried tubing is constantly at risk from cultivation of the soil, and often a plugged emitter is not found until the plant it serves is dead. These shortcomings require constant vigilance and correction by maintenance gardeners. In addition to the above problems, the tubing and emitters in projects open to the public, such as plazas and parks, are prey to children and pets, who may pull them out of the ground or break them. The supply lines should also be drained in winters with freezing temperatures.

These two systems are the most commonly used in roof gardens at this time. By careful design either or a combination of both can be satisfactorily used. For aesthetic and practical reasons, both systems should be as inconspicuous as possible.

Supply and lateral lines for both systems should be installed directly on the waterproofing or, if one is used, on the concrete protection slab. These systems should be controlled by an electric clock especially designed to supply water for specific amounts of time and volume on a day to day or other selected schedule. Also available are moisture sensors, which automatically signal the system to operate when the moisture level in the soil drops below a certain point. A wide range of irrigation equipment is available.

Optima System

The Optima system, one of the most widely used in Europe, provides irrigation, fertilization, and drainage from *below* the surface of the soil. A layer of water is kept on the roof at all times; it rises upward through the planting medium via capillary action. The water passes through layers of expanded shale pellets, graduated in size from large, in the water on the roof, to small, where it changes to the soil-based growing mixture developed by the manufacturer (fig. 4-30). The depth of the water layer is kept uniform at all times by overflow standpipes connected to the building's drainage system. If the water level drops because of insufficient rainfall, evaporation, or absorption by plants, a float valve releases water from the building's water system onto the roof's surface (fig. 4-31). The valve automatically turns off the water when the proper level is reached. Liquid fertilizer can be injected into the replacement water from the building source. An overhead sprinkler system is not needed. (See the Social and Recreation Building and the Farmers' Insurance roof gardens, both in Hannover, Germany, and the Allianz Versicherungs-AG project in Stuttgart, Germany, in the portfolio of international gardens, for examples of Optima in use.)

The Optima system also uses a growing medium consisting of biologically inert ingredients, which are not subject to decay. Soil shrinkage is thus not a problem, and no organic matter needs replacement. This system is a long-term solution to the problem of soil shrinkage, overcoming most of the shortcomings of soil amendments. In addition, the elimination of an overhead sprinkler system yields long-term cost savings.

The Optima system is currently not available in the United States, but more information about it can be obtained from the manufacturer (see Appendix B).

ZinCo System

The primary component of the ZinCo system is a manufactured modular unit marketed under the trade name Floradrain (fig. 4-32). Floradrain units are high-profile panels made from recycled polyethylene. A series of water-retention troughs and air-ventilation holes on top of the panels ensure water retention (for supplemental irrigation) for a longer period of time, as well as necessary ventilation of the soil layer. A multidirectional channel system beneath the panels allows excess water to drain from the system. A rot-proof filter sheet made of polypropylene fibers is laid over the Floradrain units to prevent soil particles from being washed from the system.

The soil mix, which is placed directly over the filter fabric, has been developed by the manufacturer and is an integral element of the system. It

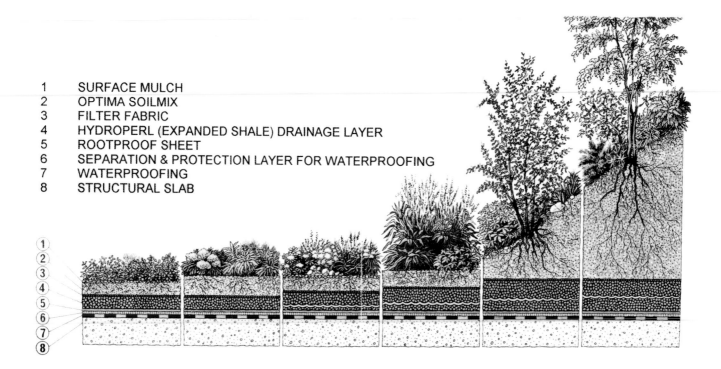

1 SURFACE MULCH
2 OPTIMA SOILMIX
3 FILTER FABRIC
4 HYDROPERL (EXPANDED SHALE) DRAINAGE LAYER
5 ROOTPROOF SHEET
6 SEPARATION & PROTECTION LAYER FOR WATERPROOFING
7 WATERPROOFING
8 STRUCTURAL SLAB

4-30. Extensive (left) and intensive (right) roof planting can both be accommodated with the Optima system. Greater depths of material are simply used for larger plants. (Courtesy of Optima)

contains a special mixture of minerals and organic material, based on extensive research and development by ZinCo. The special soil design ensures the proper amounts of air, water, and nutrients are present to sustain plant growth while at the same time keeping the total weight of the system lower than if conventional materials were used. The ZinCo system is currently not on the market in the United States.

Floradrain is, however, available in the United States as one component of a system called the Garden Roof Assembly, produced through a cooperative venture between ZinCo and American Hydrotech, a well-established American manufacturer of roof membranes. The Garden Roof Assembly is a complete roof and garden system that is installed over the roof slab (fig. 4-33). For intensive planting it consists of a monolithic, high-endurance waterproof membrane of rubberized asphalt (American Hydrotech's MM6125EV). This membrane is a fluid elastomer that is painted on in a single coat. The membrane is topped by a protection layer and root barrier (Hydroplex RB). Styrofoam insulation is next, then a moisture-retention mat and Floradrain, which stores water for the system. A lightweight soil that serves as a planting medium tops the system. A system for extensive roof

4-31. The continuous permanent water level maintained by the Optima system is achieved with overflow standpipes, which allow excess water to overflow to drains. Conversely, a built-in float valve is activated when the surface of the water reaches a preset low level. (Courtesy of Optima)

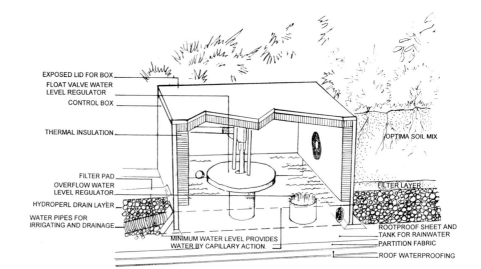

EXPOSED LID FOR BOX
FLOAT VALVE WATER LEVEL REGULATOR
CONTROL BOX
THERMAL INSULATION
FILTER PAD
OVERFLOW WATER LEVEL REGULATOR
HYDROPERL DRAIN LAYER
WATER PIPES FOR IRRIGATING AND DRAINAGE
MINIMUM WATER LEVEL PROVIDES WATER BY CAPILLARY ACTION.
OPTIMA SOIL MIX
FILTER LAYER
ROOTPROOF SHEET AND TANK FOR RAINWATER
PARTITION FABRIC
ROOF WATERPROOFING

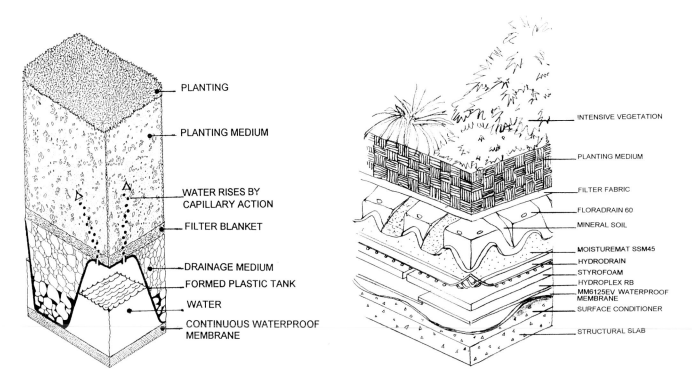

Labels for left diagram:
PLANTING
PLANTING MEDIUM
WATER RISES BY CAPILLARY ACTION
FILTER BLANKET
DRAINAGE MEDIUM
FORMED PLASTIC TANK
WATER
CONTINUOUS WATERPROOF MEMBRANE

Labels for right diagram:
INTENSIVE VEGETATION
PLANTING MEDIUM
FILTER FABRIC
FLORADRAIN 60
MINERAL SOIL
MOISTUREMAT SSM45
HYDRODRAIN
STYROFOAM
HYDROPLEX RB
MM6125EV WATERPROOF MEMBRANE
SURFACE CONDITIONER
STRUCTURAL SLAB

planting, using the same components, but of lighter and thinner materials and without the root barrier (which is not necessary when large trees and shrubs are omitted), is also available. See Appendix B for sources of information about the ZinCo system and American Hydrotech's Garden Roof Assembly.

ROOF AND GARDEN SYSTEMS

In Europe, where the installation of roof gardens is not considered merely a nicety but is, in a number of places, mandated by law for environmental reasons, manufacturers have addressed various aspects of roof garden construction in an effort to improve the materials and processes involved. Although a number of their innovations focus on individual components of the garden itself, several manufacturers have developed systems that encompasses both roof and garden construction. Two are described below. The Garden Roof Assembly, which is an American and German product, is another such system; it has just been discussed, under "ZinCo System."

The Bauder System

Paul Bauder GmbH and Company of Stuttgart, Germany, has devised a roof garden system available only in Europe, that is highly regarded in Germany by many landscape architects because it prevents root penetration of the waterproof membrane and because it is lightweight and long-lasting. Bauder recommends that the entire system be installed by a single contractor to ensure quality control throughout. The system's profile is shown in figure 4-34, and its components are described below, starting from the bottom of the section at the concrete roof deck.

The first layer, the *primer,* is a cold bitumen-based liquid that is applied directly to the surface of the roof deck to provide a good bond between the deck and the next layer, the vapor retardant. (Because the Bauder system does not use a protected-membrane roof but instead has the insulation *below* the membrane, a vapor retardant is needed to prevent warm, moist air inside the building from being trapped in the insulation, where the moisture would condense and saturate the insulation.) The vapor retardant is a 4-millimeter-thick (0.15-inch) torch-on sheet made of elastomeric modified bitumen, with a base of highly flexible aluminum film plus a film of fiberglass. In addition to being a vapor retardant, it can also serve as temporary waterproofing during construction.

Placed above the vapor retardant is the *insulation,* consisting of polyisocyanate foam board

4-32 (left). Section of a roof garden that includes ZinCo's Floradrain units for irrigation.

4-33 (right). Section of the Garden Roof Assembly, a joint venture between ZinCo and American Hydrotech.

with seamed joints. It has high pressure resistance and is heat resistant and resistant to hot bitumen.

The system employs two layers of *waterproofing*. The layer directly above the insulation is a 5-millimeter-thick elastomeric modified bitumen with a polyester base that is extremely flexible and puncture resistant. The upper, second layer of waterproofing protection is a 5-millimeter-thick (0.2-inch) torch-on membrane of elastomeric modified bitumen with a base of copper sheet. The thin layer of copper sheeting between these membranes bars the penetration of roots, as well as water, through the membrane. Controlled testing of this system for over twenty years in German laboratories, as well as its actual use in over 2 million square meters (21 million square feet) of roof gardens, has proven fairly conclusively that roots cannot penetrate this layer.

Above the membrane is a double layer to separate the roof construction from the garden above it. Bauder believes that there is a need for a non-slip flexible connection of the roofing system to the built-up layers above. For example, if an ice dam forms in the drainage or water reservoir layer that leads to roof damage, even years after planting, the upper layer can be removed, and the roof will still have a functioning waterproof layer at the lower level. The damaged part of the roofing can be repaired without loss of leak protection.

Protection of the membrane from construction damage by other trades must be provided.

Damage from storage, traffic, and building materials must be prevented to ensure that the membrane is not compromised. Bauder recommends using polyurethane rubber, available in 8-millimeter-thick (⅓-inch) sheets and 6-millimeter (¼-inch) rolls, as a protection layer.

The standard Bauder *drainage layer* consists of polystyrene supplied in rolls. This economical solution for drainage is extremely light, resistant to wear, able to withstand high air and water pressure, and is rot resistant and easy to install. The correct thickness depends on the design of the whole system. This drainage layer has a water-storage capacity equal to 30 percent of its volume.

An alternate drainage system provides for a water-storage layer, which can hold more or less water as needed, for example, during drought periods. This system is created by adjusting the drains to allow a higher depth of water to remain in the drainage layer. Overflow openings, drain openings, and a canal system underneath are responsible for immediate drainage. This alternative is made of polystyrene foam, which is lightweight and pressure resistant, so that wheelbarrows can be moved about atop it, even at its joints. It is available in several thicknesses, to hold more or less water in reserve.

The *filter layer* prevents soil or other growing media from entering and clogging the drainage layer. The filter fabric allows for easy passage of water and is chemically neutral and rot resistant. It is also capable of wicking water from the water-storage layer below into the growing medium above.

Completing the system, Bauder also prepares soil mixtures to suit the type and size of planting desired

This system is currently not available in the United States, but further information about it can be obtained from the manufacturer (see Appendix B).

The Sopranature System

This system, designed by the Soprema Company of France, is intended to support extensive roof planting on relatively flat or slightly sloping roofs. The plant materials recommended are wildflowers, annuals, perennials, and low-growing, hardy succulents. The system, shown in sec-

4-34. The components of the Bauder system of roof and garden construction. (Courtesy of Paul Bauder GmbH and Co.)

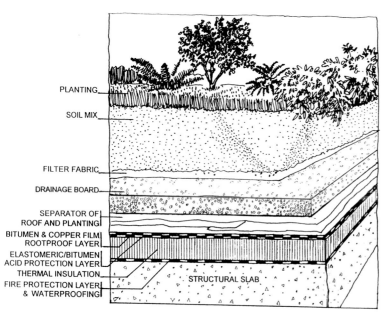

PLANTING

SOIL MIX

FILTER FABRIC

DRAINAGE BOARD

SEPARATOR OF ROOF AND PLANTING

BITUMEN & COPPER FILM ROOTPROOF LAYER

ELASTOMERIC/BITUMEN ACID PROTECTION LAYER

THERMAL INSULATION

FIRE PROTECTION LAYER & WATERPROOFING

STRUCTURAL SLAB

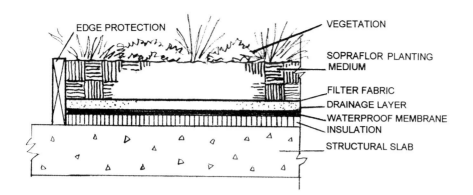

4-35. The components of the Sopranature system of roof and garden construction.

EDGE PROTECTION — VEGETATION

SOPRAFLOR PLANTING MEDIUM

FILTER FABRIC
DRAINAGE LAYER
WATERPROOF MEMBRANE
INSULATION
STRUCTURAL SLAB

tion in figure 4-35, consists of a layer of Sopralene Flam Jardin waterproofing atop the structural slab. This membrane contains root-repelling agents that prevent root penetration. Covering the membrane is a drainage layer, consisting of cellular polystyrene, mineral aggregate, or drainage geotextile, depending on the degree of slope of the roof. The drainage material is protected by Soprafilter, a nonwoven synthetic geotextile that serves as a filter fabric. Finally, the Sopraflor substrate, or planting medium, is designed to achieve optimum water retention, permeability, density, and resistance to erosion, to support healthy vegetation on the roof. Because it is laid over large expanses of roof, any slump in the planting medium is not as obvious as in a raised planter, where its surface can be compared to the top of the surrounding wall.

The Sopranature system is available in the United States and Canada; see Appendix B for sources of supply.

BUILDING THE GARDEN

Every roof garden has individual construction requirements that demand site- and design-specific solutions. It is impossible to outline all of the possible ways of putting the garden in place, but a look at some of the equipment and techniques that have been used can be instructive. Three construction case studies, of Kaiser Center in Oakland, Kaiser Resources in Vancouver, and Thoreau Hall in Davis, California, illustrate how roof gardens were added to these places.

A note about lifting devices: despite the seemingly impossible locations to which building

4-36 (bottom left). To move small loads over short vertical distances and in tight spaces difficult for larger equipment to reach, this collapsible hand-operated steel lift is often all that is needed.

4-37 (bottom right). An endless belt attached to a truck delivers soil mix over the roof parapet into a garden, while a front-end loader fills the hopper at the street end of the belt.

4-38 (top left). Many types of motorized lifts, with various capabilities and sizes, can be used to place materials and plants on roofs. This one can reach the roof of a high first floor.

4-39 (top right). An endless belt machine throws soil mix into a planter bed on the third-floor roof of a new office building for the Oakland Port Authority.

4-40 (bottom). The roof of the Kaiser Center before its roof garden was added.

materials for roof gardens must be delivered, a number of machines commonly used in the construction industry can reach almost anywhere on a building under construction, thereby making a roof garden considerably less costly to construct. Some of these, shown in figures 4-36, 4-37, 4-38, and 4-39, are often already on the job site for other purposes when the roof garden is being built.

KAISER CENTER CONSTRUCTION, 1959–60

See figures 4-40 through 4-50. The Kaiser Center in Oakland, California, five to six floors above the street, presented some new problems to its landscape construction contractor in 1959. As the first major private roof garden to be built in California after World War II, it required original and imaginative construction techniques. Fortunately,

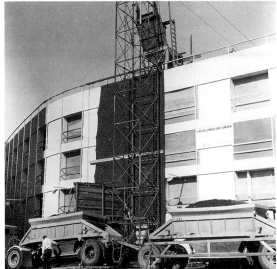

4-41 (top left). A row of holly oaks, *Quercus ilex*, waits in line to be lifted by crane to the roof of the Kaiser Center.

4-42 (top right). Loose materials, such as soil mix, gravel, and wet concrete, are lifted by a construction elevator with a tipping bucket that will fill a vehicle on the roof. The material is delivered in hopper trailers and blocked up to permit clearance for bottom-loading of the elevator box.

4-43. This early view of the Kaiser Center roof garden shows the initial layout of bracing for curb forms, the finished curbing for the pond, irrigation lines (many not hooked up), and the beginning of walk construction in the upper part of the photo. Boxed trees are being raised to the roof by a crane at the lower right. A rubber-tired tractor delivers the trees to their final location.

4-44 (top left). Below the surfaces of roof gardens are unseen systems that make the garden's beauty possible. These are the conduits and junction boxes for the lighting system at Kaiser Center.

4-45 (top right). What appears to be a major piece of concrete construction is actually a future raised planting bed and metalwork for a curved recessed wooden bench, much of which will be covered with planting mix.

4-46 (bottom left). Braces, two-by-four stakes, and crushed rock (for stabilization) provide support to the forms for the concrete paving.

4-47 (bottom right). A crane with a 60-foot (18-m) reach raised the 36-inch (91-cm) boxed olives to the roof garden.

equipment from other types of projects was available. Elevator hoists, 60-foot (18-m) cranes, and rubber-tired tractors and dollies were assembled to transport the materials to the roof. Because of weight restrictions, vehicles on the roof could not drive off of the grid lines indicating the location of supporting columns. Only rubber-tired vehicles were allowed on the roof. Field-surveying instruments were used to lay out the basic design directly onto the roof's concrete surface.

Trees in 36-inch (91.5-cm) boxes were trucked in from as far away as Los Angeles and Indio, a desert town east of San Diego, and raised to the roof. With the recent exception of an infestation of insects similar to phylloxera in grapes that killed several of the garden's olive trees, almost all of the original trees are still on the roof, and the garden as a whole has thrived since its completion in 1960. Figure 4-21, earlier in this chapter, shows the garden as it looks today; see also the portfolio of American roof gardens for more information about it.

KAISER RESOURCES CONSTRUCTION, 1978

See figures 4-51 through 4-63. This garden was built on an eighteenth-floor roof that, at first review, appeared unable to support anything more than its own weight and a snow load. Its slab, 32 by 150 feet (9.7 by 45.7 m), is supported only at its outer edge, with no vertical columns within its area. The construction of this garden presented formidable challenges, requiring techniques never before used in roof gardens. Constraints included a roof-load limitation of 68 pounds per square foot, or 332 kg per square meter (after the roof's protective concrete slab had been removed), high winds, difficult access, inadequate drainage, and the need to provide 8 feet (2.5 m) of clearance along the building's edge for a rolling window-washing machine.

4-48 (top left). A boxed specimen olive tree is placed on a rubber-tired dolly to be moved to its final location, previously marked on the roof surface.

4-49 (top right). The tree has been moved from the crane site (upper right) to its predetermined location, next to forms for a concrete walk.

4-50 (bottom). A row of boxed holly oaks is at its final location, over columns in the garage below. Note the wide cracks in the boxes, which allow the roots to grow into the surrounding soil. The boxes will be left in place.

A combination of design and construction solutions resolved these problems. Most of the garden was designed to be sheltered from the winds on two sides by the building walls, with an arbor and fence added on a third side to serve as both a windscreen and a place to store the window-washing machine. The clearance needed to use that machine was provided by incorporating an 8-foot (2.5-m) buffer area of paving and lawn along the building's outer edge.

The problem of access was twofold. The garden's site initially had no means of access, including no elevator access, which raised the question of how to transport the construction materials

4-51 (top). The roof for the Kaiser Resources garden before construction. The window-washing machine had to remain on the roof. A new fire exit, improved access, and a railing were all code-required additions to come.

4-52 (middle left). All materials were delivered to the twentieth-floor roof and then lowered to the eighteenth-floor site for installation.

4-53 (middle right). A temporary exterior construction elevator lifted all materials from the street to the twentieth-floor roof.

4-54. Workmen install irrigation lines and set drains in a continuous layer of plastic drainage material.

and design elements from the ground to the eighteenth floor. A temporary exterior elevator, already in place for the building's construction, was used to hoist the materials to the building's roof on the twentieth floor, from which they were then lowered to the eighteenth. In addition to construction access, an entrance to the garden from the building's interior of course also had to be provided. Windows were cut down to the floor and replaced by a door to provide such access; a second fire exit, required by building codes, was added at the far end of the garden. The 42-inch (106.7-cm) teak-and-Plexiglas railing at the garden edge was also added to meet code requirements.

The challenge of providing adequate drainage for the garden was complicated by the load constraints and the window-washing machine. The subsoil medium had to be light enough to meet the load restrictions but strong enough to support the weight of the machine. Grass-Cel, a

4-55 (top). One-foot-square (30.5-cm) interlocking units of Grass-Cel were used for the drainage system, along with metal drains with surface and side grilles.

4-56 (bottom left). After the installation of Grass-Cel, the plan of the roof garden is marked with tape.

4-57 (bottom right). Lightweight artificial rocks, delivered from Los Angeles to Vancouver by truck, will be lifted to the roof for the waterfall.

4-58 (top left). Parts of artificial rocks for the waterfall are hoisted into place for gluing.

4-59 (top right). As the garden nears completion, workers labor in close quarters to finish construction.

4-60 (bottom left). The pond, soil, and plants are on the roof, awaiting the assembly and completion of the deck and storage structure for the window-washing machine.

4-61 (bottom right). Workers attach two-by-four sleepers to the steel frame, The final two-by-four redwood decking, placed at right angles, will be fastened to the sleepers with brass screws.

product developed in the late 1970s to support turf parking lots, met those requirements. Grass-Cel consists of perforated hexagonal cells, made from high-strength but relatively lightweight plastic, that fit together like the cells of a honeycomb. It was used as the drainage layer for the entire roof garden. To prevent the loss of soil as excess water drained, a ⅛-inch-thick (3.2-mm) sheet of water-permeable, rotproof, nonwoven polypropylene batting (Supac) was placed atop the Grass-Cel before the soil was added. To complete the drainage system, new drains were installed in the ceiling of the space below the garden to carry off excess runoff.

The load constraints necessarily affected the selection of every element in the garden, dictating the choice of lightweight concrete, a light soil mix, plastic plant containers, a plastic irrigation

4-62 (above). Completion of planting, lawns, and the finished surface of the deck remain.

4-63 (left). With the completion of the deck, the garden is finished. Furnishings add the final touch.

system, custom-designed spun-aluminum light fixtures, and aluminum furniture. In addition, the pond's depth was limited to 4 inches (10.2 cm), and all trees were restricted to a maximum ball height of 20 inches (50.8 cm). And yet, one of the garden's focal points is a massive-looking stone waterfall that seemingly belies the need to consider load constraints. Only close examination reveals that these apparently huge boulders are actually remarkably convincing hollow cement-and-fiberglass copies of rocks from nature, cast from latex impressions and stained to imitate natural rock formations.

THOREAU HALL CONSTRUCTION, 1989

See figures 4-64 through 4-75. The roof garden of Thoreau Hall and its first floor are one-half floor above the surrounding grade. The garage below is a full floor lower and is entered by a ramp leading down. A parking area located at the front of the building permitted delivery of almost all

4-64 (left). The layout of the horizontal shape of Thoreau Hall's garden is drawn on the surface of the concrete roof.

4-65 (above). Curb and raised-bed construction reinforces the drawn layout and serves as points of departure for future work on the roof garden.

4-66 (right). Heavy precast material for the pergola columns is lifted over the building by a crane at street level. The cartons are stored on the deck for later assembly.

4-67 (top left). Precast pool curbs and the fountain are placed before mechanical work on the fountain begins.

4-68 (top right). The raised beds are water-proofed.

4-69 (middle left). Filter fabric has been secured to the plastic drainage layer of Enkadrain, which has been placed on the bottom and sides of the planter after waterproofing has been applied. The drain in the center of the bed and the plastic irrigation pipes penetrate the roof to the drainpipe and water supply hung in the ceiling of the garage below.

4-70 (middle right). A front-end loader places soil mix on an endless belt for delivery to the interior court.

4-71. A jointed endless belt, running from the street in front of the building to the garden court, delivers a continuous supply of soil to the planting area.

4-72. Laborers spread soil mix in a planter bed by hand as it is delivered by the endless belt.

4-73 (top left). The sand bed is screed in preparation for laying the precast paving.

4-74 (top right). On the smooth bed of sand, workmen lay bricks and precast concrete slabs in a specified pattern.

4-75 (bottom). Seven years of growth with good maintenance has resulted in a roof garden with luxuriant greenery.

materials by truck. The exceptions were soil, concrete for paving, pallets of precast ornamental columns, fountain units, bricks, and concrete blocks. The concrete was pumped in through flexible hoses, and the soil was transported via conveyor belt. The pallets of precast units, bricks, and large plants were delivered from the parking area to the roof deck by crane.

WALK A BIT FARTHER
A PORTFOLIO OF INTERNATIONAL ROOF GARDENS

KAISER RESOURCES

VANCOUVER, BRITISH COLUMBIA, CANADA

LANDSCAPE ARCHITECT: Theodore Osmundson and Associates, with Gordon Osmundson, associate

ARCHITECT: Rhone and Iredale

CLIENT: Kaiser Resources

OWNER: Crown Life Insurance

This roof garden is owned by Kaiser Resources, a Canadian coal-mining firm that leases the top four floors for its headquarters in the Crown Life Centre, located in downtown Vancouver. Despite its severe load limitation of 65 pounds per square foot (317 kg per square meter), limited access, and a need to provide space for window-washing equipment, this site had a number of advantages that many other roof gardens do not have. They included excellent protection from prevailing winds (two additional building floors rise above its entrance end and along its back), sufficient length to provide a separate storage area for the window-washing gondola, and options for improving access and meeting egress codes. Perhaps most important were the magnificent views

Above: Before any work began, the roof was empty except for the window-washing machine and its gondola.

Left: The same view several years after the roof garden was completed.

of the harbor and downtown Vancouver, visible from all parts of the roof, eighteen floors above the street.

To take advantage of these assets, the roof was divided into three basic areas: (1) the deck, pond, and waterfall near the main entry; (2) the window-washing storage structure; and (3) the secondary sitting area at the far end of the roof. These were all connected with convenient walkways.

Starting with this design framework, Kaiser's chief executive officer, Edgar Kaiser, Jr., was presented with three designs, from which the best elements were chosen; using these, the final design was agreed upon and built.

On an underpinning of Grass-Cel drainage, the main redwood deck is elevated to take advantage of the view over the new 42-inch (106-cm) teak and Plexiglas railing. One-foot-square (30-cm) tiles and smooth concrete constitute the hard-surfaced paving, and lightweight simulated stones are used in informal walks. The balance of the flat surfaces, also atop Grass-Cel, is lawn. The window-washing storage structure provided another means of sheltering the main deck and gave additional wind protection at the far end of the roof. With the addition of a low waterfall over natural-appearing fabricated rocks, a 4-inch-deep (10-cm) fiberglass pool extending a short distance beneath the deck, an additional fire door, and carefully selected plant materials, garden furniture, and potted flowering plants, a very pleasant gardenesque setting was created.

New floor-to-ceiling sliding glass doors make the garden visible from indoors and readily accessible to the office occupants. A small cafeteria is available on the same floor for light lunches.

For more details about the construction of this garden, see the discussion near the end of chapter 4.

Top: Eighteen floors above the street, the garden has its back to the prevailing wind and looks toward a magnificent view of the downtown and harbor.

Bottom: The patio deck, with the waterfall and building in the background. The step down from the deck is removable, to allow a full 8 feet (2.4 m) of clearance for the window washer.

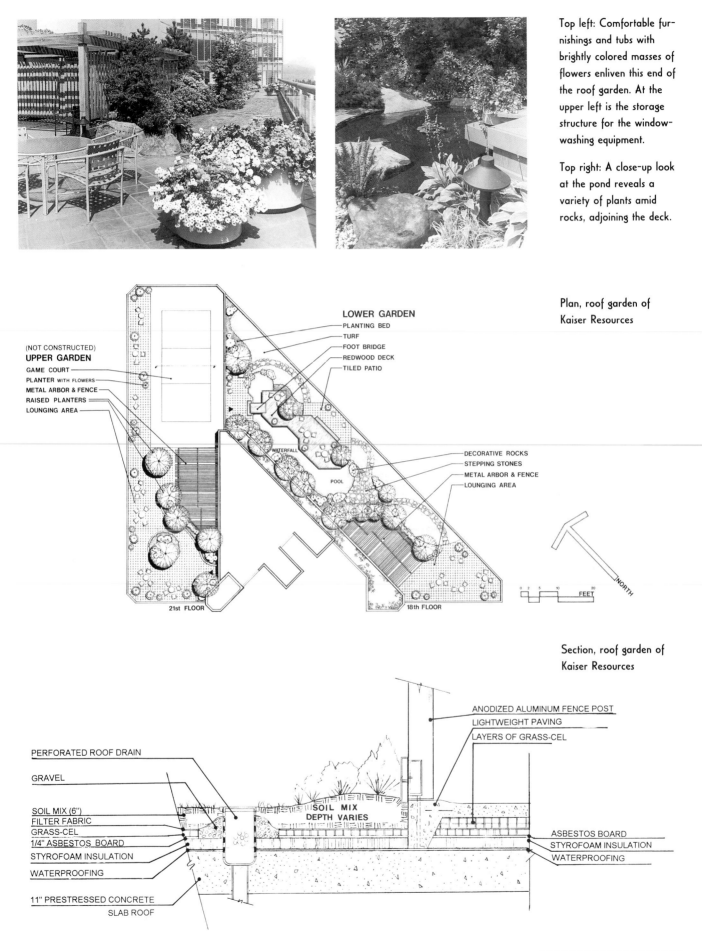

Top left: Comfortable furnishings and tubs with brightly colored masses of flowers enliven this end of the roof garden. At the upper left is the storage structure for the window-washing equipment.

Top right: A close-up look at the pond reveals a variety of plants amid rocks, adjoining the deck.

Plan, roof garden of Kaiser Resources

LOWER GARDEN
— PLANTING BED
— TURF
— FOOT BRIDGE
— REDWOOD DECK
— TILED PATIO

(NOT CONSTRUCTED)
UPPER GARDEN
GAME COURT
PLANTER WITH FLOWERS
METAL ARBOR & FENCE
RAISED PLANTERS
LOUNGING AREA

WATERFALL

POOL

— DECORATIVE ROCKS
— STEPPING STONES
— METAL ARBOR & FENCE
— LOUNGING AREA

21st FLOOR

18th FLOOR

0 2 5 10 20 FEET

NORTH

Section, roof garden of Kaiser Resources

ANODIZED ALUMINUM FENCE POST
LIGHTWEIGHT PAVING
LAYERS OF GRASS-CEL

PERFORATED ROOF DRAIN

GRAVEL

SOIL MIX (6")
FILTER FABRIC
GRASS-CEL
1/4" ASBESTOS BOARD
STYROFOAM INSULATION
WATERPROOFING

11" PRESTRESSED CONCRETE
SLAB ROOF

SOIL MIX
DEPTH VARIES

ASBESTOS BOARD
STYROFOAM INSULATION
WATERPROOFING

Top left: The sheltered redwood deck extends over the pond. With its comfortable outdoor furniture and flowers, it is an ideal space for quiet conversation.

Above left: The turnaround space required to access the window-washing machine from its storage shelter created an opportunity for a colorful secondary sitting area with comfortable furniture.

Top right: The roof garden as seen from the twentieth-floor roof of the building.

Bottom right: The redwood deck and 8-foot-wide (2.4-m) window-washer setback, looking toward the machine's "garage." Tie-downs for the equipment are in the paving and lawn.

BONAVENTURE HILTON INTERNATIONAL (FORMERLY LE BONAVENTURE WESTIN)

MONTRÉAL, QUÉBEC, CANADA

LANDSCAPE ARCHITECT: Sasaki Associates
ARCHITECT: Affleck, Desbarats, Dimakopoulos, Lebensold, and Sise
CLIENT: Westin International Hotels

The Bonaventure Hilton in Montréal, which occupies the top three floors of the enormous Place Bonaventure multiuse exhibition hall, has a 2-acre (0.8-hectare) roof garden that serves as a kind of outdoor corridor for its top floor, seventeen stories above the street. The spaces on the interior of the garden are public rooms, while those on the exterior perimeter are guest rooms; hence, the maximum number of people can enjoy the outdoors between. The garden is divided into quadrants, which are linked by winding paths and a continuous watercourse. The water flows in a stream that varies from narrow waterfalls to broad expanses of virtually still ponds. So skillfully is this design handled that one is hardly conscious that the water is only 2 inches (5.1 cm) deep and is moving on a flat roof. The corridor is punctuated by outdoor common sitting areas,

one with a swimming pool, as well as by small nooks for private enjoyment near guest rooms.

Montréal's cold climate produces severe freeze/thaw cycles, causing significant problems with expansion and contraction of building materials. To counteract these problems, the entire garden rests on 8 to 14 inches (20 to 36 cm) of drainage gravel above a base membrane over the structural slab. Heavy snows and drifting are also concerns in Montréal; to support the loads, a panel-loading distribution system was used. Allowable loads range from 130 to 400 pounds per square foot (635 to 1,953 kg per square meter).

Plant materials were carefully selected to withstand the bitter winters of Montréal. Trees are located where structural columns support the roof.

In its early years, the garden, though densely planted, had not yet grown full, making the continuous, ever-changing stream the garden's dominant feature.

Plan, roof garden of
Bonaventure Hilton Inter-
national

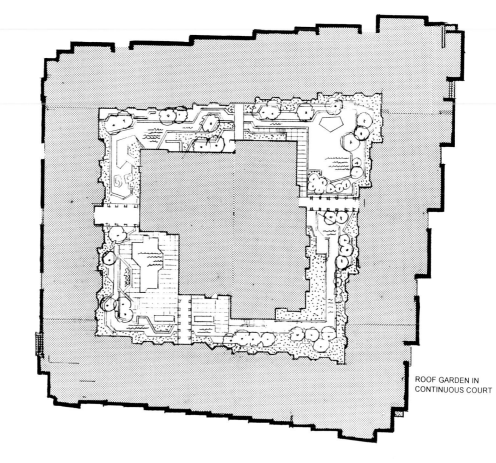

ROOF GARDEN IN
CONTINUOUS COURT

Below left: Waterfalls are
one of the key points of
interest in the stream as it
flows around the entire
roof.

Below right: Walks that
parallel the stream pro-
vide a place for guests to
stroll or jog.

After almost three decades, the full growth of trees has created a bower for outdoor dining. (Courtesy Sasaki Associates)

Even the areas of little activity have become verdant walkways alongside the streams. (Courtesy Sasaki Associates)

The water feature, after almost thirty years, is still an important element but is no longer dominant. (Courtesy Sasaki Associates)

FOUR SEASONS MEXICO CITY HOTEL

MEXICO CITY, MEXICO

LANDSCAPE ARCHITECT: Eliseo Arredondo Gonzalez of Espacios Verdes
ARCHITECT: Sergio Alvarez Aleman and Patrick Garel
CLIENT: Immobilaria Nacional Mexicana (Four Seasons hotel chain)

Unlike Mexico's coastal areas and low-lying interior, Mexico City, located on the country's high central plateau, has a very moderate climate, with high temperatures of 70°F to 80°F (21°C to 26°C) and lows of 40°F to 50°F (4°C to 10°C) year-round. Such a climate is ideal for roof gardens and their visitors, and the garden featured here takes full advantage of it.

Opened in 1994, one of Mexico City's newest hotels, the Four Seasons, on the Paseo de la Reforma, has a traditional central courtyard, or patio, at ground level, built over an underground parking garage. As is the case with many such roof gardens, one is barely aware of being above a garage in this space. Because the patio is the central space of the hotel, most of the rooms have a direct view into the garden. The formal design solution required the consideration of perspec-

tives from ground level as well as from the rooms above. Other problems, including weight on the structure, drainage, and sun and shade, also had to be addressed.

This 13,620–square foot (1,265–square meter) patio is a so-called living patio, or outdoor living room, a feature common in Spanish Colonial–style buildings. The open terrace located on the south side of the patio is an outdoor extension of the hotel's specialty restaurant and looks north across the garden to the lobby. The patio is surrounded by arcades serving public areas of the hotel.

Vegetation includes such trees as *Lagerstroemia indica* (crape myrtle), *Magnolia grandiflora* (southern magnolia), *Ficus benjamina* (weeping fig), *Cupressus sempervirens* (Italian cypress), and *Citrus aurantium* (Seville orange).

The plan of the patio shows its formal design. (Courtesy Eliseo Arredondo)

Shrubbery includes azaleas, *Camellia japonica* (camellia), *Viburnum suspensum* (Sandankwa viburnum), and *Strelitzia reginae* (bird-of-paradise); *Liriope* (mondo grass) is used as ground cover. Flowering perennials and annuals give the garden exciting splashes of color.

The soil in the garden is 1 foot (30 cm) deep, except where it has been mounded for trees. It consists of 40 percent sand, 40 percent topsoil, and 20 percent leaf mold. It rests on 4 inches (10 cm) of drain rock that is covered with polypropylene filter fabric.

From the outdoor areas, the walks converge on the sparkling fountain. (Courtesy Eliseo Arredondo)

The fountain is ornamented with pots of yellow chrysanthemums at its corners. (Courtesy Eliseo Arredondo)

RMC GROUP SERVICES INTERNATIONAL HEADQUARTERS

RUNNYMEDE BOROUGH, SURREY,

GREAT BRITAIN

LANDSCAPE ARCHITECT: Derek Lovejoy Partnership
ARCHITECT: Edward Cullinan Architects
OWNER/CLIENT: RMC Group Services

One of the most difficult places to obtain permission to build new offices in England is in the Green Belt around London. It was particularly true for this site, partly in a designated Conservation Area, which already contained a historical Georgian house and stable block listed as a national landmark and an attractive Arts and Crafts–style house. After the first design was turned down in 1986 by the Runnymede Borough Council, the owners turned to the landscape architects to advise on adapting a new building to the site.

A one-story structure with three courtyards at ground level and gardens on the roof was presented, accepted by the council, and completed in 1990. The final project was visually unobtrusive, offering no long-distance views toward or from the site of more than ¾ mile (1 km). Parking areas, entrance roads, and service areas were designed to blend into the Conservation Area. Existing trees were retained. The roof gardens cover over 48,000 square feet (4,500 square meters), or over 1 acre, making them one of the largest roof gardens in Great Britain.

In this plan of RMC Group Services International Headquarters, the color highlights the roof gardens. (Courtesy Derek Lovejoy Partnership and John M. Whalley)

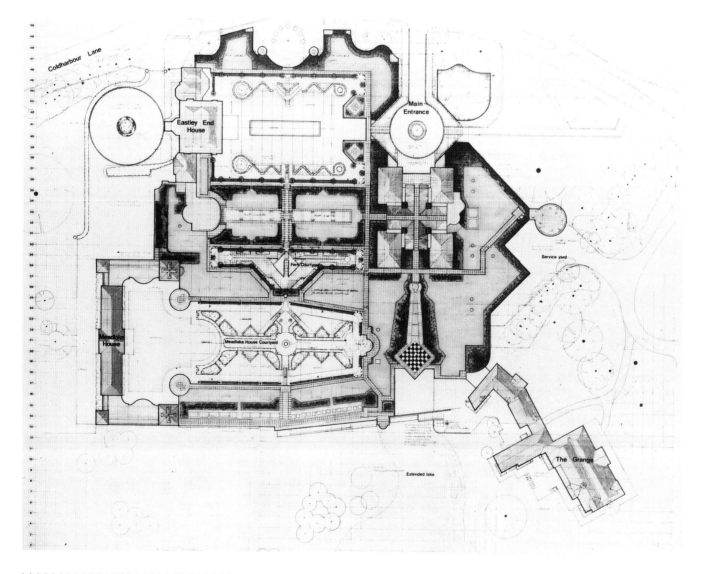

Paved roof areas are covered with 2-inch-thick (5-cm) precast-concrete paving slabs mounted on rubber paving supports. These supports are lighter in weight than a heavy sub-base and expedite drainage from the surface. Waterproofing is a three-coat asphalt system, covered by 2 inches (5-cm) of Styrofoam insulation, which provides some protection to the asphalt, maintains a somewhat consistent temperature year-round, and mitigates thermal expansion and contraction. The planting medium is field topsoil with lightweight aggregate added to aid drainage. The filter fabric, a geotextile of polypropylene, separates the planting medium from the drainage layer below, a 4-inch (10-cm) depth of Leca (lightweight expanded clay aggregate). A system of perforated pipes extends down through the Leca to the outer parapet walls and then to downspouts that lead to the ground. An automatic irrigation system includes a sprinkler system for lawns and flower beds and drip irrigation for shrubs.

Large areas of the roof are covered in lawn, bordered by yew hedges and accented by shaped holly in planter boxes. The planter boxes consist of two layers of plastic with insulation sand-

wiched between the layers. Each box is individually linked to the irrigation system. Those edges of the garden that are subject to strong, cold winds are bordered by evergreen junipers, cotoneasters, pyracanthas, and escallonia, which create a wind barrier and conceal the handrails at the edge of the roof. The topsoil under the shrubs is about 18 to 20 inches (45 to 50 cm) deep; that in the lawn area is 10 to 12 inches (25 to 30 cm) deep. Pebble or bark mulch provides additional protection for the shrubs.

The information for this project was kindly supplied by John Mason Whalley, formerly a senior partner of the Derek Lovejoy Partnership; he now practices with J. M. W. International in the United Kingdom.

Left: The gardens consist mainly of lawn, with substantial shrub borders at their outside edges to block wind and so improve the microclimate. (Courtesy Derek Lovejoy Partnership and John M. Whalley)

Below: Section, roof garden edge of RMC Group Services International Headquarters. (Courtesy Derek Lovejoy Partnership and John M. Whalley)

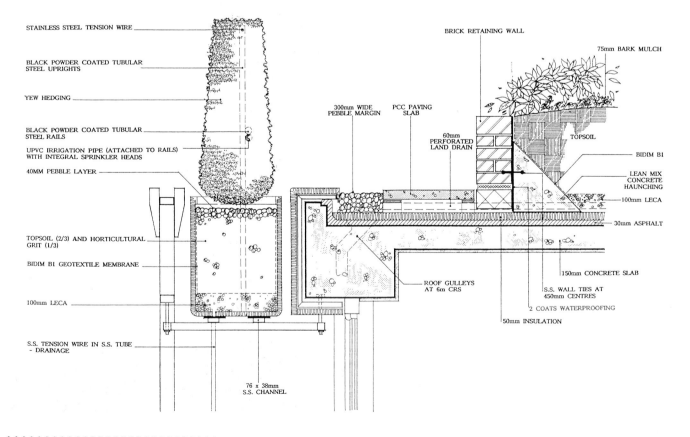

STAINLESS STEEL TENSION WIRE

BLACK POWDER COATED TUBULAR STEEL UPRIGHTS

YEW HEDGING

BLACK POWDER COATED TUBULAR STEEL RAILS

UPVC IRRIGATION PIPE (ATTACHED TO RAILS) WITH INTEGRAL SPRINKLER HEADS

40MM PEBBLE LAYER

TOPSOIL (2/3) AND HORTICULTURAL GRIT (1/3)

BIDIM B1 GEOTEXTILE MEMBRANE

100mm LECA

S.S. TENSION WIRE IN S.S. TUBE - DRAINAGE

76 x 38mm S.S. CHANNEL

300mm WIDE PEBBLE MARGIN

PCC PAVING SLAB

60mm PERFORATED LAND DRAIN

ROOF GULLEYS AT 6m CRS

BRICK RETAINING WALL

75mm BARK MULCH

TOPSOIL

BIDIM B1

LEAN MIX CONCRETE HAUNCHING

100mm LECA

30mm ASPHALT

150mm CONCRETE SLAB

S.S. WALL TIES AT 450mm CENTRES

2 COATS WATERPROOFING

50mm INSULATION

SOCIAL AND RECREATION BUILDING

HANNOVER, GERMANY

LANDSCAPE ARCHITECT: Ruprecht Dröge

This recreation building has a lounge terrace and garden off its second-story gaming rooms. The 1-foot-thick (30-cm) layer of soil mix contains an Optima irrigation system and low plantings of shrubs and perennials.

At roof level the experience is akin to being in a garden, with some very pleasant views across a lake in a park. Visitors are protected by a railing in the sitting area, but the greater width of the planting bed is the only source of protection in the adjacent space. In the United States, only maintenance personnel would be permitted in this area.

From ground level the roof garden appears to be only edge planting.

At roof level the experience is of being in a garden. Visitors are protected by a railing in the sitting area, but the width of the planting bed alone is relied upon for safety where the bed is wider.

FARMERS' INSURANCE

HANNOVER, GERMANY

LANDSCAPE ARCHITECT: Joachim Adam

At the time these photos were taken, Germany was suffering though a prolonged drought. The courtyard area of the office building was irrigated by an overhead system, and its supply was limited as a public conservation measure. The plant material there clearly reflected its lack of water. However, the roof garden above offices in the building, which was irrigated with the Optima system, was able to thrive, relying on the water-storage capacity of that system to supplement the reduced irrigation schedule.

The employees' patio, plantings, and ornamental pool are on the roof of an underground garage. The upper level, atop offices, is not used as an outdoor space for employees.

A view of the central roof garden from the office roof.

The office roof garden was installed with the Optima system, which guaranteed a supply of water. This garden was not affected by prolonged draught.

Above: The courtyard roof garden was designed with details similar to those typically used in the United States. This garden suffered during the drought.

Left: The central courtyard fountain, with short sculptural granite pylons and river stones in a paved area of granite sets.

UNISYS CORPORATION (FORMERLY SPERRY UNIVAC)

FRANKFURT, GERMANY

LANDSCAPE ARCHITECT: Hans Dorn
ARCHITECT: Meid and Romeick, Frankfurt
CLIENT: Sperry Univac

The employees' dining area looks out directly onto a lush 8,500–square foot (790–square meter) garden in the central open space of this American company's branch office in Frankfurt, one of Germany's largest cities. Although the site is directly over a parking garage, archives, and offices in the basement of the building, no trace of this fact is evident at garden level.

The wide tiled walks winding through the garden enable easy pedestrian circulation. In addition, such generous widths provide ample space to arrange the portable white plastic stools, designed by the landscape architect, into informal groupings in good weather. A sparkling design feature when not in use, they complement the white light globes when arranged decoratively. These stools, however, supply the only seating in the garden. Located as it is next to the employees' cafeteria, the garden would benefit from more comfortable seating, along with tables.

The planting medium in the garden is Novoflor, a German product sold by Frankische

This view into the garden from an upper floor of the building shows its overall plan. (Courtesy Hans Dorn)

Rohrwerke. It is 30 inches (76 cm) deep for the trees, *Cedrus atlantica glauca* (blue Atlas cedar) and *Crataegus monogyna* (English hawthorn). Shrubbery consists mostly of rhododendrons and azaleas.

Specially designed tiles were arranged in the shape of Sperry Univac's logo, permanently embedded in the paving. A fountain, composed of two square, elevated concrete basins, splashes into a bed of round river stones nearby.

Recently the garden was closed to visitors for security reasons.

Looking across the garden, toward its main entrance, one can see the portable white plastic seats in the foreground.

The fountain at left consists of two concrete basins, one above the other, from which water falls to a bed of river stones below.

INDUSTRIE-KREDIT BANK CONFERENCE CENTER

FRANKFURT, GERMANY

LANDSCAPE ARCHITECT: Hans Dorn
ARCHITECT: Kleine Handling (garage)
CLIENT: Industrie-Kredit Bank

The renovation of a palatial residence into a guest house and conference center for visiting bank officials required the provision of additional parking facilities on the site. Because space for such facilities was limited to land immediately adjacent to the building and because of the quiet nature of the activities to be carried out in the building, it was decided that a twenty-car underground garage topped by a roof garden would be built.

The landscape architect designed a low-key, almost residential garden, using lawn surrounded by shrubs and large trees, with a fountain feature at the end farthest from the street. The plantings consist mostly of lawn, with rhododendrons and azaleas in shady spots and roses, kolkwitzia, pyracantha, and boxwood in sunny places. The fountains are four amphora-shaped vessels of dark granitelike material called Diabas, which was specially carved for this garden. Water overflows to circles of hard-set ornamental pebbles and small tiles at their base. In the center of the lawn, just off the end of the building, is a simple bronze sculpture of a seated nymph with outstretched arms, entitled *Goldmary*.

A native mixture of sand and loess soil, to which soil amendments, 20 percent by volume, were added, was placed to a depth of 20 inches (50 cm) for planting. A 1-inch-thick (2.5-cm) layer of drainage sheets, called SF-Drain and produced by Frankische Rohrwerke, was placed directly atop the waterproofing and then covered by filter fabric to prevent soil from entering the drainage layer.

Top: This view of the garden looking toward the street shows the broad expanse of lawn bordered by trees and shrubs.

Middle: The amphora fountains adorn the far end of the garden.

Bottom: A close-up of the featured bronze sculpture on the lawn.

ALLIANZ VERSICHERUNGS-AG
STUTTGART, GERMANY

LANDSCAPE ARCHITECT: Hans Luz and Partner, Stuttgart
ARCHITECT: Brümmendorf, Müller, Murr, and Reichmann, Stuttgart
OWNER/CLIENT: Allianz Versicherungs-AG

The regional headquarters of this insurance company has been in the heart of Stuttgart's historical center for over one hundred years. When the company needed to enlarge its office space, its executives decided to retain the existing site and buildings, blending them with new construction. The architects succeeded in combining the old and the new with an almost seamless design solution.

In keeping with a widely accepted trend throughout Germany, the greening of roofs was a highly important consideration. The architect and landscape architect worked together to provide two series of stepped-down roofs atop offices surrounding the large courtyards of the main buildings. All other roofs, including those adjacent to offices around the courtyards and those on the tops of the new buildings, are planted, giving the roofs a handsome, soft, green appearance.

Plan, Allianz Versicherungs-AG; all dark areas except the trees at street level are roof gardens

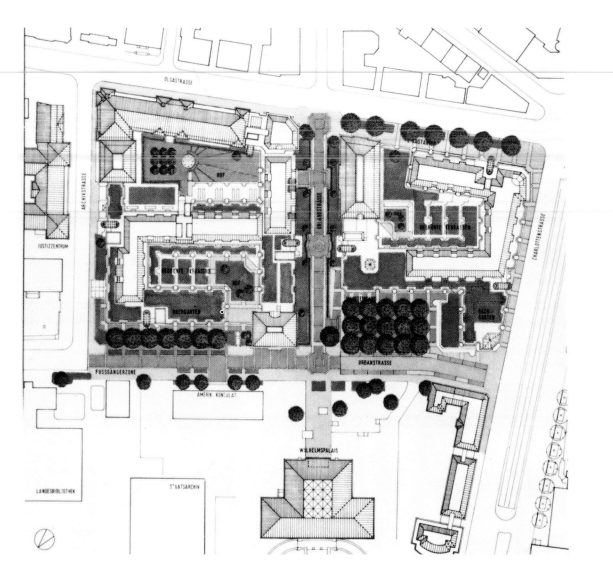

Throughout the roof garden the Optima system of continuous self-watering by capillary action was used.

Planting was limited to low-growing species, to permit views across the gardens and to reduce the weight on the roofs. The plants are primarily perennials and ornamental grasses, such as *Lavandula angustifolia* (English lavender), *Epimedium pinnatum* 'Elegans' (Persian epimedium), *Hemerocallus citrina* (daylilies), *Pennisetum compressum* (fountain grass), *Stripa pennata* (feather grass), *Rudbeckia fulgida* 'Goldsturm' (black-eyed Susan), and *Deschampsia caespitosa* 'Bronzeschleir' (tufted hair grass).

Although the plantings appear to be intensive, the courtyards are designed to be ornamental only and are not accessible. An exception are the gardens for the company's apartments on the highest roofs. Here the plantings are very residential in tone and include flowering cherries, forsythia, *Magnolia soulangeana* (saucer magnolia), tea and polyantha roses, and extensive lawn.

Above: A planted terrace outside a row of offices.

Right: A stepped-down roof garden on one of the new buildings. All of the offices surrounding the courtyard have views of this space.

GATE TOWER PARK
REUTLINGEN, GERMANY

LANDSCAPE ARCHITECT: Eppinger and Schmid, Leonberg
ARCHITECT: Hagenlocher and Nölle, Stuttgart
SCULPTOR: Rainer Hantschke
CLIENT/OWNER: City of Reutlingen

The need for additional parking for shopping and town-hall areas near Reutlingen's medieval gate tower inspired city officials to adopt an ambitious plan for a 1¼-acre (0.5-hectare) park at grade above a two-story underground garage for four hundred cars. A pedestrian bridge, starting at the gate tower and crossing over the adjacent, busy Lederstrasse, was part of the project. The garage is entered via ramps from Lederstrasse. The project's landscape architect and architect, selected through a city-sponsored design competition, combined these elements into a highly functional and attractive design. The architect designed the bridge, and the landscape architect, its approaches and the park and plaza at street level. Construction of the project was completed in 1984.

Easy maintenance was an important factor in the layout of trees and shrubs; for example, consideration was given for the cutting width of riding mowers. The park is maintained by the city's Recreation and Park Department. No leaks, soil problems, or root penetration of the roof has developed. No commercial roof garden system was used in the park; the system was custom-designed by the landscape architect using high-quality components.

Plantings include the trees *Platanus acerifolia* (London plane tree), *Crataegus carrieri* (apple hawthorn), *Acer platanoides* (Norway maple), *Catalpa bignonioides*, and *Plerocarya fraxinifolia;* and the shrubs *Amelanchier canadensis* (serviceberry), roses, *Kolkwitzia amabilis* (beauty bush), *Kerria japonica*, and *Hypericum* 'Hidcote Gold' (Saint John's-wort).

The walks are of granite-set pavers, concrete-set pavers, and asphalt. The fountain is all cut and polished granite.

The shops and cafés near the old city wall have direct access to the well-maintained city park, which has eating areas along its northern edge. These park areas, away from the traffic along Lederstrasse, are heavily used by pedestrians, shoppers, and nearby office workers.

This view of the park is from the pedestrian bridge over Lederstrasse.

This new city park is the result of a municipal program to provide parking for the downtown commercial area at left.

Below: The sculpture/fountain feature marks the turning point on the broad paved landing between the old medieval city gate and the bridge over the street.

Right: From the old city gate and park, access from the busy adjoining street is by broad paved steps and landings leading from the bridge, at the upper right. The roof over the garage has become a verdant outdoor park.

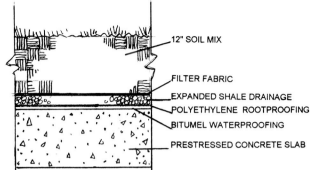

12" SOIL MIX

FILTER FABRIC

EXPANDED SHALE DRAINAGE
POLYETHYLENE ROOTPROOFING
BITUMEL WATERPROOFING

PRESTRESSED CONCRETE SLAB

SECTION THROUGH LAWN AREA

Top left: Visitors make good use of the pleasant out-door dining areas in front of cafés along the edge of the new park.

Top right: Section, lawn area of Gate Tower Park

Left: The park extends at grade right to sidewalks bordering pre-existing shops and cafés. Amenities include tables and chairs and phone kiosks conveniently nearby.

Below: Plan, Gate Tower Park

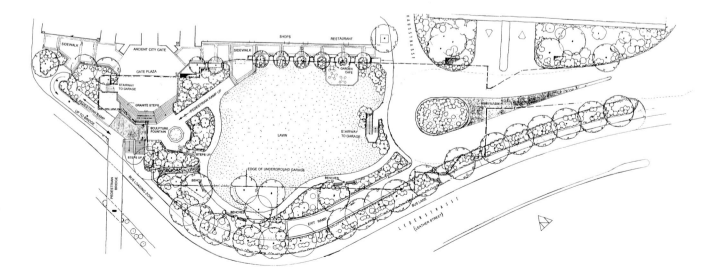

UNIVERSITY OF VIENNA

VIENNA, AUSTRIA

LANDSCAPE ARCHITECT: Wolfgang Saiko

The University of Vienna, which dates back to the fourteenth century, had no central campus but was instead spread throughout the city in numerous separate buildings. The search for a new site for the university resulted in the use of the air space above the city's railroad terminal. A new structure was built over the railway complex, covering the existing buildings as a roof. Not only are there gardens on this roof, but entire buildings are there as well.

In addition to extensive ornamental plantings, the gardens include a wide variety of vegetables and flowering plants, for this part of the university houses its biological sciences department, which uses the plants for study and research. All plantings are in raised beds that were waterproofed both to protect the occupied space below and to prevent leaks through the sides of these concrete beds.

The section shows that two layers of filter fabric and two layers of drainage are used. Such doubling is excessive and unnecessary: the upper layers of filter fabric and drainage could have been omitted.

Top: The university's elevated podium makes a sharp, clean break with the railroad yards below.

Middle: Research of plants growing in water is carried out on the roof in waterproofed concrete beds.

Right: This courtyard is a central space in the biological sciences section of the campus. The structures in the foreground are cold frames for starting plants; in this case the plants being tested are flowering annuals and perennials. The large-leaved plants are castor beans.

Section, roof garden of
University of Vienna

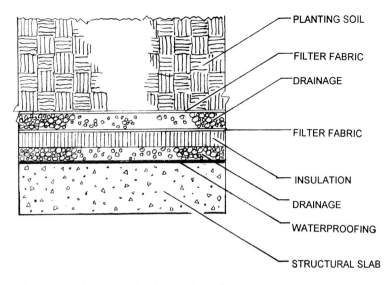

PLANTING SOIL

FILTER FABRIC

DRAINAGE

FILTER FABRIC

INSULATION

DRAINAGE

WATERPROOFING

STRUCTURAL SLAB

Left: A narrow bog covered with water is another test area. Even the cracks in the pavement are allowed to keep their "weeds" for research.

Below: This more extensive planting area contains corn, cabbage, and other vegetable crops, surrounded by castor beans. Note the street below in the upper corner.

GROSSE SCHANZE PARK
BERN, SWITZERLAND

LANDSCAPE ARCHITECT: W. Liechti, City of Bern
Parks Department
CLIENT: City of Bern

This public park in Switzerland's capital city demonstrates how idle urban space can be transformed into a multiuse development with some innovative thinking. The site originally held a retaining wall that supported the slope fronting the University of Bern. Below grade ran a railroad, which tunneled beneath the slope. The city replaced the retaining wall with a four-story structure housing the railroad station below grade (with the original train platforms a level farther below), a parking lot and passenger drop-off zone at street level, and garage and office space on the upper two floors.

Atop the structure, adjacent and connected to the university grounds, is a gorgeous public park designed by the city's staff landscape architect. The garden, built in 1964, features a paved plaza with fountains and sculpture, a wide expanse of lawn dotted with large trees, a life-size chess game, and a seasonal restaurant open to summer

Top: The view of the Bernese Oberland from the promenade of the roof garden is spectacular.

Above: This nineteenth-century building, part of the University of Bern, is the dominant structure along the rear of the rooftop park.

Right: The rooftop plaza features a fountain and bronze sculpture. The restaurant and university building are in the background.

The huge trees are poplars, grown in sunken planter boxes built atop the building's steel structural columns.

The city maintains outstanding floral plantings in season next to the terrace restaurant.

A restored statue in the rooftop park seems to stand guard over the life-size chess being played on the pavement nearby.

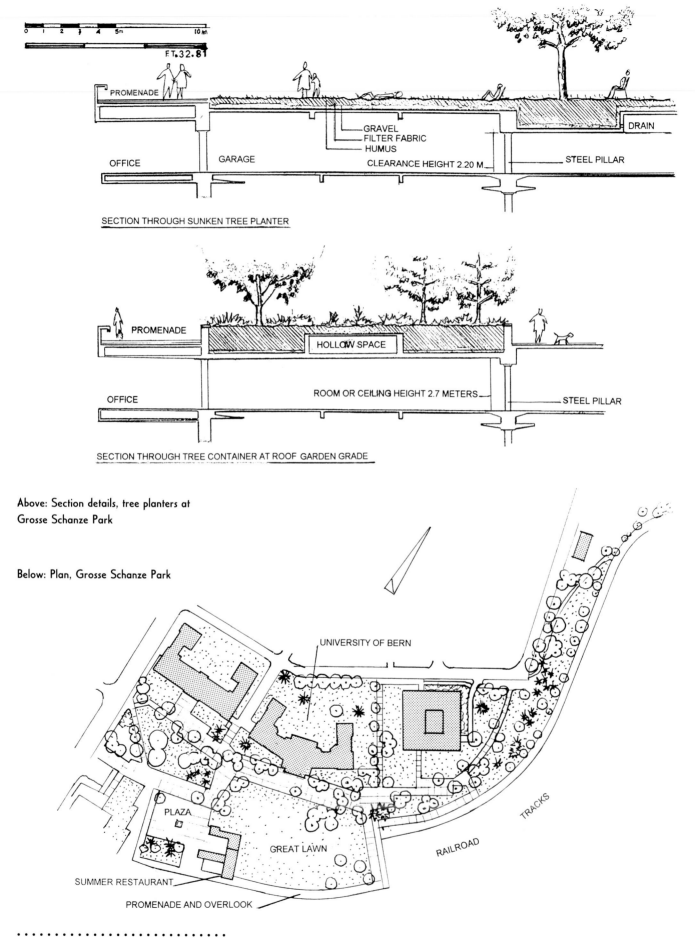

F.T. 32.81

PROMENADE

GRAVEL
FILTER FABRIC
HUMUS

DRAIN

OFFICE   GARAGE   CLEARANCE HEIGHT 2.20 M.   STEEL PILLAR

SECTION THROUGH SUNKEN TREE PLANTER

PROMENADE

HOLLOW SPACE

OFFICE   ROOM OR CEILING HEIGHT 2.7 METERS   STEEL PILLAR

SECTION THROUGH TREE CONTAINER AT ROOF GARDEN GRADE

Above: Section details, tree planters at
Grosse Schanze Park

Below: Plan, Grosse Schanze Park

UNIVERSITY OF BERN

TRACKS

RAILROAD

PLAZA

GREAT LAWN

SUMMER RESTAURANT

PROMENADE AND OVERLOOK

visitors. Access to the park is via elevator and stairs from inside the building as well as from the university grounds. A promenade extending along the entire front edge of the park provides spectacular views of the Bernese Oberland (highlands) in the distance.

Right: Section detail, garden at Grosse Schanze Park

Below: The wide promenade offers a means of traversing the park as well as glorious views of the mountains in the distance.

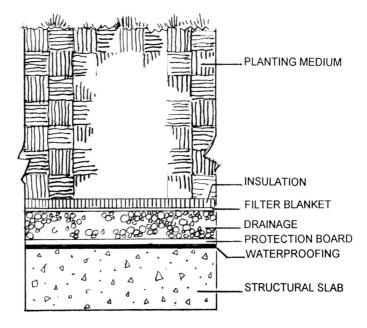

PLANTING MEDIUM

INSULATION
FILTER BLANKET
DRAINAGE
PROTECTION BOARD
WATERPROOFING

STRUCTURAL SLAB

Section, Grosse Schanze Park

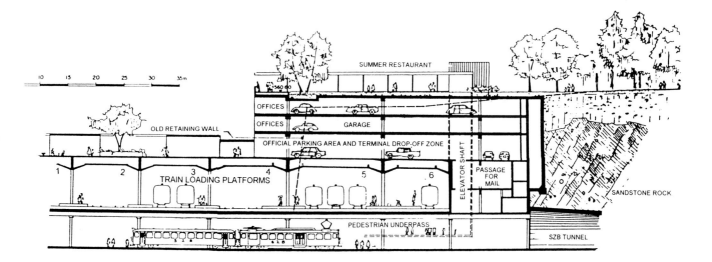

HOTEL EXCELSIOR
VENICE, ITALY

LANDSCAPE ARCHITECT: Sasaki Associates

CLIENT: CIGA Hotels

The Excelsior is a venerable seaside hotel built in 1907 on the Lido of Venice. Its design draws heavily on Moorish influences to create a festive and exotic atmosphere. In undertaking restoration of the hotel, the client's goal was to enhance its unique characteristics while providing a more comfortable and attractive environment. In 1991 the central court, Corte Moresca, replaced a bleak utility yard that was below the first-floor level; the court was designed as part of the larger renovation program. The first floor was extended over the basement and strengthened to accommodate the weight of the garden.

The courtyard design reflects the hotel's Moorish theme, with a garden that is reminiscent of those at the Alhambra in Granada, Spain. Corridors opened at each end were transformed into arcaded loggias, while a room on each side was eliminated to form vestibules that provide greater visibility, as well as access from adjacent corridors.

Low fountains at each vestibule and loggia are linked by stepped water runnels that flow to a central reflecting pool, which contains a large fountain of Carrara marble in a traditional lotus design. Fragrant fruit trees, shrubs, and vines help to make the Corte Moresca a "paradise garden" for hotel guests throughout the tourist season.

Above: At garden level the sound of fountains and water runnels and the odor of fragrant flowers fill the air. (Courtesy Sasaki Associates)

Right: The Moorish arches opening onto building vestibules, the fountains surrounded by formal gardens, and the use of ornamental tile—all create a sense of restrained opulence. (Courtesy Sasaki Associates)

Above: Before renovation, the Corte Moresca (Moorish Court) had been an unkempt outdoor storage area at basement level. (Courtesy Sasaki Associates)

Left: The court exemplifies the traditions of Moorish and Islamic landscape architecture, with its strict symmetry and use of water as a focal point. (Courtesy Sasaki Associates)

Below: Plan, Corte Moresca, Hotel Excelsior

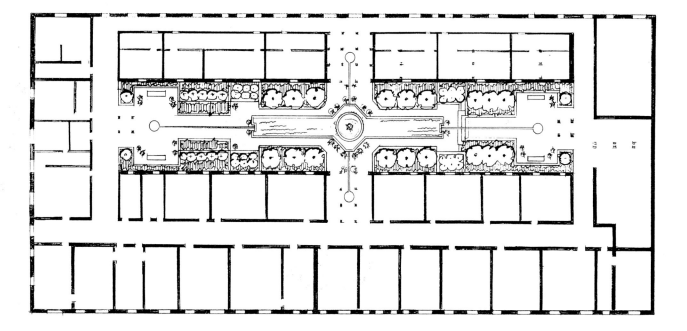

SHINJUKU MITSUI BUILDING
TOKYO, JAPAN

LANDSCAPE ARCHITECT: Toyo Landscape Construction
ARCHITECT: Hohon Sekkei Company
OWNER: Mitsui Development Company

This plaza, atop two floors of office space and just below the entrance to the Mitsui Building in the Shinjuku District in Tokyo, has many of the attributes of a well-designed roof garden. Adjacent to a busy street, it is easily accessible, from both the street area, via broad staircases, and from upper levels of the office building, via a graceful spiral staircase. Because the plaza is below the street grade, it is sheltered from the noise and commotion of Tokyo traffic. A fountain that flows down stepped bricks to a pool near the street further masks the street noise; its geometric design also provides visual interest. The plaza's paving, of warm red brick in circular patterns, mirrors the brick tree wells, which house full-grown zelkova trees that supply ample shade. The inspired use of zelkovas, one of Japan's most familiar and handsome shade trees,

Above: A spiral staircase connects higher floors of the building to the plaza below. Full-grown zelkova trees were planted to provide instant shade and scale.

Right: The main entrance to the plaza consists of broad steps down from the street's sidewalk. Most of the roof garden is to the left of this stairway.

A waterfall flows over a series of brick steps. The street is at the top; the plaza, at the right.

Below left: A smaller supplemental fountain wells up in a recessed brick pool.

Below right: Here, the seating has been arranged more formally for a special event. Shade from the trees makes umbrellas almost unnecessary. Note the brick paving pattern, as seen from above.

transformed this hot, south-facing plaza into a shady, comfortable space, a haven during Tokyo's oppressive summers. Movable tables and chairs provide plenty of seating for informal lunches and coffee breaks, as well as for more formal gatherings alongside a small elevated stage. In addition, the wide stair steps, fountain edges, and brick borders around plantings offer opportunities for seating away from the plaza's center.

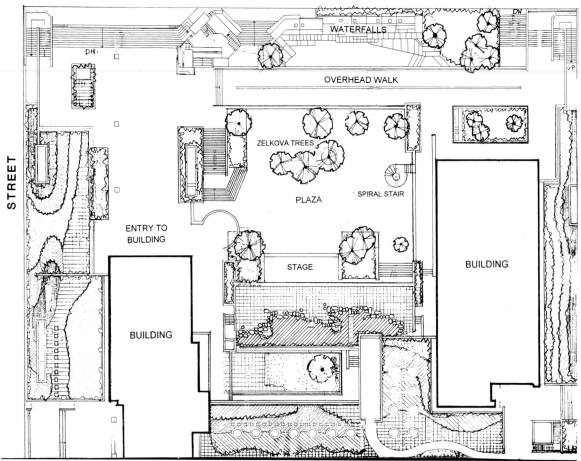

Plan, roof garden of Shinjuku Mitsui Building

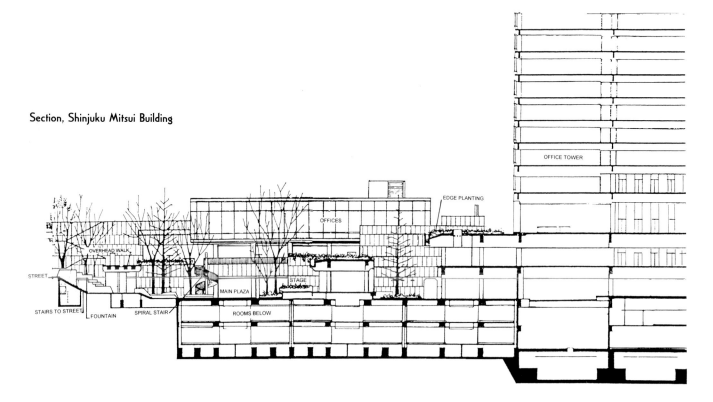

Section, Shinjuku Mitsui Building

TAISHO MARINE AND FIRE INSURANCE COMPANY

TOKYO, JAPAN

LANDSCAPE ARCHITECT: Araki Landscape Architecture
ARCHITECT: Yoshioki Gogura, Nikken Sekkei Company
OWNER: Taisho Marine and Fire Insurance Company

This fine building consists of a multistory office tower with a base that literally bridges the entrance to a great court. Low-rise offices are connected to and extend behind the tower in a horseshoe shape, enclosing three sides of the court. The main gardens are on the roof of this lower part of the building.

From the ground, the gardens appear to be merely edge planting. Upon entering them from the tower, however, one can see they are a separate private garden, connected by informal paths of concrete slabs that are pleasantly interrupted by wooden benches for quiet meditation. The paths wind their way through carefully selected plantings that include pachysandra, hosta, mondo grass, geraniums, ferns, dwarf yew, and *Ternstroemia*. A smaller part of the building near the entrance also has a very imaginative combination of plant materials.

The courtyard below the gardens contains an hourglass-shaped pool surmounted by a large red metal sculpture, created by Kyubi Kiyomizu, that is popularly known as the "Red Dragon."

Above: From the courtyard the main roof is visible atop the lower part of the building. The "Red Dragon" sculpture and pond are in the foreground.

Left: The tower is entered through an open space at ground level. The great court is beyond this entrance. A roof garden atop a small wing of the building can be seen at left.

Paths lead visitors through the carefully designed gardens. Benches, such as that shown here, offer quiet spaces for rest and contemplation.

Plan, roof garden of Taisho Marine and Fire Insurance Company

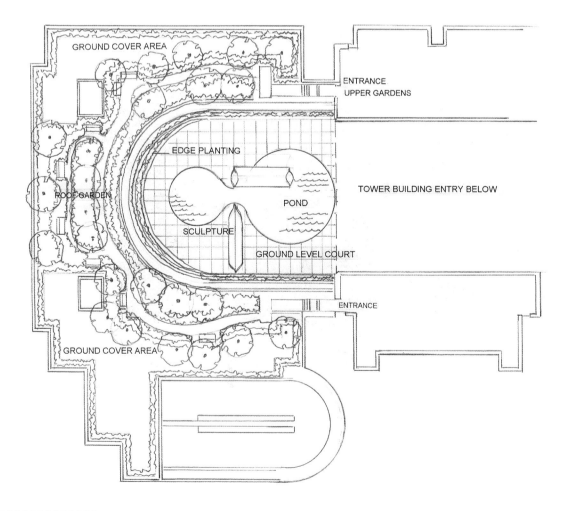

GROUND COVER AREA

ENTRANCE
UPPER GARDENS

EDGE PLANTING

ROOF GARDEN

TOWER BUILDING ENTRY BELOW

POND

SCULPTURE

GROUND LEVEL COURT

ENTRANCE

GROUND COVER AREA

Top right: Low-level garden lighting is provided by granite fixtures.

Top left: The small building wing at one entry corner of the complex has a flanking green garden on its roof.

Middle: A ground cover of dark mondo grass forms the background for variegated geranium, hosta, ferns, and dwarf yew, backed by *Ternstroemia*.

Bottom: A planting of pachysandra and hosta in a ground cover of young mondo grass.

ARAKAWA NATURAL PARK
TOKYO, JAPAN

LANDSCAPE ARCHITECT: Kenzo Ogata
CLIENT: Tokyo Sewage Office

The development of roofs atop municipal, industrial, and commercial facilities has created exciting new opportunities for designing recreation areas. This public park in Tokyo, built above a huge sewage-treatment plant, is an excellent example. The park includes a large natural pond and overlook, children's play areas, a swimming pool, a natural-looking stream running through a rocky streambed, and a walk system, all set among extensive plantings. Sculpture has been inserted at key locations throughout the park.

Approximately half of the treatment plant is in a completely enclosed building, over which the park was built. The other half of the plant has no structure atop it. Changes in the surrounding natural grade allow some entrances to be approached at grade, while others are accessed via ramps.

Top: The overlook structure for the large pond is flanked by a white pedestal supporting a bronze sculptural group.

Above: The structure containing part of the treatment facility appears to be a typical industrial building except for the planting visible on the roof. The ramp at left approaches one of the entrances to the park.

Right: Visitors encounter sculpture as soon as they enter the park.

The wide expanse of the pond looks so natural that it is hard to believe it rests atop a roof. The water is 18 to 24 inches (45.7 to 61 cm) deep. The overlook is at right.

Children's playgrounds are another of the park's attractions.

Below left: This rocky stream, with boulders as perches, offers another spot for contemplation.

Below right: Glass-block skylights bring diffused daylight down to the equipment rooms below.

The grand stairway widens to monumental proportions at its base.

This view of the waterfall at one end of the plaza is from the grand stairway. To the right of the falls is a golden sculpture.

ARK HILLS CENTER
TOKYO, JAPAN

LANDSCAPE ARCHITECT: Nishita and Carter ASLA, San Francisco
ARCHITECT: Atsume Kawase
CLIENT: Mori Building Company

This huge complex comprises four multistory towers and a number of low-rise buildings. Included in the development are a concert hall, offices, apartments, and shops, all surrounding a large paved plaza. The gardens, atop the smaller buildings, are accessible by grand staircases. Half of the plaza can be shaded, as necessary, by a huge moving roof on tracks; a small permanent shelter is also provided to shade individuals and small groups. The principal feature of the plaza is a large, curved fountain waterfall at the unshaded

end of the plaza. The volume and shape of the falls are controlled by a changing electronic program. In addition to the traditional view of the falls from the plaza, visitors can also walk behind them, to enjoy a different view, through the sheet of falling water. Access to the roof areas from the street is possible only through the building complex, via hallways or corridors; with no direct street access, street noise does not disturb those on the plaza.

The gardens at the upper levels, both formal and informal, are quiet spaces with large trees. Their paving recalls the design of the plaza below. The gardens above the waterfall offer views of the entire plaza.

Top: This informal garden space is one of several atop the low-rise buildings in the complex. It has no visitor access and is for viewing only.

Left: The shade structure slides on tracks to shelter the plaza below when necessary. The smaller permanent shade pavilion is at the lower right.

Above: Access behind the waterfall allows one to view the plaza through falling water.

Top left: This more formal garden, also atop a low-rise structure, has the same paving as that of the main plaza.

Top right: Built-in seating is provided on the plaza just below the edges of the upper gardens. A secondary set of stairs, at right, also leads up to the gardens.

Below: Perspective, ARK Hills Center; gardens are on the lower roofs

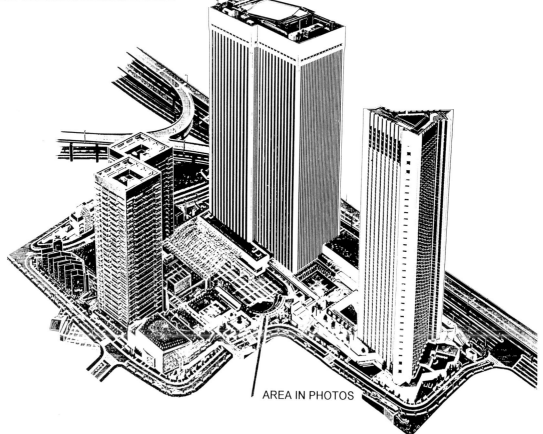

AREA IN PHOTOS

NEW OTANI HOTEL AND GARDENS

TOKYO, JAPAN

LANDSCAPE ARCHITECT: Sentaro Iwaki

The New Otani Hotel in Tokyo, one of the finest and largest in Japan, has the most spectacular roof garden in the world. Built in 1965 on the site of a villa and garden that once belonged to a Japanese daimyo, or feudal baron, much of the magnificent 10-acre (4-hectare) garden was preserved and adapted to the needs of the new hotel. The garden is dominated by a magnificent waterfall fed by a large pond level with the first floor of the hotel. The waterfall is probably the largest roof garden waterfall in the world. The pond at the right of the falls and its garden rest on the roof of an underground garage, but so deftly are the lip of the waterfall and the transition from upper to lower levels of the garden handled that the overall impression is of a single unified space, with no trace of a seam between the original garden and the roof garden.

The careful manipulation of raked gravel, rocks, selected plants, and water to create a balanced natural landscape, so typical of traditional Japanese gardens, is masterfully demonstrated

Above: A footbridge across a small pond near the waterfall forms part of the walkway through the upper garden.

Left: The waterfall, as seen from the hotel's bar and dining room, is the most spectacular of any roof garden in the world.

Above left: A traditional Japanese sand garden can also be found on the upper level of the garden.

Above right: The pond's water cascades over the stone lip of the waterfall.

Below: A red wooden bridge crosses the upper pond and leads to another area of the roof garden. The pond is alive with golden and silver carp.

here. Unlike the lower, original garden with its pine woods and torrential stream, the rooftop garden uses these more human-size components, which require a relatively shallow layer of soil and drainage. Paths throughout all levels of the garden enable hotel guests to enjoy its beauty.

SHINJUKU N.S. BUILDING

TOKYO, JAPAN

LANDSCAPE ARCHITECT: Araki Landscape Architecture
ARCHITECT: Nikken Sekkei Company
CLIENT: Shinjuku N.S.

This high-rise building, flanked on both sides by elevated streets, is fronted by a single-story gallery of shops opening onto a paved court. Atop the gallery is a handsome roof garden, extending from one elevated street to the other. The garden is bisected by the building's entrance, but the walkway through the garden continues around it, connecting the two parts of the garden and serving as a balcony that looks down on the building entrance below. Access to the garden, as well as to the paved court in front of the shops and building entrance, is from the elevated streets alongside the building, as well as from the high-rise.

The gardens contain carefully selected groups of permanent plantings that include broad-leaved and coniferous shrubs, some dwarf, in a range of colors. The choice of different-colored long-lived plants obviates the need to replant every season with annuals to add color.

The structures below the roof garden, flanking the building entrance, house shops.

Left: When viewed from the neighboring Keio Plaza Hotel, the plan of this roof garden is very clear. The interruption of the garden directly over the high-rise building's entrance transforms part of the transverse walkway into a balcony.

Above: The unusual selection of coniferous plants and variegated holly lend permanent color.

The walkway on the roof level, which can be entered from the elevated street slightly below, is paved with tiles; rich plantings line the path.

SUNSHINE 60 BUILDING

TOKYO, JAPAN

LANDSCAPE ARCHITECT: Araki Landscape
Architecture
ARCHITECT: Mitsubishi Jisho
CLIENT: Shintoshi Kaihatsu Center

The tallest building in Japan, this sixty-story office/commercial complex, completed in 1978, includes two major roof gardens.

The first, at ground level atop an underground garage, itself consists of two parts. Upon entering the front section from the adjacent street and sidewalk, one encounters formal rows of trees separated by symmetrical walkways. A small paved plaza separates this formal space from the second part of the roof garden. This back section, which is also at ground level, is startling, but only because it is so different from the first. It is a natural scene, with a series of wide waterfalls dropping over low rocky walls, surrounded by

Above: At ground level the water appears to be a vast sheet interrupted only by short stone walls over which the cascade flows.

Below: The dense ground-level formal bosque of trees is in the upper left corner. The natural and the formal converge just short of the long seat between the two.

The narrow planting of pines of the upper plaza is at the left. The larger formal plantings of evergreens are out of view to the right.

camellias, large boulders, and full-grown trees, including *Sequoia sempervirens* (coast redwood), *Taxodium distichum* 'Rich" (bald cypress), and *Myrica rubra* 'Sieb.' (red wax myrtle). At its nadir the water spreads over the concrete paving, flooding it until flowing almost unnoticeably into flat drains in the pavement. It is then silently pumped back to the waterfall's zenith by large pumps, hidden in the garage below. The pumps can move 3 tons of water per minute from 30-

Below: Plan, roof garden of Sunshine 60 Building

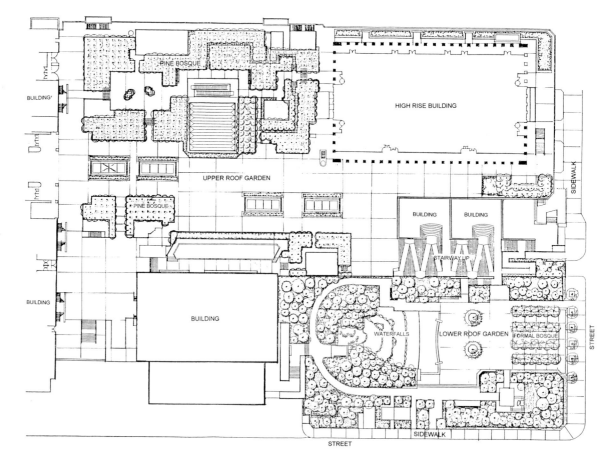

ton-capacity tanks. The roof was designed to support 3 tons per square meter (or square yard). The soil in the upper areas of this street-level garden is as much as 6 feet deep (1.8 m).

The second roof garden is accessible both from the building's elevators and via broad stairways leading up four floors from the street below. This garden plaza is all formal, consisting of heavy plantings of *Myrica rubra* 'Sieb.' in rectangular raised beds. The paved plaza serves as an alternate means of access to the building's upper floors, as well as providing an outdoor space for relaxation and conversation. Benches throughout provide ample seating. Strong tile paving patterns and retaining walls of the Indonesian wood *serauganbatu* add visual interest to the plaza.

The upper roof garden is accessible via stairs from the street

RIHGA ROYAL HOTEL
OSAKA, JAPAN

LANDSCAPE: Araki Landscape Architecture
ARCHITECT: Isoyu-Yoshida
CLIENT/OWNER: RIHGA Royal Hotel (formerly Osaka Royal Hotel)

The RIHGA Royal Hotel, one of the finest hotels in Osaka, has one of its most beautiful roof gardens. Built in 1965, the garden can be viewed only from the lobby of the hotel: it is inaccessible to visitors. The meticulously maintained landscape features a number of waterfalls of different sizes set among many plants, giving the impression that the falls are in a natural woodland setting. These spectacular waterfalls, when viewed within the context of their relatively small site by guests inside the hotel, seem far larger than they actually are. Unfortunately, their sound cannot be heard through the heavy plate-glass windows. But then, if the roar of the water was audible in the lobby, conversation would be impossible to hear in that space.

A ledge of the garage structure is used as the overflow point for one of the larger waterfalls. The floor below the waterfall's pond is used as storage space by the hotel.

Top: The seating in the cocktail lounge at a far corner of the long lobby has a full view of the roof gardens and their waterfalls. A stream, inches below floor level, flows through the lobby and into the garden, to the pool below the waterfalls.

Above and right: The spectacular waterfalls of different heights are lit at night so that guests can enjoy them from the lobby's lounge during the evening as well as during the day.

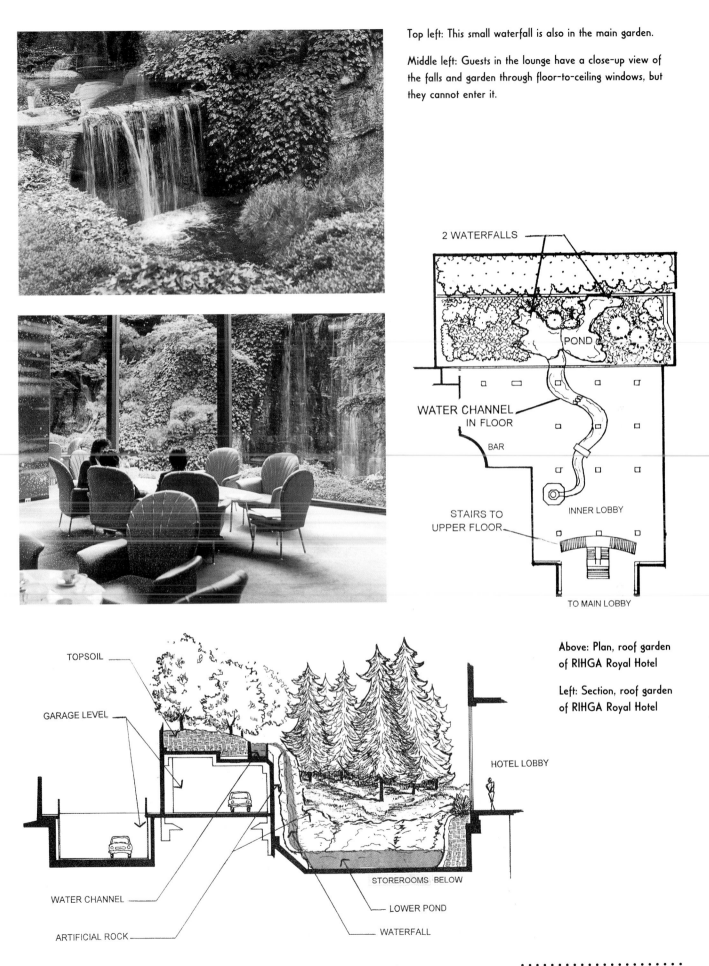

Top left: This small waterfall is also in the main garden.

Middle left: Guests in the lounge have a close-up view of the falls and garden through floor-to-ceiling windows, but they cannot enter it.

2 WATERFALLS

POND

WATER CHANNEL IN FLOOR

BAR

INNER LOBBY

STAIRS TO UPPER FLOOR

TO MAIN LOBBY

Above: Plan, roof garden of RIHGA Royal Hotel

Left: Section, roof garden of RIHGA Royal Hotel

TOPSOIL

GARAGE LEVEL

HOTEL LOBBY

WATER CHANNEL

ARTIFICIAL ROCK

STOREROOMS BELOW

LOWER POND

WATERFALL

KITAKYUSHU HOTEL
KITAKYUSHU, JAPAN

Although "modernism" or Western-style design has greatly influenced Japanese landscape architecture, the traditional "stroll garden," designed for the enjoyment of visitors walking through the garden, and the garden designed strictly for viewing from specific vantage points still exist. Although it is a large city on the northern coast of the island of Kyushu, Kitakyushu is not a typical destination for Westerners. Its public spaces, including hotels, favor traditional styles, and this includes its garden art and design. The Kitakyushu Hotel's rooftop garden exemplifies such a place.

This garden, located in a quiet nook off second-floor meeting rooms, has a single means of access, from a hallway that leads directly into that part of the garden from which it is to be viewed. There are no paths or benches, only five stone blocks (a slight bow to Western culture), set in paving of the same material, to sit upon and contemplate the arrangement of stones, raked coarse sand, sheared azaleas, and flowering cherries, with a screen terminating the view. The flat gravel

Above: From an upper floor of the hotel, one can see the layout of the entire garden, with the city in the distance.

Right: This view of the garden includes the accessible sitting area and the more distant sand area, which passes around to the right and beyond the tiny hillock in the garden's center.

surface (representing water) sweeps around to the right past a planted mound (an island), giving the impression that the garden continues in that direction. But the full garden can be seen only through the floor-to-ceiling glass walls of a meeting room to the left of the viewer. Open to the sky, the garden is flooded with southern sunlight most of the day. Surrounded on three sides by the hotel's walls, it seems private yet spacious; the walls enclose but do not suffocate.

Much of the garden is not accessible and can be viewed only through floor-to-ceiling windows in adjacent conference rooms. Here, a view through a window shows the entry to the garden and sitting area.

From the same position as in the photo above, one can turn and look directly into the main part of the sand area.

CENTRAL PARK

PERTH, AUSTRALIA

LANDSCAPE ARCHITECT: Landscan, Perth
ARCHITECT: Forbes and Fitzharding
CLIENT: Government Employees
Superannuation Board

Located in downtown Perth, the capital of the state of Western Australia, this verdant open space of approximately 1 acre (0.4 hectare) is quite different from the paved urban plazas so common in the United States. Built in 1994 atop a three-floor parking structure designed for twelve hundred cars, the park is flush with the adjacent streets on two of its sides. The garden is dominated by expanses of lawn sheltered by shrubs and trees, making the space less visible to the passing crowds beyond. It is indeed an urban oasis, located just steps away from three sophisticated high-rise buildings. With foodservice available on the first floor of one of these buildings, the garden is very popular at lunch time.

Most of the planted areas have at least 4 feet

(1.2 m) of growing medium for shrubs and trees, which include plane trees and locusts. The growing medium consists of 32 inches (81 cm) of clean topsoil with a high sand content, topped with 16 inches (40.6 cm) of an organically enriched mixture of nine parts screened sand (no fines), one part chicken manure, two parts brewery sludge, three parts organic peat, and two parts sawdust. Because almost half of this mixture is decomposable organic material, as much as half of its volume may shrink over time. Drainage beneath the soil consists of 2-inch-thick (5.1-cm) perforated hard plastic called Nylex, covered with filter fabric made from polypropylene.

Opposite:

Top: The open spaces of this privately owned downtown park are separated from the sidewalks only by short shrubs. Benches are provided in the small paved plaza, but most "brown-baggers" sit or lie on the lawns. A restaurant is located at ground level in the building from which this photo was taken.

Bottom: Lawns and planting provide a green haven in the midst of the city.

Above: Although the space is visible from the busy downtown sidewalks, the feeling within is that of a green park.

Left: Plan, Central Park, Perth

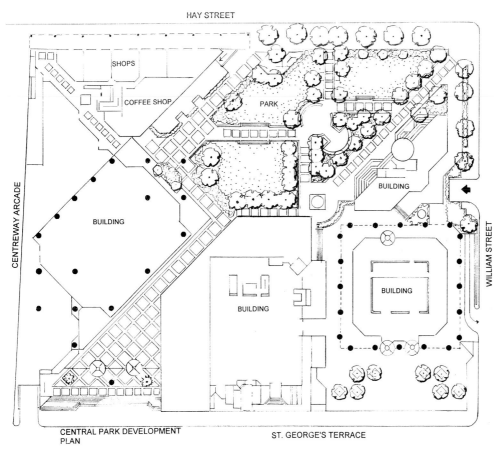

CENTRAL PARK DEVELOPMENT PLAN

TRANSPERTH BUS DEPOT (PERTH CITY COUNCIL CARPARK)

PERTH, AUSTRALIA

LANDSCAPE ARCHITECT: TRACT
ARCHITECT: Cameron, Chisolm and Nichol
CLIENT: TransPerth

The city transportation authority in Perth constructed this building as the main transfer point in the city. Its roof garden, which lies directly below the recently built high-rise towers in downtown Perth, serves both as a pleasant vista for those in nearby office buildings and as a rendezvous point for train passengers meeting friends. A café at one end of the garden makes it an attractive dining spot as well.

The roof garden is divided into two equal parts bisected by a linear roofed shelter that extends from a covered bridge (leading to the main terminal) to the restaurant at its far end. Each half of the garden includes lawns and planted areas, as well as a rivulet or rill water feature running parallel to the roof shelter. The garden was completed in 1990, and the plants, largely Australian natives, have established themselves well.

Native topsoil was not used. Instead, the soil mix in the garden is a sand base enriched with organic matter (such as pine bark). Its depth ranges from 6 inches (15 cm) in the lawn areas to 24 to 28 inches (61 to 71 cm) in the mounded garden beds. The soil mix rests on polypropylene filter fabric that covers a bit more than ½ inch (1.3 cm) of gravel for drainage. Perforated pipe helps carry excess water to the roof drains.

Above: One of the large lawn panels surrounded by trees and shrubs. At the far right, the soil is deeper to accommodate tree roots.

Right: The main terminal is connected to the roof garden of the bus-transfer building via this covered pedestrian bridge.

The rivulet and rill features are each fed by a water source at the far end.

Plan, roof garden of TransPerth Bus Depot

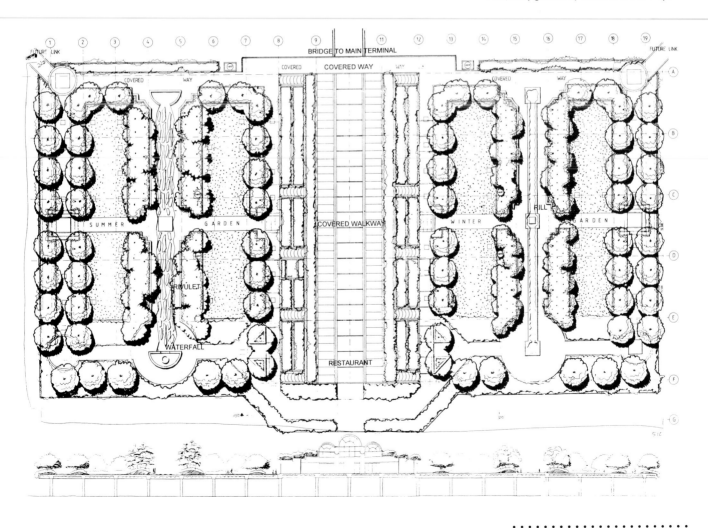

SAINT GEORGES SQUARE
PERTH, AUSTRALIA

LANDSCAPE ARCHITECT: Elizabeth Adams
ARCHITECT: John Collier

This public garden is at the rear of the new Saint Georges Square development, on the roof of the high-rise structure's adjacent four-hundred-car underground parking garage. The rectangular rooftop parterre is divided into quadrants, containing symmetrical beds created with lawn outlined by small shrubs. Within each quadrant are two fountain jets, accented by swirling ornaments, created by carving the design from the lawn and filling the resulting relief with Western Australian pea gravel. The parterre is bisected by a reflection basin that extends the length of the garden, fed by a small waterfall near the rear entrance to the high-rise. The waterfall is topped by sculpture created by a local artist. The basin is bridged at several spots, allowing visitors to cross from one quadrant to another. The wide paths that separate the quadrants, forming the parterre, are also paved in Western Australian pea gravel, a locally quarried smooth, round, red pebble that ranges from ⅛ to ¼ inch (3 to 6 mm) in size.

Top: The entrance to the parking garage below the roof garden is not visible from the garden space.

Above: The elevated portion of the roof garden is paved entirely with local red gravel and is planted with potted specimen plants.

Right: At the center of the parterre is this small pool, bisecting the reflecting basin that runs the length of the garden. Notice the bridges on either side. The residence in the distance is the historical Alexander Forrest House.

At the terminus of the path that bisects the parterre crosswise is a small ornamental pool and fountain, backed by a tree-sheltered sculpture, also created by a local artist. A few wooden benches line the path in front of the pool, facing the parterre. The parterre itself has no seating, nor does it have any shade trees, although shadows cast from the high-rise do help to mitigate the high summer temperatures. Foodservice is available on-site, but the limited seating allows little opportunity for alfresco dining.

Three restored early-nineteenth-century houses, the Alexander Forrest House, Bishop's House, and Saint Georges House, are just beyond the roof garden. Both Bishop's House and Forrest House are accessible from the roof garden. Bishop's House, outside the area of the garage structure, is occupied by the property's developer and has a substantial garden of its own.

The bridge leading over the reflecting basin eases circulation throughout the garden.

Plan, Saint Georges Square

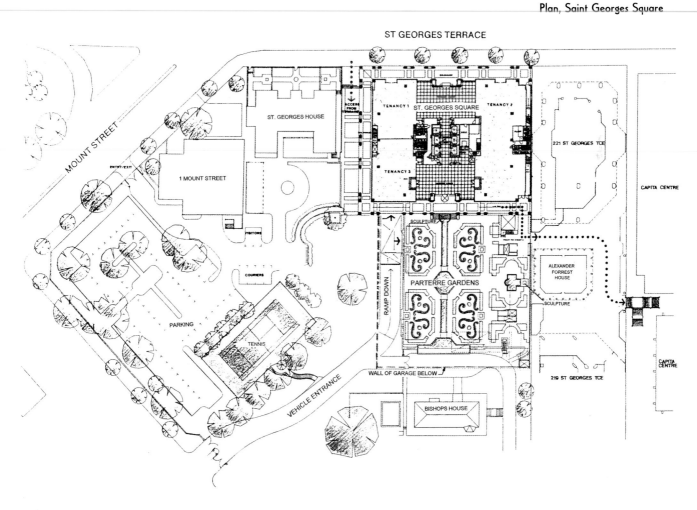

Top left : One of the tiny fountain jets in the parterre

Top right: From the rear of the Saint Georges Square high-rise building, one can see the entire length of the parterre garden and reflection basin. The Bishop's House is in the distance.

Left middle: This waterfall topped by sculpture is at the rear entrance to the Saint Georges Square high-rise. It supplies the water to the reflecting basin in the parterre.

Left bottom: The view from the pool to the parterre garden steps, which lead to an elevated area of the roof garden.

Right bottom: This ornamental pool and sculpture, outside the parterre proper, form the terminus for its transverse path. The Alexander Forrest House is directly behind the water feature.

DESIGN ELEMENTS

The variety of design elements that can be used in a roof garden is limited only by the imagination. Almost anything that can be installed on the ground can be included in a roof garden. This chapter looks at some of the more common features of roof gardens and offers suggestions on choosing and installing them. A sense of the range of design features available can also be gained by examining the portfolios of American and international roof gardens, following chapter 1 and chapter 4.

PLANTS AND PLANTING

True roof gardens, by definition, must have plant materials in more or less liberal quantities. The intensive garden should be able to support a whole range of plants, from lawns, ground covers, perennials, and annuals to shrubs and trees of considerable height. Such a combination requires consideration of weight, soil depth, drainage, soil consistency, ultimate height, ultimate spread of roots and crown, type and extent of root system, resistance to drought and overwatering, potential life span, the mix of plant types, and the ease or difficulty of replacement. Moreover, all of these factors must be carefully examined with regard to the aesthetic effect desired and the intended use of the garden. This planning process may well test the experience and reasoning of even a highly experienced landscape architect to the limit.

Categorizing individual plants according to their suitability for roof gardens would be a gargantuan task, undertaken largely in vain. Each garden has its own particular requirements with regard to function, microclimate and climate, soil, water availability, cost, maintenance, and aesthetics. Plants that are ideally suited for a small private garden in San Francisco might not survive six months in a public garden in Boston. Moreover, a plant that has some disadvantages might nevertheless have more important strong points that make its choice appropriate. For example, although crab apples can be messy trees that drop both flowers and fruit, their small size, quick maturity, hardiness, and ornamental nature might supersede their weaknesses in a particular space. Landscape architects should consider the necessary characteristics of trees, shrubs, and plants in roof gardens that are described below and then apply this information in determining plant selections that are appropriate for a particular garden design in a specific location. Local consultants, such as horticulturists, county extension services, and nurseries, can provide advice on choosing species well suited to a site's climate. Many books are devoted entirely to describing and illustrating the features of different plants. Relatively new on the market are computer software programs that will list species based on the designer's chosen parameters. In short, there are many sources of information for choosing suitable plants for individual gardens; this discussion will describe only the general plant characteristics that should be considered in roof garden design.

In a roof garden, ground covers, lawn, and ornamental annuals and perennials are chosen using essentially the same criteria as in ground-level gardens. Trees and woody plants require more careful consideration, for they should be the longest-lived and are the most costly. They also weigh the most, require the most adaptation to roof garden settings, and have the strongest visual effect in the garden. Trees and woody shrubs should flourish for a period of twenty to sixty years, with as few replacements as possible. (For all plants to live equally long is virtually

5-1 (right). Root penetration of the waterproof membrane, as shown here, compromises the building's waterproofing and results in costly repairs. (Courtesy of Dr. Hans-Joachim Liesecke)

5-2 (below). These palms on the roof of 444 South Flower in Los Angeles demonstrate that, with special care, large trees can be successfully planted on roofs. Here, the trees are protected from high winds, and the soil depth at the base of the tree has been increased. The tree type, with its ball-shaped root structure and limited foliage, also is important.

impossible, however, and replacement of dead plants should be considered an ongoing cost in any maintenance budget.) Characteristics to be considered when choosing these plants include root invasion and penetration of the membrane, excessive leaf and fruit drop, self seeding, reaction to acid and alkaline soils, resistance to drought and tolerance for overwatering, surface rooting, acceptance of root pruning, and ability to survive the drying out or freezing of roots.

Invasive Roots

Some trees are well known for their invasive root habits. For example, poplars, willows, alders, and sweet gums are notorious surface feeders that will seek out any water source within their reach and beyond. On the West Coast, this brief list also includes the eucalyptus and acacias. Many woody shrubs also have invasive roots. Such plants will quickly fill a planting bed with roots, draw down the water supply of other plants, and generally dominate the planting. Trees with invasive root habits will also likely seek out openings in waterproofing, where water has penetrated the membrane (fig. 5-1). As noted in chapter 3, roots may also compromise the membrane themselves if the membrane contains organic material that the roots can feed upon, as is the case with built-up asphaltic roofs. Although inclusion of barriers to root penetration in the garden's design can eliminate these problems, for extra safety as well as to ensure the survival of all plants in the vicinity, trees and shrubs with invasive root habits should be avoided.

Size of Trees

The height of the tree's crown and its spread in relation to the spread of its roots are important characteristics to consider to prevent the tree from overturning in high winds (fig. 5-2). A tree planted with soil mounded up to the top of the root ball, so that the surface gradually slopes away to a flat area of a foot or more in depth, will develop a suitable root flange that anchors it to the garden. A wide root flange is the best means of preventing windthrow; however, limited space may prevent adequate root spread. The tree should also be braced when planted, and the braces should be left in place permanently, allowed to rot away underground as the roots grow horizontally and the tree matures. Two such methods of bracing are shown in figures 5-3 and 5-4.

Although inadequate soil depth and area can restrict a tree's root system and thus prevent it from attaining full size, tall species should not be planted on roofs. Such trees, even when stunted by a limited root system, are susceptible to windthrow, exceed weight limits, and appear oversized. A reasonable range of height should be from 10 to 15 feet (3 to 4.5 m) for small trees and 20 to 25 feet (6 to 7.6 m) for the largest. In most roof areas close to buildings, these sizes appear to be in good scale relative to their surroundings.

Weight of Trees

When the weight of a mature tree is computed, it should be remembered that weights on roofs are figured as concentrated loads, that is, in weight per square foot at each contact point on the roof. If a 3-foot boxed tree is in a 3- by 3- by 3-foot container, the weight is computed based on 3 by 3 feet, or 9 square feet, of contact surface on the roof. In other words, the overall weight of the tree and ball is divided by 9 to determine load. A tree in such a container that weighs 300 pounds would therefore convey a load of 33 pounds per square foot on the roof surface. As the root system and the tree's superstructure grow outward, the overall weight will be spread out over a larger surface area. It is even possible that the point load weight of the tree could decrease as the tree grows, if it has enough horizontal area over which its roots can spread.

Fruit and Leaf Drop

All trees and woody shrubs drop fruit and leaves as a natural part of healthy growth. On roofs this is a concern only of degree and location.

The inclusion of paved paths, patios, plazas, benches, and similar hard surfaces in a design can

---

LANDSCAPE ON TOP OF UNDERGROUND GARAGES
Philip Hicks, A.A. Dip., ARIBA, Dip. L.D.

American research has shown that 97% of the roots of trees and shrubs occur in the top 4' of soil although a few go as deep as 10' to 12'. . . . It is likely that the greater part of the root is to be found in or near the humus where the tree finds most of its food.

On the west coast of Scotland, near Glen Mama, trees in naturally-regenerating oak forest are growing in soil depths of as little as 9" to 12" on top of rock. Their heights vary from 30 feet to 50 feet and trunk diameters reach two feet. While it is true that climatic conditions for these particular trees are unusually favorable, the depth of soil is very small.

It is almost certain that the depth is not so important as the quality of the soil. Top soil used for tree planting on top of underground garages should be the best available with a high humus content, but however good the initial soil, the well being of the trees and their ultimate dimensions will depend entirely on its being fed and maintained all the year and every year.

With regard to anchorage, it appears the depth of rooting is not so important as the development of a full "plate" of roots—i.e. the ideal theoretical root system is an even spread of roots through 360 degrees round the trunk of the tree so that it can resist gales from whatever direction they blow. In practice, however, this rarely happens because of natural obstructions, but the system is capable of considerable adaptation by root strengthening, provided the trees are not growing too closely together.

From *Landscape Design*, November 1965, the journal of the Landscape Institute.

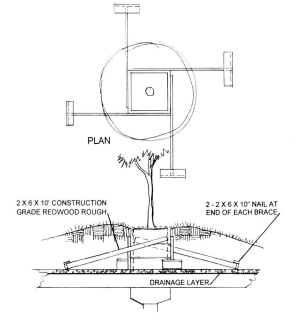

PLAN

2 X 6 X 10' CONSTRUCTION GRADE REDWOOD ROUGH

2 - 2 X 6 X 10" NAIL AT END OF EACH BRACE

DRAINAGE LAYER

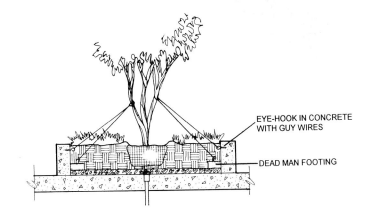

EYE-HOOK IN CONCRETE WITH GUY WIRES

DEAD MAN FOOTING

5-3 (left). Underground bracing of a tree to prevent guying. The wooden braces and tree box are allowed to rot away, with root growth replacing them for support.

5-4 (above). Guying or bracing a tree aboveground to either a wall or deadman underground.

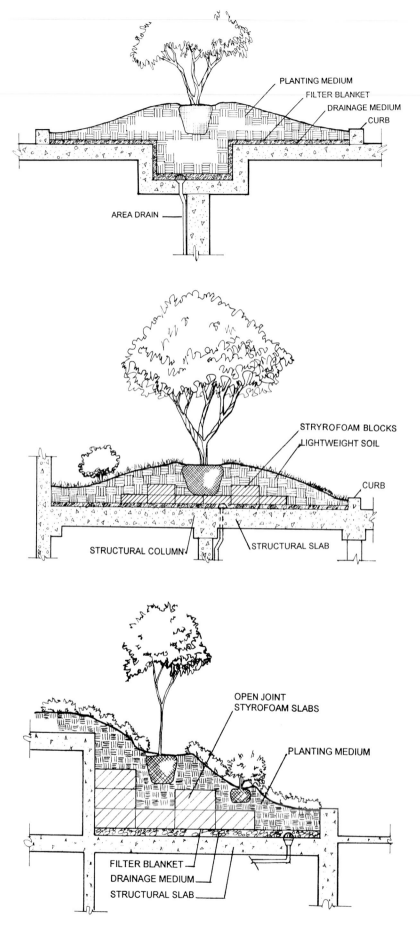

PLANTING MEDIUM
FILTER BLANKET
DRAINAGE MEDIUM
CURB

AREA DRAIN

STRYROFOAM BLOCKS
LIGHTWEIGHT SOIL

CURB

STRUCTURAL COLUMN
STRUCTURAL SLAB

OPEN JOINT
STYROFOAM SLABS

PLANTING MEDIUM

FILTER BLANKET
DRAINAGE MEDIUM
STRUCTURAL SLAB

make fruit drop a messy problem in rooftop development. If possible, flowering plums, crab apples, cherries, female ginkgos, olives, tree pittosporums, and other heavily fruiting trees should not be planted near paving, furnishings, and water features. Some fruits can permanently stain hard surfaces where they fall.

Leaf drop occurs largely in deciduous trees and shrubs, but coniferous and broad-leaved evergreen plants also drop leaves at varying times of the year, for differing lengths of time. This is a natural part of the annual cycle of plants and is generally enjoyed as part of the colorful change of the seasons. To maintenance gardeners, it can mean heavy work at times. Trees that drop their leaves over long periods of time are looked on with less favor than those that drop them, say, all within a week or so. Short periods of leaf drop can be cleaned up in an annual short burst of energy. Deciduous trees and shrubs are predominant on the East Coast and in the Midwest, making leaf drop a greater concern in these places than in the South and West, where there are a great many broad-leaved evergreens from which to choose. But the splendid spring bloom of deciduous plants more than compensates for the extra maintenance.

Soil Depths

With notable exceptions, such as the Enid A. Haupt Garden at the Smithsonian Institution in Washington, D.C. (which has soil depths of up to 8 feet [2.5 m]; see the portfolio of American gardens following chapter 1), the ultimate size of trees must be limited because soil depth is limited in roof gardens. Where the overall depth of

5-5 (top). To increase soil depth, the roof below the tree can be lower than it is beneath other parts of the garden.

5-6 (middle). Soil can be mounded around a tree to provide greater depths. The Styrofoam blocks reduce the amount of soil needed, thus also reducing weight and cost.

5-7 (bottom). Styrofoam slabs below the planting medium can vary the soil depth, making a range of depths for a variety of plants possible.

soil must be low, in the range of 6 to 10 inches (15 to 25.4 cm), it is possible to mound soil higher over stronger points in the structure, such as columns, to depths of 30 inches (76.2 cm) or more. Using raised beds, the bottoms of which are dropped below the surface of the roof, can increase total soil depth to 5 to 6 feet, or 1.5 to 1.8 m (figs. 5-5 and 5-6). Clearly, such an arrangement must be planned and designed as part of the building's architecture. For other areas where shrubs, ground covers, and lawn but no trees are to be planted, depths ranging from a minimum of 6 inches (15 cm) for lawns rising to 24 inches (61 cm) or more for shrubs are possible (fig. 5-7).

PLANT CONTAINERS

Plant containers such as pots, tubs, and boxes are used universally on decks, balconies, and porches. They can also be indispensable on a roof that has a severe load restriction or has waterproofing that requires periodic replacement (to replace waterproofing, all objects must be moved from the working area, even if only from one point to another on the same roof). In such cases plant containers, though some can be quite heavy, are often the only answer to having any planting at all. Even in roof gardens with less stringent

weight restrictions, plant tubs can have a very useful purpose in enhancing plant material as design accents, as temporary homes for colorful annual flowers, and as places to grow flowering shrubs and trees that function as handsome structural elements in nonflowering seasons (figs. 5-8, 5-9, 5-10, and 5-11).

It should be noted that stationary plant containers that remain in place year-round are generally only appropriate in areas that experience

5-8. Large-scale containers can be used to define functional areas as well as the overall design of a roof plaza. At Crocker Terrace in San Francisco, a strong pattern is established by the containers and trees, the scale of the containers, and the tile and concrete paving.

5-9. The important trees at Embarcadero Center in San Francisco grow in large precast concrete planters. No trees are planted in raised beds in this part of the development.

mild winters. In northern climes, freezing and/or the freeze/thaw cycle will cause many containers to crack, regardless of material. If container planting is desired in such areas, containers can be used in spring, summer, and fall and then stored in a protected interior space during the winter.

Plant containers have some of the same requirements as larger raised beds do. They should be able to retain moisture in the soil and yet have good drainage to prevent souring of the soil. A soil mix that will not decay and be lost in drainage is just as important here as in a bed (see chapter 4). A ½-inch (1.3-cm) layer of pine, redwood, or fir bark mulch is needed to slow drying. But container planting also has unique requirements that can be difficult to resolve, irrigation and drainage being the most acute.

Materials

Unlike ornamental residential containers, which can be considered temporary, roof garden plant containers should be considered permanent design elements and therefore should be as durable as possible. Replacement, particularly if irrigation piping has been installed, can be both difficult and costly. Concrete (which is very heavy), terra-cotta, and UV-resistant plastic containers last the longest and will retain their shape

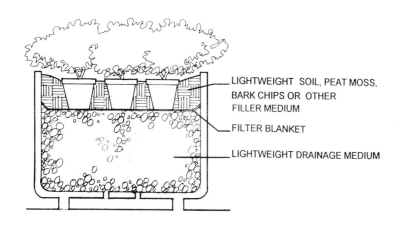

LIGHTWEIGHT SOIL, PEAT MOSS, BARK CHIPS OR OTHER FILLER MEDIUM

FILTER BLANKET

LIGHTWEIGHT DRAINAGE MEDIUM

5-10 (top). At the Pacific Telesis Center in San Francisco, oversized saucer containers add scale and definition to the open space.

5-11 (middle). To reduce the amount of planting mix used for potted flowering plants that are changed seasonally, small pots are grouped in a larger container. Lightweight drainage medium fills most of the container, providing support as well as drainage. A backfill of lightweight organic fill, such as soil, peat, or bark chips, conceals the flower pots. Filter fabric between the two media prevents loss of the organic fill through drainage.

5-12 (bottom). This commercial/office complex in Stuttgart has roofs greened with plants in plastic containers produced by the Brecht company. Trees are simulated with pipe standards supporting stacked containers with trailing plants.

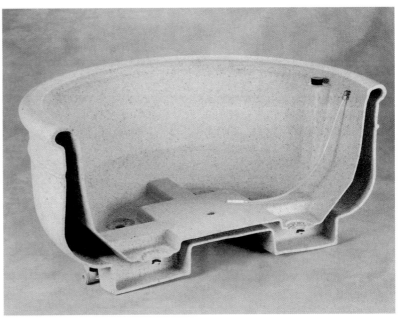

and color. Redwood, cedar, and teak are durable but should be lined with copper or galvanized iron to prevent the inside of the container from rotting. A ½-inch (1.3-cm) drainage pipe should be soldered into the bottom of the liner for drainage.

In Europe a system based on polystyrene containers is fairly popular. The Brecht roof system consists of lightweight polystyrene boxes that are approximately 7 to 14 inches (17.8 to 35.5 cm) high. Their limited depth prohibits their use for large plants such as trees, but they are very useful for low ground covers or low shrubs (fig. 5-12). Their design is functional for mobility, drainage, and extended storage of water for irrigation. The system is widely used for roof planting where access to the roof is limited to maintenance personnel.

Irrigation

There are few alternatives for supplying water to a plant container placed on ornamental paving during dry periods. The first is to have water piped to the container and brought up through the soil, where it can be distributed by a bubbler or other short-throw sprinkler head. A difficulty with this method is in bringing the water to the plant without the pipe being visible on the pavement. If the container is to be placed next to a building wall, the pipe can be laid on the surface where the wall and pavement meet. The pipe can

be seen but is not obtrusive. A connection or tee can bring the pipe under the container and up through the soil to its surface.

A second and more difficult method is to hang the water-supply pipe in the ceiling of the space below the roof and bring it up through the structural slab and paving at the specific location where the container will be permanently placed. This penetration must be carefully and permanently sealed to prevent leaks later in the space below. The supply is then brought to the surface of the container soil, where it can be sprayed or bubbled onto the plants. With this system the containers must remain permanently in their original position.

Another method is the obvious one of hand watering, which involves the labor-intensive (and messy-looking) use of hoses that must be dragged across the paving from hose bibbs. Obviously, if one or more hose bibbs can be installed near the containers, this method requires less work.

Recent innovations in container configurations have made container irrigation somewhat less difficult. The Mona Plant System (MPS) of irrigation, which relies on the transmittal of water via capillary action from reservoirs at the base of the container, is available for individual planters as well as raised beds (fig. 5-13). Another possibility is the Container Watering System sold by the company Planter Technology (fig. 5-

5-13 (left). The Mona self-watering system for plant containers includes a plastic reservoir that rests on the bottom of the pot. Its removable top is perforated to allow excess water from rainfall to penetrate the tank. The ring in the center is the top of a permanent probe that holds a small part of the potting soil, which stays wet and permits water to rise into the main planting mix above it by capillary action. The reservoir is refilled through the flexible plastic pipe. The depth of existing water in the tank is determined by inserting a dipstick into the refill tube.

5-14 (right). A cutaway view of the Seacrest series planter from Planter Technology. The outer wall of the container is a hollow reservoir. Irrigation is facilitated by capillary action. (Courtesy of Planter Technology)

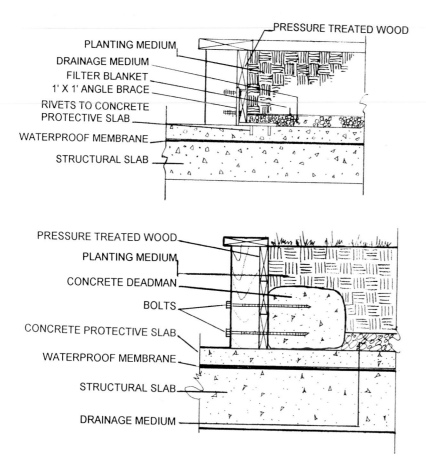

PLANTING MEDIUM
DRAINAGE MEDIUM
FILTER BLANKET
1' X 1' ANGLE BRACE
RIVETS TO CONCRETE
PROTECTIVE SLAB
WATERPROOF MEMBRANE
STRUCTURAL SLAB
PRESSURE TREATED WOOD

PRESSURE TREATED WOOD
PLANTING MEDIUM
CONCRETE DEADMAN
BOLTS
CONCRETE PROTECTIVE SLAB
WATERPROOF MEMBRANE
STRUCTURAL SLAB
DRAINAGE MEDIUM

5-15 (top). Angle braces riveted to the concrete protection slab are one means of supporting wooden walls for planting beds.

5-16 (bottom). Wooden container walls can also be bolted to a deadman for support.

14). These very handsome plant containers are sold in a range of sizes for use both indoors and outdoors. The planter and its water reservoir are integral. Water is held in the hollow walls of the plastic container itself, which is filled by opening an airtight cap on its upper rim. When the cap is replaced and tightened, a vacuum is created above the water level. When the soil becomes dry, a moisture sensor located at the upper root level of the plant connected by a tube to the vacuum chamber allows air into the vacuum chamber. The water in the tank walls is released and moves down to the bottom of the container, where it rises by capillary action through the soil to the plant roots. When the soil around the roots becomes saturated, the sensor closes the water-feed valve. The vacuum is reestablished, preventing more water from moving to the container. A petcock near the outside bottom of the container allows draining of the wall tank and disposal of water containing excess salt and of excess rainwater. Depending on existing conditions, the tank can supply water for two to four weeks before refilling is needed.

Drainage

The difficulty with drainage in container planting is not with the draining of the container, which is handled in the same way as a planting bed, but in dealing with the water after it drains from the container. Drainage itself is fairly straightforward. A layer of drainage material, such as ½-inch (1.3-cm) drain rock or a drainage material such as Enkadrain or Geotech, should cover the inside bottom of the container. Polypropylene filter fabric should cover the drainage material on the upper, or soil, side. When the water leaves the container, it will drain onto the surface beneath and should flow to the nearest catch basin. If the container is on a paved surface or the route to the catch basin is paved, decaying humus, salts, and other material in solution in the drain water will stain the paving. A simple way to prevent this problem is to install a 2-inch-deep (5.1-cm) long-lasting copper pan under each container. The pan should be deep enough to hold any excess water. It should be emptied regularly to ensure that it does not overflow and that the water in it does not become fetid or become a breeding place for mosquitoes.

Wooden Planter Walls for Raised Beds and Containers

When less sophisticated gardens, such as community gardens, are desired on building roofs, low wooden walls are often used to frame the planting beds, instead of the more typical brick, stone, or concrete. The material is easily brought to the roof in the building's elevator. Although building codes generally prohibit the use of wood in steel-frame buildings, there seems to be some acquiescence in permitting this type of construction. The wood, for longevity, should be seasoned redwood or cedar or wood that has been pressure-treated with preservative. The walls may be attached to the roof, either with metal angle braces attached to the wall and protective concrete slab (fig. 5-15) or with concrete deadmen poured after the wall has been built (fig. 5-16). A drainage medium should be added before the beds are filled with planting medium. If the bed is large enough, the weight of the soil may be enough to hold the bed in place, and the angle braces may not be necessary.

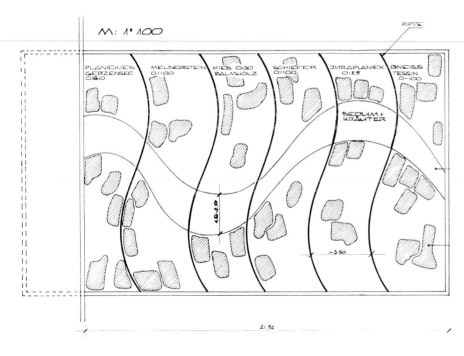

5-17 (top left). Adjacent to the East Bay Municipal Utility District's offices in Oakland, California, this simple gravel and tile pattern provides a graceful transition between the employees' roof deck and the neighboring gardens below.

5-18 (top right). The roof below the civic plaza in the country of San Marino is covered with a pattern of trimmed perennials, including *Stachys lanata* (lambs' ear), *Lavandula officinalis* (English lavender), and other drought-resistant plants.

5-19 (left). This simple roof pattern was designed for the roof of an elementary school in Bern, Switzerland, by Franz Vogel. The pattern is created mostly from various colors of gravel, with black S-shaped lines of dark gravel showing above the adjacent colored material. An undulating strip of *Sedum* sp. meanders from one end of the roof to the other. (Courtesy of Franz Vogel)

ROOF PATTERNS

The appearance of buildings with weak roofs and those that are unsuitable for gardens can be substantially improved by applying simple, permanent materials such as colored gravels. Gravel is very commonly used as ballast on flat built-up bituminous roofs to protect the membrane from ultraviolet light and physical wear, to prevent wind uplift of the membrane, and to improve the membrane's fire resistance. When such roofs are lower than, and so, visible from the occupied floors of neighboring buildings, they can be made more attractive by applying two or more

5-20. Varicolored bricks create an interesting paving pattern for a quiet patio area off the main lounge building at Thoreau Hall on the campus of the University of California at Davis.

5-21. Concrete paving can be poured directly on the surface of drain rock if filter fabric is placed as a barrier to prevent wet concrete from filling rock voids.

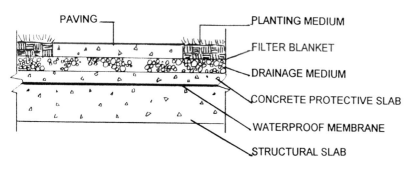

colors of gravel in a planned pattern for almost the same cost as a single color (fig. 5-17).

Patterns created from low durable ground covers, such as *Sedum acre,* a hardy silver-green succulent, are also an alternative under some circumstances. These have been successfully used in Germany, Switzerland, and other European countries (figs. 5-18 and 5-19). Good drainage is necessary, and an irrigation system would be needed in areas of the United States where seasonal rainfall is scarce or erratic.

PAVING

Although hard surfaces on roof gardens serve the same purposes as those in gardens at ground level, in at least two respects they deserve special attention. In most cases roof gardens are viewed from the higher floors of adjacent buildings in downtown areas. The appearance of paving thereby assumes a far greater importance and demands stronger and more careful design.

In addition, the amount of shade provided by trees on top of buildings is restricted by the lack of size and spread of mature trees in this artificial environment. If people are to sit outside in sunny areas, the paving must reflect a minimum of unpleasant glare. Plain concrete paving, for example, reflects considerably more uncomfortable glare than, say, red brick pavers do. Nonreflective paving choices are extensive and range from deep-colored concrete to fine tile and brick (figs. 5-20 and 5-21). Colored concrete with deep-colored exposed aggregate, cut flat fieldstone, granite sets, concrete interlocking, and sandstone are all nonreflective. (Concrete and fieldstone, however, are not good choices in areas where rapid freezing and thawing occurs, as they are vulnerable to cracking under these conditions.) There are many variations within each of these general types of paving, and the combinations of such materials are limited only by one's imagination and good taste.

On wood-frame buildings with structurally weak roofs, removable pallets provide a good surface for furniture and potted plants. They are lightweight and allow good access to the drains and membrane for repairs and maintenance.

Not recommended in public roof gardens is loose gravel, which, if kicked about, can cause mowing and clean-up problems. Gravel is also an uncomfortable walking surface, and it is difficult to maneuver wheeled vehicles, such as strollers and wheelchairs, on it. Dust on the surface of decomposed granite walks may be blown about by high winds; if carried inside on the bottoms of shoes, it may scratch fine flooring. Asphalt is usually impractical or impossible to install because it must be rolled with heavy equipment to obtain its final finish; its use is feasible only if access is directly available from the street and weight limitations permit.

When choosing paving materials, particularly those for elevated gardens on existing structures, consider how they will be transported to the site. It is, for example, easier, cleaner, and less expensive to transport bricks in an elevator in an existing building than it is wet concrete. In a building under construction, of course, cranes and exterior elevators are capable of lifting almost any material equally well.

Pedestal Paving

It is sometimes desirable to use a system of prefabricated pedestals to mount paving squares or rectangles above the surface of the roof. Such paving units can be easily removed to repair or clean the roof surface below. Water enters the cavity formed between the paving and the roof through spaces between the paving slabs and is carried away via the sloping roof and drains (fig. 5-22). The insulation lies beneath the concrete slab. Pedestals should never rest directly on the waterproof membrane.

It is also possible to use open-joint paving units without pedestals, providing the roof surface is pitched at no more than ³⁄₁₆ inch per foot. Protection board or a concrete protection slab is placed on the surface of the waterproof membrane, and the drain is covered with filter fabric. A layer of drainage medium is placed over all, its surface is leveled, and it is then covered with filter fabric. Open-joint prefabricated paving units are placed on the surface with ¼-inch (6.4-mm) spaces between them (fig. 5-23).

FURNISHINGS

If an outdoor space is uncomfortable, it will not be used unless it offers an attraction that greatly outweighs comfort. William F. Whyte has proven rather conclusively through long observation and study that people-watching on a busy downtown street will attract and hold people's attention, even if only a concrete ledge or wall is available as seating. If the wall is too high to sit on, people will sit on the sidewalk and lean against the wall if other people are doing it and there are plenty of passersby to watch. However, Whyte's observations only prove that people will insist upon using a space despite discomfort if it has compensating benefits. It does not prove that people would not prefer comfort or that all places are used even when they are not comfortable.

Private roof gardens should be well furnished and as comfortable to use as possible, as should privately owned gardens that are open to the public. The roof gardens of hotels, where access is somewhat limited, are almost universally well furnished, adding greatly to their use and guests' enjoyment of them. To prevent vandalism or theft of furniture in a more accessible space, the garden might require the employment of a guard on duty during the garden's visiting hours.

Furnishings should be weather resistant so that they can be left in place during warm seasons. Plastic-covered steel or aluminum frames with an all-weather coating are both very good. Wood furnishings, because of their bulk and weight as well as their easily loosened joints, are less desirable for public use. As noted in chapter 3, care should be taken during windy weather to remove lightweight, nonstationary furnishings to prevent them from causing damage or injury if they are blown about.

A garden table 3 feet (1 m) square or round with four chairs requires a circle of space 9 to 10 feet (3 m) in diameter to provide access and a degree of privacy (figs. 5-24, 5-25, and 5-26). Umbrellas are almost a necessity in bright sunny spaces. A maintenance person should be available on the premises to lower the umbrellas on windy days, so that they do not tip over.

If only permanent benches are to be provided, they should have arms, should have seat backs made of wood or resilient metal, and should be

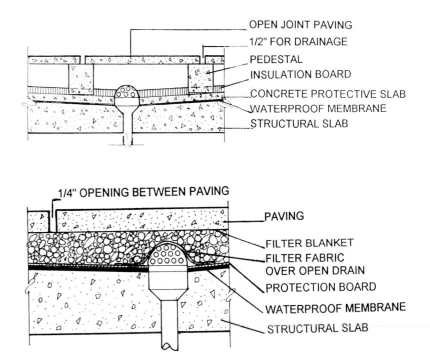

OPEN JOINT PAVING
1/2" FOR DRAINAGE
PEDESTAL
INSULATION BOARD
CONCRETE PROTECTIVE SLAB
WATERPROOF MEMBRANE
STRUCTURAL SLAB

1/4" OPENING BETWEEN PAVING

PAVING
FILTER BLANKET
FILTER FABRIC OVER OPEN DRAIN
PROTECTION BOARD
WATERPROOF MEMBRANE
STRUCTURAL SLAB

5-22 (top). Paving blocks placed and leveled on permanent pedestals permit good drainage to the sloping roof below and protect the membrane from sunlight.

5-23 (bottom). Slabs with ¼ inch (6.4 mm) of drainage space between them can be placed directly on the drainage layer. This detail is for a garage roof, where insulation is not needed.

5-24 (top left). Plenty of lightweight comfortable furnishings make this roof terrace at the Donatello Hotel in San Francisco a relaxing space for guests; Mario Gaidano, architect.

5-25 (top right). A wide curb/seat around the tree grate adds additional seating to the ample furnishings provided at the Mitsui roof garden in Tokyo.

5-26 (middle right). Furnishings can serve many functions. At these shady tables in San Francisco's Yerba Buena Gardens, visitors can relax, enjoy a snack, and play a game of chess.

5-27 (bottom left). This semicircular bench at Crocker Terrace in San Francisco permits a number of visitors to relax and eat singly or with others. Small groups can chat without the inconvenience of twisting to see one another.

5-28 (bottom right). The benches around the periphery of the Cambridge Center roof garden in Cambridge, Massachusetts, are metal with a baked-on finish.

designed to fit the contours of the back properly. With all the back troubles from which people suffer, there is no reason to settle for less in outdoor benches. A number of such well-designed benches are commercially available; check for comfort before specifying or purchasing them (figs. 5-27 and 5-28). Well-designed trash receptacles and drinking fountains should be provided at convenient locations throughout the garden (figs. 5-29, 5-30, and 5-31).

An example of a roof garden that could be more popular if it were better furnished is the Kaiser Center roof garden in Oakland, California. Open to the public five days a week, the garden has never had movable furnishings, and this lack, along with confusing access, has almost certainly contributed to its relatively low public use. Visitors sit on built-in backless concrete benches like that shown in figure 5-32 or on the low concrete edges of raised planter beds. This policy has persisted for many years, even though a security officer had been on duty while the garden was open until just recently. In this case, the difficulty of access alone would greatly decrease the threat of vandalism or theft. Plenty of outdoor furniture, including weatherproof tables, chairs, and umbrellas, adequate and tastefully done signage to direct visitors to the roof garden, and the availability of light refreshment during the lunch hours (perhaps from a cheerfully designed small kiosk) would greatly improve the enjoyment of

5-29 (top left). One of the many small but attractive refuse receptacles at the Federal Reserve Bank's roof garden in Boston.

5-30 (top middle). Convenient water fountains are a welcome comfort. This one was designed especially for the Pacific Bell roof garden in Sacramento.

5-31 (top right). This drinking fountain at the Kaiser Center roof garden in Oakland offers fountains suitable for both adults and children.

5-32 (bottom). Permanent and durable, benches are basic seating in roof gardens, but additional comfortable and portable garden furniture is necessary if the space is to be enjoyed fully. Unfortunately these benches are the only seats available at the Kaiser Center in Oakland.

this otherwise splendid and well-maintained privately owned downtown roof garden.

LIGHTING

No effect in a garden is more dramatic than when the space is lit at night. To see what was blackness appear suddenly highlighted or flooded with carefully focused light adds a new and spectacular dimension to the plantings and garden structures that can be achieved in no other way. Indeed, lighting can give the garden owner two quite different gardens, one by day and one by

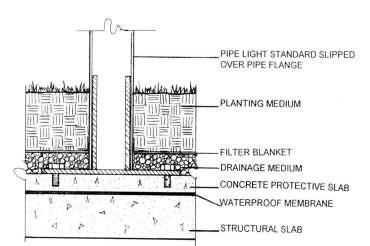

PIPE LIGHT STANDARD SLIPPED OVER PIPE FLANGE

PLANTING MEDIUM

FILTER BLANKET

DRAINAGE MEDIUM

CONCRETE PROTECTIVE SLAB

WATERPROOF MEMBRANE

STRUCTURAL SLAB

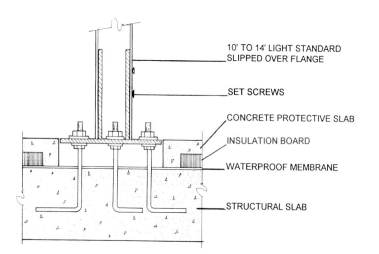

10' TO 14' LIGHT STANDARD SLIPPED OVER FLANGE

SET SCREWS

CONCRETE PROTECTIVE SLAB

INSULATION BOARD

WATERPROOF MEMBRANE

STRUCTURAL SLAB

5-33 (top left). These handsome light standards at the roof garden at the Christian Science Center in Boston are beautiful as well as practical and are a strong design element; Sasaki Associates, landscape architects.

5-34 (middle left). Lights can be anchored to the concrete protection slab by attaching the flange with set screws or bolts to expansion shields in the concrete or by shooting bolts into the slab.

5-35 (above). A pipe with flange placed on the concrete protection slab makes a firm base onto which a short light fixture can be fitted. Secure the low-level light with set screws.

5-36 (bottom left). Tall light standards must withstand heavy winds. Bolts should be securely anchored into the structural slab while the slab is still wet and must be carefully sealed to prevent leaks.

night. Moreover, light fixtures themselves can be decorative as well as functional design elements (fig. 5-33). In addition, lighting can improve the security of a garden.

A roof garden is least costly to light when lighting is planned during its design, so that electrical wiring can be installed during construction. Like the irrigation system, electrical conduits and the necessary junction boxes, outlets, and other elements can be installed before the placement of the planting medium, eliminating the cost of digging or trenching later. At the general location where lighting is desired, the individual wiring and fixtures can be connected to the outlets, and the lighting effect can be fine-tuned. The conduits are installed on the roof surface, hidden under the drainage and planting medium. If open plastic drainage materials, such as Enkadrain or Grass-Cel, are used, the conduits and irrigation lines are placed on the surface of the drainage material and backfilled with planting medium.

Special attachments are needed for light standards atop roofs where the waterproof membrane should not be punctured. Path lighting with short standards can be attached to the concrete protective slab as shown in figure 5-34. A flanged pipe is attached to the slab with short bolts (fig. 5-35). Taller light standards that must resist the pressure of high winds require a strong attachment to the roof's structural slab. Their supports thus will penetrate the waterproof membrane. Such openings must be carefully

sealed. Bolts are set into the structural slab, and a steel flange with a pipe attached is set at the height of the concrete protection slab. A tall light standard is slipped over the vertical pipe flange and is held in place by set screws (fig. 5-36).

SCULPTURE

Sculpture is an important feature in almost any garden and is especially useful to highlight a feature or create a focal point in roof gardens (figs. 5-37, 5-38, and 5-39). No practical reason prevents the use of such works of art except for the excessive weight of heavy pieces. If the roof garden is designed before the building is built, the roof structure can be designed to receive such concentrated loads. Otherwise, care should be taken to assess the weight of the sculpture and, if necessary, to locate the piece over a column or other strongly reinforced part of the roof. Partic-

5-37 (top left). Sculpture can serve as an eye-catching focal point. These pieces are featured at Pershing Square in Los Angeles; Hanna/Olin, landscape architect.

5-38 (top right). A fountain and sculpture on the roof of a shopping center in Stuttgart, Germany.

5-39 (bottom). San Francisco's ordinance requiring 1 percent of construction costs to be spent on art in publicly financed buildings allowed SWA, the landscape architects for Embarcadero Center, to design its roof garden to include sculpture.

pose of a garden is to house such artwork. One example of such a place is the sculpture garden of the Museum of Modern Art in New York (figs. 5-40 and 5-41). Designed by Philip Johnson and opened in 1966, part of the garden at the east end is atop a roof, while the rest was built over broken rubble and old foundations of brownstone houses. Hence, it is settling unevenly, and that portion above the roof has had problems with leaks. Tentative plans have been made to remove the garden as part of an extensive renovation and to restore it to its original size and condition on top of an underground extension of the basement, thus creating a new and complete roof garden.

WATER FEATURES

The use of water on roofs is restricted only by weight and strong winds. It is possible to have reflection pools, waterfalls, streams, fountains, sculpture, and moving water in unlimited design configurations (figs. 5-42, 5-43, 5-44, 5-45, 5-46, and 5-47). If water features are planned well in advance of a building's construction, the landscape architect can compute the weight requirements and work with the building's structural engineer to ensure the roof can support the water feature. The water supply can be designed and installed easily in the ceiling of the floor below.

Although flat expanses of water are not affected by strong winds, fountains and sprays can be a problem, as wind blows the water before it reaches the basin below, possibly causing floods in planted areas, puddling on pavement, and an annoying and unexpected showering of visitors. Wind sensors that turn off the fountain when wind velocity reaches a certain level can be installed to prevent this problem.

If a water feature is to be added after the structure is underway or completed, the building's established weight limitations must be met. Nonetheless, even with severe weight restrictions, highly imaginative water features can be constructed. Most water effects occur on the surface of the water only. Still water rippled by a small jet or a waterfall or fountain need only a 4-inch-deep (10.2-cm) pond to achieve the same effect as great depths of water in a pool or basin. Water recirculated by a pump can give the impression of an

ular attention is needed if additional weight from water is added to the load when ponds or fountains are part of the feature. If a garden has a restrictive load limit, the material for the sculpture can be adjusted to lighten its weight; hollow metal or plastic are two possibilities. A great many sculptures can be easily accommodated on a roof that has been designed to carry the weight of a roof garden. In all cases a structural engineer should be consulted.

Gardens are such ideal spaces in which to feature sculpture that occasionally the primary pur-

5-42 (top left). Atop the Sunshine 60 building in Tokyo, these low, flat rock formations form the framework for waterfalls. The water ultimately flows across the paving in the foreground and is recirculated to its source at the upper right.

5-43 (top right). The 16-inch-deep (40.6-cm) pond at the Kaiser Center in Oakland has functioned successfully since 1960. The surfaces below the water are painted black to create the impression of greater depth.

5-44 (middle left). Ponds need not have edges of uniform width, as this one at the Kaiser Center demonstrates. The pool edge was built in accordance with the section shown in figure 5-51. Any of the four methods would have produced the same final appearance.

5-45 (middle right). Large masses of concrete underlie the waterfalls in the principal water feature at Freeway Park in Seattle.

5-46 (bottom left). Water flooding over stepped bricks against a vertical wall also creates a wall of sound that buffers the Mitsui roof garden in Tokyo from street noise.

5-47 (bottom right). The use of water as a decorative element is limited only by imagination, weight, and cost. It can move or remain still, depending on the desired effect. This fountain at the Stamford Center in Connecticut is the simplest way of including moving water. Underwater jets force the water up from the pond's surface.

5-48 (top). Section show-
ing concrete pond base
poured directly atop the
membrane, with re-bar
used at the curb wall.

5-49 (middle). Section
showing concrete curb wall
poured atop preinstalled
re-bar. A second mem-
brane is placed atop the
concrete protective slab,
then the concrete pond
base is poured.

5-50 (below). Section
showing concrete pond
base poured as part of the
concrete protection slab.

5-51 (bottom). Section
showing pond that is to be
tiled or finished decora-
tively with other materials.

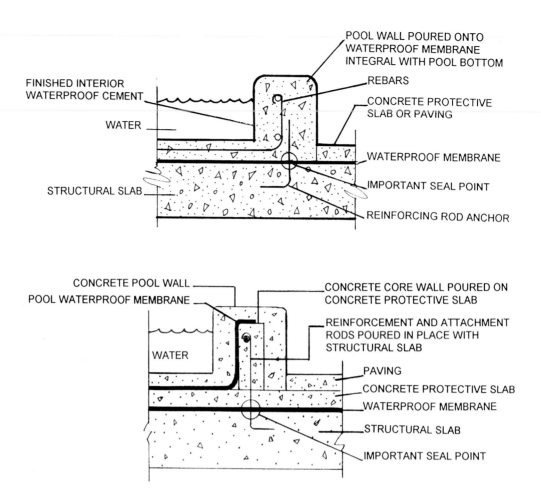

POOL WALL POURED ONTO
WATERPROOF MEMBRANE
INTEGRAL WITH POOL BOTTOM

REBARS

CONCRETE PROTECTIVE
SLAB OR PAVING

FINISHED INTERIOR
WATERPROOF CEMENT

WATER

WATERPROOF MEMBRANE

IMPORTANT SEAL POINT

STRUCTURAL SLAB

REINFORCING ROD ANCHOR

CONCRETE POOL WALL
POOL WATERPROOF MEMBRANE

CONCRETE CORE WALL POURED ON
CONCRETE PROTECTIVE SLAB

REINFORCEMENT AND ATTACHMENT
RODS POURED IN PLACE WITH
STRUCTURAL SLAB

WATER

PAVING

CONCRETE PROTECTIVE SLAB

WATERPROOF MEMBRANE

STRUCTURAL SLAB

IMPORTANT SEAL POINT

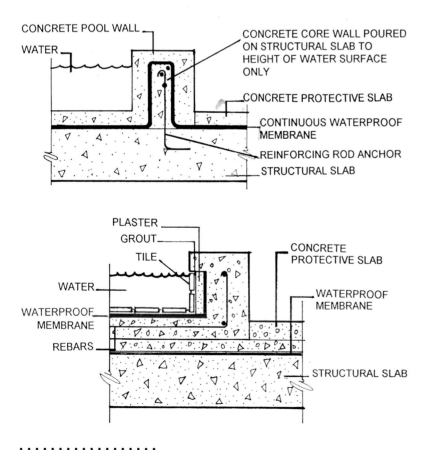

CONCRETE POOL WALL

WATER

CONCRETE CORE WALL POURED
ON STRUCTURAL SLAB TO
HEIGHT OF WATER SURFACE
ONLY

CONCRETE PROTECTIVE SLAB

CONTINUOUS WATERPROOF
MEMBRANE

REINFORCING ROD ANCHOR

STRUCTURAL SLAB

PLASTER
GROUT
TILE

CONCRETE
PROTECTIVE SLAB

WATER

WATERPROOF
MEMBRANE

WATERPROOF
MEMBRANE

REBARS

STRUCTURAL SLAB

endless stream. Although some water will be lost
through evaporation in a circulating water system, it can be easily replenished by using a float
valve attached to the building's water system
(water is supplied from pipes in the ceiling of the
floor below). For a natural rocky setting, adroit
placement of field stones above load-bearing
locations such as columns, with lighter material
placed in the weaker areas between columns, can
be as effective as covering the entire roof with
heavy materials. In limited space, the heavier elements, if placed directly over a structural column,
can serve as the entire setting for the garden.

Creating a body of water on a roof presents
special waterproofing concerns, for leaks onto
the roof must be prevented. The edge of a large
body of water, such as a reflecting pool, can be
built in a number of ways using formed concrete
curb walls. Regardless of which method is used,
the water is shallow, and this is reflected in the
height of the curb wall. Ten to fifteen inches (25.4
to 38.1 cm) of water is usually sufficient to give

an impression of depth if the interior surface is painted black. Any of the following methods can be used as shown or can be adapted as conditions warrant. (To simplify matters, the methods and illustrations that follow all assume the building below is uninsulated, as would be the case for a parking garage roof. The second method can also be used for protected-membrane roofs, in which the insulation is laid atop the roof membrane.)

One of the simplest ways of constructing a waterproof curb wall is to pour the concrete pool bottom directly on the surface of the waterproof membrane, forming a curb wall at its outer edge with steel reinforcing (fig. 5-48). The inside faces of the curb wall and the pool bottom are painted with a waterproof cement or other similar material. This method requires repainting of the pool over time and so is less preferred than other methods.

A second method is simple and practical. It can be used after the roof and its waterproofing have been completed, provided reinforcement and attachment rods were inserted in the structural slab when it was poured in place. A concrete core wall is then formed and poured atop the concrete protection slab. After it sets, a second waterproof membrane is laid on the surface of the concrete protection slab within the perimeter of the pool. This membrane is brought up and over the top of the core wall (fig. 5-49). The top of the core wall must be slightly higher than the surface of the water will be. The bottom of the pool and final curb wall are then poured in one operation and are finished.

With a third method, the pool bottom and the concrete protective slab are one and the same. Before pouring the curb wall and the protective slab, a core wall is poured over reinforcing rod anchors that have been placed in the structural slab. Waterproof membrane is laid continuously over the structural slab within the pool area, the concrete core wall, and the structural slab outside the pool area. The concrete protective slab, inside and outside the pool area, and the concrete curb wall are then poured and finished (fig. 5-50). No waterproofing need be applied to the inner surface of the pool.

If tile or other applied material is to be used on the interior of the pool, the construction of

the pool and curb wall and their waterproofing may be accomplished as shown in figure 5-51. The concrete pool bottom and curb wall are built as an integral unit, with reinforcing rods or bars as shown, leaving space to apply a second membrane inside the pool, plaster, grout, and tile or other finish materials. The second waterproof membrane is applied to the pool and curb wall, as shown, and brought to a height above the intended surface of the water in the pool.

Precast fiberglass shells can be used for small ponds (fig. 5-52). The flat-bottomed pool shell should be placed on a level surface of drainage medium that has been covered by filter fabric.

If an elaborate water feature is desired on a relatively low strength roof, a combination of shallow water and precast artificial rocks is a possibility (fig. 5-53). Lightweight concrete and fiberglass can be poured into plastic forms molded from natural rocks in the field to make realistic-looking boulders and outcrops when permanent coloring is applied (fig. 5-54). A whole new world of water and rock effects is thus possible in roof gardens. Although some may object to the use of artificial elements in the landscape, it should be noted that gardens on roofs have many artificial elements, such as soils, light, and irrigation. Even their location is artificial! To produce a garden on a roof, one must occasionally rely on artifice to achieve a natural appearance. This is

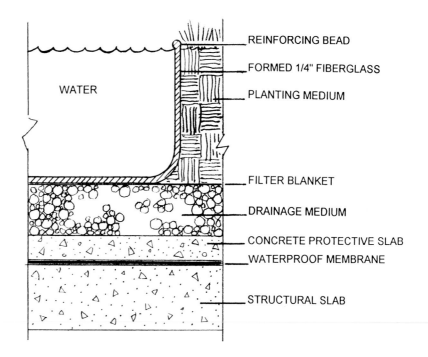

REINFORCING BEAD
FORMED 1/4" FIBERGLASS
PLANTING MEDIUM
FILTER BLANKET
DRAINAGE MEDIUM
CONCRETE PROTECTIVE SLAB
WATERPROOF MEMBRANE
STRUCTURAL SLAB
WATER

5-52. A lightweight pond container can be prefabricated off-site from fiberglass. The bead at the top stiffens the edge.

WINDSCREENS, SHELTERS, AND OTHER STRUCTURES.

It may seem that including a built structure in a roof garden is in conflict with the whole concept of greening roofs. But in intensive roof gardens, that is, those that mimic designed gardens at ground level, certain structures are as appropriate on the roof as they would be in a local park. As noted in chapter 3, such structures are functional in moderating the effects of climate and weather. A small shelter can serve as a windscreen as well as a place for people to congregate during a cloudburst. Sheltered structures can also alleviate the effects of heat and glare.

As design accents, they provide visual interest. A seating area, for example, is more memorable when it is shaded by a vine-covered trellis. Small structures are especially effective at the terminal point of a path or as the focal point of a view.

Such features can take on even more meaning when they are planned as the central element around which the rest of the garden is designed. They become the focus of the garden visually and the center of the garden's activities literally. Figures 5-55, 5-56, 5-57, and 5-58 are but a small indication of how these structures can add interest and variety to a garden space.

UTILITIES

Like most designed spaces, roof gardens require the inclusion of assorted utilities to be functional. Potable water should be available from threaded faucets or quick couplers. These should be on separate valves so that hand watering is possible should the automatic irrigation system be shut down for repair. Fresh water can also be convenient for outdoor dining and parties.

Electrical outlets should be conveniently located along with junction boxes for the installation of outdoor garden lighting, sound equipment, fountain motors, electric-powered garden equipment, and automatic clocks and sensors for irrigation. All electrical switches and outlets should be weatherproof.

Last, but very important, convenient jacks for telephones should be provided.

5-53 (above). Well away from the waterfall feature at the Kaiser Resources roof garden in Vancouver, the water seems to disappear under the wood deck. Lightweight artificial boulders complete the natural effect.

5-54 (right). This fragment of concrete "stone" has been reinforced with fiberglass cast from nature. Notice the fine detail of the stone's texture.

not a blanket endorsement of using artificial elements everywhere; the practice of replacing real plants with plastic facsimiles, for example, is abhorrent. In some cases, however, practical considerations prevent the achievement of a spectacular effect if only natural materials are to be used. The combination of rock and water may be such an effect; their inclusion in a roof garden should not be rejected out of hand.

WINDOW-WASHING EQUIPMENT

Although they are not design features of the roof garden per se, the devices used to wash a building's windows frequently must be considered when planning the garden. There are many such devices, and almost all are too large and cumbersome to remove and replace every time the building's windows need cleaning. They must instead be stored on the roof, and space along the roof's edge must be kept clear to allow horizontal movement of the wheeled machine to complete its section of the windows below. In addition, because of the leveraged pull of the cables and workman's platform over the railing and down

5-55 (top left). Lightweight buildings, such as this finely designed greenhouse at the offices of the Champion Paper Company at Stamford Center in Connecticut, are fairly easy to accommodate on roofs.

5-56 (top right). This sheltered sitting area is a strong architectural feature of this roof deck landscape at the Amoco headquarters building in Chicago; Jacobs/Ryan Associates, landscape architect.

5-57 (bottom left). An ornamental garden structure can define the boundary between a roof garden and an adjacent structure or area. This design, at the Bechtel Engineering Center at the University of California at Berkeley, also provides shaded sitting areas for students and raised beds for plants.

5-58 (bottom right). This covered walk between the restaurants and the Performing Arts Center at the Yerba Buena Gardens in San Francisco provides shelter in a light and playful way.

the face of the building, the machine must be temporarily anchored to hooks embedded in the roof (fig. 5-59). These must remain permanently accessible. When not in use, the ungainly machine must be stored on the roof, out of sight.

Some of these devices move on tracks, and some move on rubber tires. The architect chooses this equipment, and its selection should be coordinated with the landscape architect's design of the garden. The rubber-tired machines can usually be stored and concealed without loss of garden space along the building's edge. Those with tracks require that the garden area give up 5 feet (1.5 m) or more next to the building's railing, to allow space for the permanent steel tracks. Decorative screens and even specially designed building structures are often designed for concealment (figs. 5-60 and 5-61).

5-59 (top right). Tie-downs for window-washing machines with gondolas must remain accessible within the roof garden system. This one, at Kaiser Resources in Vancouver, is covered with an easily removable metal lid.

5-60 (top left). The window-washing equipment in the roof garden at 555 Market Street in San Francisco is concealed by an ornamental screen.

5-61 (right). Structures to hide permanently accessible window-washing cranes and gondolas need not be obtrusive. This wide-doored storage shelter provides top and side concealment, and its double doors provide turning access to the areas along the building's edge so the windows below can be reached.

. . . .

DESIGN DETAILS

The photographs that follow provide close-up views of some of the design elements just described in chapter 5. Each demonstrates an outstanding example of incorporating into a roof garden a distinctive element that acts almost like a signature, yet blends perfectly into the garden's design.

PLANTING VARIETY

Central Headquarters, Church of the Latter-Day Saints, Salt Lake City; Hare and Hare, landscape architects

CONTAINERS

Union Bank Square, Los Angeles; Eckbo, Dean, Austin and Williams, landscape architects

PAVING AND WALKING SURFACES

(Above) Equitable Plaza, Pittsburgh; Simonds and Simonds, Collins, landscape architects

(Top right) Yerba Buena Gardens, San Francisco; Mitchell, Giurgola and Associates, architects

(Middle right): ARK Hills Center, Tokyo; Nishita and Carter, landscape architects

(Bottom right): Munich Hospital, Munich; Gerhard Teutsch, landscape architect

FURNISHINGS

(Above) Four Seasons Mexico
City Hotel, Mexico City; Eliseo
Arredondo, landscape architect
(Courtesy Eliseo Arredonda)

(Left) Shinjuku Mitsui Building,
Tokyo; Toyo Landscape Construction, landscape architects

Yerba Buena Gardens, San
Francisco; Mitchell, Giurgola
and Associates, architects

SHELTERS

(Top) Amoco Headquarters,
Chicago; Jacobs/Ryan, landscape
architects

(Bottom) North Linden Housing
Project, Hannover, Germany;
Ruprecht Dröge, landscape
architect

SCULPTURE

(Above) Embarcadero Center, San
Francisco; SWA Group, landscape
architects

(Top right) Embarcadero Center, San
Francisco; SWA Group, landscape
architects

(Middle right) Arco Headquarters,
Chicago

(Bottom right) Embarcadero Center,
San Francisco; SWA Group, landscape
architects

SCULPTURE

Cambridge Center, Cam-
bridge, Massachusetts;
SWA Group, landscape
architects

WATER

(Right) Golden Gateway,
San Francisco; SWA Group,
landscape architects

WATER

(Top) Pernas International Hotel, Kuala Lumpur, Malaysia

(Middle left) Ghirardelli Square, San Francisco; Lawrence Halprin and Associates, landscape architects

(Middle right) Thoreau Hall, University of California at Davis; Theodore Osmundson and Associates, landscape architects

(Bottom) 444 South Flower Terrace, Los Angeles; Lawrence Halprin and Associates, landscape architects

WATER

(Above left) Tokyo Municipal Center, Tokyo, Japan.

(Above right) Grosse Schanze Park, Bern, Switzerland; W. Liechti, landscape architect

(Right) Constitution Plaza, Hartford; Sasaki Associates, landscape architects

CHAPTER SIX

MAINTENANCE

Effective maintenance is the key to the growth and development of healthy and beautiful roof gardens. Although the maintenance of roof gardens is fundamentally different from that of ground-level gardens, once the basic requirements are satisfied, the care of roof garden plants is similar in scope to the care of ground-level plants.

The problem of maintenance in roof gardens can be easily understood by comparing a roof garden to a potted plant. Anyone who has kept a plant on a patio or deck has learned quickly that the plant is subject to stress from several sources. First and foremost, the small quantity of soil in the pot dries out rapidly because of quick drainage, the plant's usage, and evaporation. With no subsoil to draw water from, the plant must be watered at least every two days, or it will wilt. If neglected longer, it will die.

Moreover, the planting mix in the pot contains a limited supply of nutrients to feed the plant, and the constant watering causes the nutrients to leach out of the bottom. This is particularly true for nitrogen, which is needed by leaves and stems. Leaching, combined with the plant's own feeding, can cause the soil to become sterile in a very short time.

Healthy potted plants also eventually outgrow their pots. If they are not transplanted to a larger container, their growth may be stunted, and their roots may grow through the drainage holes in search of additional space and nutrients.

Transfer these concerns to a planting bed on a roof: the same conditions prevail. The planting areas on a roof are like large pots and must be maintained in the same way. Drainage, evaporation, leaching, and plant usage deplete water and nutrients, requiring constant supplements of both to replace what is lost or used. Plant growth must be monitored to ensure the plants do not try to grow beyond their containers. To neglect these needs risks loss of the plants.

IRRIGATION

Plants vary in their inherent tolerance of drought conditions, but none can withstand dry soil for long. If the least tolerant show wilt, it is time to water.

Automatic irrigation systems can deliver water regularly through the use of electrically controlled timers, providing an optimum amount of water consistently, with full coverage over all planting areas. Soil-moisture sensors are available to signal dangerously dry conditions and activate the irrigation system. The discussion of irrigation systems in chapter 4 describes several different types of automatic systems, including some innovative methods now in use in Europe. In chapter 5 the discussion of plant containers examines several means of providing water to these smaller plant holders.

Unlike ground-level gardens, roof gardens usually cannot be overwatered. Good drainage, a necessity in planted areas of roof gardens, prevents a backup of water in planting beds. However, the more water applied to the beds, the greater the leaching of soil nutrients will be. In addition, in many places water is not an insignificant cost, and allowing a roof garden to be overwatered is tantamount to throwing dollars down the drain. Moisture sensors that signal dryness can also indicate when the soil has enough water, to prevent overwatering.

FERTILIZATION

A regular program of fertilization is essential to healthy plant growth and long-term maintenance. Actively growing plants constantly absorb these additives through their roots and use them for growth, flowering, and other functions. It is important to be aware that fertilizers, as well as nutrients naturally within the soil, leach from the porous soils used in roof gardens, washed away by rainfall or irrigation into the drainage system. They must be systematically and repeatedly replaced. Anything that can slow this process, keeping the nutrients in the soil mix and available to the plants for a longer time, is a great advantage. The discussion of planting mix in chapter 4 suggests several soil amendments that can improve nutrient retention.

Application of fertilizer should be on a programmed schedule, with consistent amounts of balanced fertilizer applied at regular times throughout the year. Generally fertilization should take place in early spring (April), when most plants are beginning their active growth period, again in midsummer (July), and finally in early fall (September), well before winter begins. No fertilization is needed during winter, when most plants are dormant and any new leaf or twig growth stimulated by fertilizer could be frost-killed. This schedule is a general recommendation; some plants will require more or less fertilizer. The maintenance gardener should research each plant type to determine the appropriate formulation, quantity, and timing of fertilizer application. It should be noted that too much fertilizer, which "burns" the plant, can be as harmful as too little.

In seeking advice from local experts, the maintenance gardener should carefully explain the type and content of the soil, its depth, the drainage system, and whether dry or liquid fertilizer will be used. These factors, which are quite different from conditions in ground-level gardens, affect the fertilizer's formula, amount, schedule, and method of application.

Plants requiring acid-supplemented fertilizers, such as azaleas, rhododendrons, kalmias, and camellias, should be fed separately from other plants.

All planting areas on roofs should have their growing medium tested at least annually to determine the degree of nutrient loss that has occurred over the previous year. Tests reveal the presence or absence of important plant nutrients and other chemical elements necessary for healthy plant growth. Once identified and quantified by a competent laboratory, these needed elements can be conveniently replaced or added as needed. Many county extension services do soil testing, as do private soil laboratories. Kits for do-it-yourself testing are also available from nurseries and garden-supply stores.

Budgetary reductions that reduce the amount of money available for fertilizer over time are a classic case of being penny wise and pound foolish. Failing to meet the plants' nutritional needs in order to save on maintenance costs may well result in spending far more, to replace a sickly or dead garden.

Types of Fertilizer

Two forms of balanced fertilizers are widely available, and they are so successful that they are likely to be standard supplies for planting for a long time to come. They are both so reasonable in cost, easy to handle in dry form, and effective that they have virtually superseded every other form of fertilizer in larger-scale landscaping projects.

The older of these fertilizers is the group of fast-acting mixtures, which readily go into solution and are thus absorbed with the water the plant needs. These fertilizers contain varying percentages of nitrogen, phosphorus, and potassium. Small quantities of elements such as iron, calcium, magnesium, and sulphur are usually included for highly important specialized functions, such as changing the existing pH of the soil, acting, with nitrogen, to form new cells, and in the case of alkaline soils, enabling the soil to absorb other elements such as zinc, iron, and manganese. This type of applied complete fertilizer is especially valuable for new plantings, where the soil has been tested and found deficient in one or more of the necessary elements, as well as to encourage immediate growth in the plants' new growing medium. It is also useful for periodic fertilizing. Its advantage of going into solution quickly can also be a disadvantage, in that it also leaches out of the soil rather quickly, especially in porous roof garden soil mixes. This type of fertilizer is available in dry pellet or liquid form and in bulk.

The second type is slow-release fertilizer, used

both in establishing new plantings and in the long-term maintenance of plants. These fertilizers usually contain higher percentages of the three basic elements; because of their slow release, they can be used without danger of burning or otherwise damaging the plants with, for example, too much nitrogen in one feeding. They are also used to provide continuous feeding over a longer period, thereby reducing the amount of labor needed to apply the fertilizer.

Unlike fast-acting fertilizers, slow-release fertilizers are not affected by water and so will not go into solution and leach out of the planting medium. They are affected by temperature, however, and release more of their nutrients as the soil and atmosphere become warmer, conveniently when plants are most in need of nutrients. Conversely, these fertilizers release nutrients more slowly under cooler conditions, holding them back when plant metabolism has slowed and the plants are dormant. These fertilizers are available in dry pellet and pill form. The pill type must be in direct contact with the plant roots to be effective.

Generally speaking, present-day practice includes the use of both fast-acting and slow-release fertilizers. Quick-acting, usually dry, balanced fertilizers are applied to new lawns during their initial germination and growth periods and to newly planted shrubs and trees as part of the soil mix that is backfilled around the plants' root balls or around bare-root plants during planting.

Slow-release balanced fertilizer is usually applied as the soil mix is being cultivated and before planting, just before turning a newly installed project over to the owner. This provides a supply of nutrients for the new plants for six months to a year and gives the owner of the project sufficient time to establish a maintenance staff and program for long-term care. The maintenance gardener should continue the application of slow-release fertilizer periodically on a permanent basis, being careful to work the fertilizer into the soil without damaging plant roots.

At least one company, Hyponex Corporation of Fort Wayne, Indiana, currently offers a pelleted dry fertilizer for lawns with a formula of 29-4-8 that includes 4 percent of its nitrogen content in slow-release form. Combining the two types of

6-1. A commercial-grade automatic fertilizer-injection system in use at an apartment building in San Mateo, California. The injector provides controlled quantities of liquid fertilizer to the irrigation system.

fertilizer in one application without on-site mixing could result in a saving in the labor costs of application.

Automatic Fertilization

The application of liquid fertilizer can be greatly simplified by automatically injecting the liquid fertilizer into the garden's sprinkler system. Equipment is available to fertilize roof gardens of almost any size and complexity (fig. 6-1). The proper combination of elements in solution can be injected by presetting the equipment for any desired amount of fertilizer per thousand gallons of water. Used primarily for growing plants in nurseries, this system can be readily adapted for garden use. Like most mechanical equipment, it must be kept in good repair. However, the benefits to the growth and health of plants, which receive consistent amounts of nutrients without hand labor, are well worth the initial investment in this device and the time and effort involved in training its operator.

Earthworms

A different way of improving soil nutrients in a roof garden is by introducing earthworms (*Lumbricus terrestris*) into the planting mix. This species of earthworm, native to North America and Europe, can be found where the soil is not pure sand or heavy clay and is not deficient in humus. They are also unable to live in heavily acidic soil. They are rarely seen in daylight unless their burrows have been flooded by rain, preferring to come to the surface to feed at night (hence, the nickname "night crawlers"). An earthworm has the remarkable ability to move through soil by ingesting it through its mouth, passing it through its body, and egesting it through its anal passage as castings. It is through this same process that they swallow and digest organic matter such as decaying leaves. Earthworms prefer moist soil and will burrow deeper if the surface is dry or subject to extreme temperatures.

Soil structure and fertility are greatly enhanced by earthworms. Their burrowing at various levels aerates the soil and permits water to enter the growing strata. Most important, however, their castings contain nitrogen in a form readily taken up by plants.

The roof garden atop the Federal Reserve Bank in Boston has been kept in excellent growing condition for many years by using earthworms. Obviously, unless they have been accidentally introduced to a garden via field soil, earthworms will not make their way to a roof garden well above the street. The worms at the Boston bank were introduced into the soil by the head gardener with the intention of eliminating the need for nonorganic fertilizers. All the plants in this roof garden are thriving, and labor and materials for manufactured fertilizer applications have been deleted from the annual maintenance budget.

Night crawlers are often available from roadside stands and fishermen's supply stores, where they are sold as bait. They reproduce rapidly, as they are hermaphroditic (each has both male and female sex organs); therefore, obtaining worms of separate sexes is neither possible nor necessary.

ROOT PRUNING

Root pruning is regularly practiced in Europe and Japan but is less common in the United States. In the root structure of trees growing in raised beds on a roof, the large and medium-sized roots are closest to the trunk. The fine roots, at the extremities, are blocked from growing outward by the boundary of the growing area, that is, the inside face of the soil container or raised bed. After several growing seasons, these fine roots begin to build up in a mass behind the walls of the bed, causing a condition similar to the pot-bound roots of a young plant left too long in a can or container. This will not only stunt the growth and health of the tree but will also fill the area within the bed or container completely with roots, so that no other plants will grow. A desirable variety of other plants in the raised bed may then be impossible to maintain.

Root pruning is usually done in the late fall, before the tree goes dormant. Cuts are made 2 or 3 feet (61 to 91 cm) inside the walls, to the depth of the bed. The roots are removed by cutting with a sharp blade. The areas are then backfilled with planting medium, tamped, and watered in place. Any plants that were removed to accommodate this procedure are replanted, and the areas are left for new growth of fine roots in the spring and in succeeding years, until it is necessary for the process to be repeated. To balance the loss of fine roots, the upper branches of the tree are pruned at the same time.

Before root pruning is repeated, several exploratory pits are dug in the area to determine the extent of the problem. If the condition is not serious, the pruning is postponed to a later time. Root pruning is particularly needed for trees growing in small raised beds. To avoid frequent pruning, it is wise to select slow-growing trees.

MULCH

A top dressing of mulch is an important component of any roof garden, as noted in chapter 4. Mulch helps to prevent the growth of weeds, to retain soil moisture by reducing evaporation, and to moderate soil temperature. Replenishing mulch in a roof garden is a necessary part of its maintenance. To remain effective, the mulch should be checked each year for condition and depth. A ½-inch (1.3-cm) layer should be consistently maintained.

OTHER MAINTENANCE CHORES

Just as in a ground-level garden, a variety of routine maintenance tasks must be performed in roof gardens to keep them healthy and attractive. All of these chores are performed in essentially the same manner as in ground-level gardens. Included among these regular jobs are lawn mowing, weed and pest control, trimming and pruning, fruit and leaf cleanup, deadheading flowers, replacement of annuals each spring, removal and storage of bulbs in the fall, and snow removal. Even the removal of a large tree is done as it is on the ground: the limbs and trunk are sawn into small pieces but are taken via elevator to the ground for disposal. Power saws for such work are hand held and easily maneuverable in roof gardens. When the tree is removed, the large and medium roots should be removed and discarded as well. Fine roots can be left in place to rot and add humus to the soil.

MAINTENANCE CENTER

It would seem to be stating the obvious to recommend that an area be set aside on the roof to serve as a center for the daily and long-term maintenance chores of a highly visible, valuable, and naturally fragile roof garden (figs. 6-2, 6-3, and 6-4). In many roof gardens, however, it is apparent that maintenance is not considered a high-priority item. Although invariably every building has a maintenance and storage room for personnel and building supplies, these rooms are usually too inconveniently located and ill equipped to be of any use to roof garden personnel. A space is needed on the same level as the roof garden for the convenience of gardeners and maintenance people. It should be concealed from the users of the roof garden, the building's employees, and the public in adjacent buildings if possible. Ideally, the space should be large enough to accommodate a greenhouse or lathhouse; potting benches with running water; counters or tables to hold growing plants in containers; a small office space for at least the head gardener; bins to store fertilizers, soil mixes, sand, humus, and the like for starting plants; a storage area for garden tools and other equipment; and a receptacle for garden trash. It should be surrounded by a protective fence or other screen to conceal it from the public. Finally, a telephone is an obvious necessity.

6-2 (top). The roof garden atop the Federal Reserve Bank in Boston provides an excellent example of a roof garden maintenance center. It includes a greenhouse for starting plants in late winter and early spring.

6-3 (middle). The maintenance center at Boston's Federal Reserve Bank also provides outdoor space for hardening off greenhouse plants, as well as for starting plants during warmer months.

6-4 (bottom). A small office, with running water and an area for tool storage, completes the roof garden maintenance center at the Federal Reserve Bank in Boston.

EPILOGUE

· · · · · · · · · · · · · · · ·

It should be apparent to most after reading this book that extending green space to the tops of structures is a worthy enterprise. And, with the wide selection of modern materials and techniques available today, it would seem that any chance for error in the development of roof gardens could be easily eliminated.

Since 1960, roof garden design has suffered through a period of disinterest and ignorance about techniques and materials, followed by more concern, when various materials and methods were tried, with mixed success, at the client's risk. Almost everything has been used in the cross section, from large chunks of broken sidewalk for drainage to tar painted on the walls of deep planting beds for waterproofing (the latter was not a success, resulting in leaks in offices below). If this book succeeds only in demonstrating that the design and construction of roof gardens must be considered differently from that of gardens on the ground, it will be progress. From that point forward, we all can work to find unique solutions to individual design problems.

The previous chapters have explained how rooftop developments can be built successfully, with minimal possibility of failure in the waterproofing, insulation, drainage, filtration, soil, and irrigation systems, and with little risk to the roof and building below. They are based on personal experience, analysis, and common sense, tempered by a high degree of caution. Some recommendations are based on the careful field-testing of various products used in the roof garden section by interested landscape architects in Germany. Only this segment of our profession has conducted such careful tests, and only a few of these products are available in the United States.

Because new products come on the market regularly and because even established products have never been properly examined under roof garden conditions in the United States, a program of controlled field research of products and methods under rooftop conditions is urgently needed at this point. Manufacturers' claims are not enough. These products must be thoroughly tested before being used on roofs. The consequences of risk taking are too great to do otherwise. Such tests could be performed by private research firms and/or government agencies, under the guidance of landscape architects, preferably along with architects and structural engineers.

This book has highlighted a number of materials that were originally designed for use in other types of projects, such as Grass-Cel, nonwoven filter fabric, expanded shale, and elastomeric membrane that is root-proof as well as waterproof. Other products are sure to be found or developed as the demand for roof gardens grows. As new and successful materials are developed, roof gardens will be more widely accepted, and outdoor living space that was once lost to building construction will be restored, at the roof level. There may come a day when, for environmental reasons alone, the greening of roofs will be required by law in all countries, as it currently is in many German cities. That will be "the day."

· · · · · · · · · · · ·

USEFUL DATA

Table A-1

WEIGHTS OF COMMON BUILDING MATERIALS

Material	lbs/ft³	kg/m³
Granite	170	2,757
Marble	170	2,757
Slate	160–180	2,595–2,919
Limestone	155	2,514
Sandstone	145	2,352
Shale	162	2,627
Expanded shale	40–45	649–730
Grass-Cel	6	96
Fieldstone	95	1,541
Gravel	120	1,946
Pebbles	120	1,946
Pumice	40	649
Concrete		
lightweight	80–100	1,298–1,622
precast	130	2,108
reinforced	150	2,433
Concrete block: 8 in.	50–60	811–973
Brickwork (average)	115	1,865
Cast iron	450	7,297
Steel	490	7,945
Bronze	513	8,318
Timber		
hardwood (average)	45	730
softwood (average)	35	568
Sand		
dry	90–110	1,460–1,784
wet	110–130	1,784–2,108
Sand and gravel, mixed	115	1,865
Clay soil		
compacted, dry	75–100	1,216–1,622
compacted, wet	125	2,027
Loam		
dry	80	1,298
wet	120	1,946
Special commercial soil, wet	110	1,784

continued on next page

· · · · · ·

Material	lbs/ft³	kg/m³
Topsoil		
dry	80	1,298
wet	120	1,946
Peat		
dry	9.6	154.28
wet	10.3	165.53
Humus		
dry	35	568
wet	82	1,330
Water	62.428	1,013
Flagstone and setting bed	25 lb/ft²	122 kg/m²
Tile and setting bed	15–73 lb/ft²	73–353 kg/m²

SOURCE: Nicholas Dines and Charles W. Harris, ed., *Time Saver Standards for Landscape Architecture,* 2d edition. New York: McGraw Hill, 1997.

TABLE A-2

WEIGHTS OF PLANTING MEDIA

Material	lbs/ft³	kg/m³
Fine sand		
dry	90.00	1,446.42
damp	120.00	1,928.56
Cedar shavings with fertilizer		
dry	9.25	148.66
damp	13.00	208.93
Peat moss		
dry	9.60	154.28
damp	10.30	165.53
Red lava, ⁵⁄₁₆ in. (8 mm) max.		
dry	50.00	803.57
damp	53.70	863.03
Redwood compost and shaving		
dry	14.80	237.86
damp	22.20	356.78
Fir and pine bark humus		
dry	22.20	356.78
damp	33.30	535.17

continued on next page

Table A-2, continued

Material	lbs/ft³	kg/m³
Perlite		
dry	6.50	104.46
wet	32.40	520.71
Vermiculite		
coarse, dry	6.25	100.45
medium, dry	5.75	92.41
fine, dry	7.50	120.53
Topsoil		
dry	76.00	1,221.42
damp	78.00	1,253.56

SOURCE: Nicholas Dines and Charles W. Harris, ed., *Time Saver Standards for Landscape Architecture,* 2d edition. New York: McGraw Hill, 1997.

TABLE A-3

WEIGHTS OF CONTAINERS AND FIELD-GROWN PLANTS

Container size	Container grown in mushroom compost, lb. (kg)		Field-grown, lb. (kg)	
15-gal (56-L) can	80	(36)	—	—
20-in (510-mm) box	200	(90)	400	(180)
24 in (610-mm) box	400	(180)	725	(325)
30-in (760-mm) box	800	(360)	1,500	(675)
36-in (900-mm) box	1,300	(585)	2,500	(1,125)
48-in (1,220-mm) box	3,500	(1,575)	6,000	(2,700)
54-in (1,370-mm) box	4,000	(1,800)	7,000	(3,150)
60-in (1,520-mm) box	5,000	(2,250)	8,000	(3,600)
72-in (1,830-mm) box	7,000	(3,150)	12,000	(5,400)
84-in (2,130-mm) box	9,000	(4,050)	16,000	(7,200)
96-in (2,440-mm) box	12,000	(5,400)	20,000	(9,000)
120-in (3,050-mm) box	14,000	(6,300)	24,000	(10,800)

Note: All the above are shipping weights, including the box.

SOURCE: Nicholas Dines and Charles W. Harris, ed., *Time Saver Standards for Landscape Architecture,* 2d edition. New York: McGraw Hill, 1997.

WOOD WEIGHT, POUNDS PER CUBIC FOOT

Common name	Green	Dry
Ash	48	41
Aspen	43	26
Basswood	42	26
Beech	54	45
Birch, paper	50	38
Birch, yellow	57	44
Cedar, red	37	33
Cedar, western	27	23
Cherry, black	45	35
Cypress, southern	51	32
Elm	55	36
Fir, balsam	45	25
Fir, Douglas	36	31
Gum, black	45	35
Hemlock, eastern	50	28
Hemlock, West Coast	41	29
Hickory	63	51
Larch, western	48	36
Maple, hard	55	42
Maple, soft	47	35
Oak	64	44
Pecan	62	45
Pine, northern white	36	25
Pine, southern shortleaf	52	36
Poplar, yellow	38	28
Redwood	50	28
Spruce	34	28
Sycamore	52	34
Tamarack	47	37
Walnut, black	58	38

SOURCE: Timber Engineering Company, *Timber Design and Construction Handbook.* New York: McGraw Hill Book Company, 1956.

Table A-5

SIEVE ANALYSIS FOR SAND*

Sieve Size (NO.)	Weight (% PASSING)
4	100
10	95–100
18	90–100
35	65–100
60	0–50
140	0–20
270	0–7

*With no silt mixed in

SOURCE: Nicholas Dines and Charles W. Harris, ed., *Time Saver Standards for Landscape Architecture,* 2d edition. New York: McGraw Hill, 1997.

Table A-6

SUITABLE CHEMICAL PROPERTIES
OF SAND

Chemical Property	Permissible Range
Salinity (millisiemens per cm of saturation extract at 25°C)	Nil to 3.0
Saturation extract concentration of boron	Nil to 1.0
Adsorption ratio of sodium (SAR)	Nil to 6.0

SOURCE: Nicholas Dines and Charles W. Harris, ed., *Time Saver Standards for Landscape Architecture,* 2d edition. New York: McGraw Hill, 1997.

MINERAL PROPERTIES OF SOIL AMENDMENTS

Physical Properties	Percent Passing Sieve	Sieve Designation
	95–100	6.35 mm, ¼-in. mesh
	75–100	2.38 mm, no. 8, 8 mesh
	0–30	500, no. 35, 32 mesh
Source:	Nitrogen content, dry-weight basis, if nitrogen stabilized	Dry bulk density lb/y^3 (kg/m^3)
Redwood sawdust	0.40–0.60%	270–370 (159–218)
Redwood bark fiber	0.35–0.50%	250–350 (147–206)
Fir or cedar sawdust	0.56–0.84%	270–370 (159–218)
Fir or pine bark	0.80–1.20%	450–580 (265–341)
Hardwood bark	0.80–1.20%	450–500 (265–294)
Iron content	Minimum 0.08% dilute acid soluble iron based on dry weight if specified as, or claimed to be, iron-treated.	
Soluble salts	Maximum 3.0 ms/cm at 25°C as determined in saturation extract	
Organic content	Minimum 92% based on dry weight and determined by ash method	
Mineralized for incorporation.	Other mineral fertilizers or chemical amendments may be specified	
Wettability	The air-dry product shall, when applied to a cup or small beaker of water at 70°F in the amount of 1 tsp., become completely wet in a period not exceeding 2 min. Any wetting agent added to accomplish this shall be guaranteed to be nonphytotoxic at rate used.	

SOURCE: Nicholas Dines and Charles W. Harris, ed., *Time Saver Standards for Landscape Architecture*, 2d edition. New York: McGraw Hill, 1997.

TABLE A-8

MINIMUM SOIL DEPTHS

Planting	Minimum Soil Depth*
Lawns	8–12 in. (200–300 mm)
Flowers/ground covers	10–12 in. (260–300 mm)
Shrubs	24–30 in. (600–750 mm)†
Small trees	30–42 in. (750–1,065 mm)
Large trees	48–60 in. (1,220–1,525 mm)

*On filter blanket and drainage medium
†Depending on ultimate shrub size

SOURCE: Nicholas Dines and Charles W. Harris, ed., *Time Saver Standards for Landscape Architecture*, 2d edition. New York: McGraw Hill, 1997.

ROOT-KILLING TEMPERATURES OF CONTAINER-GROWN
ORNAMENTALS IN WINTER STORAGE*

Plant	°F	°C
Buxus sempervirens	27	-2.7
Cotoneaster congesta	25	-3.8
Ilex cornuta 'Dazzler'	25	-3.8
Cotoneaster dammeri	23	-5.0
Daphne cneorum	23	-5.0
Euonymus fortunei vegetus	23	-5.0
Hypericum spp.	23	-5.0
Ilex cornuta 'Nellie Stevens'	23	-5.0
Ilex crenata convexa	23	-5.0
Ilex crenata helleri	23	-5.0
Ilex crenata 'Hetzi'	23	-5.0
Ilex crenata 'Stokes'	23	-5.0
Ilex meserveae	23	-5.0
Ilex opaca	23	-5.0
Magnolia X soulangeana	23	-5.0
Mahonia bealei	23	-5.0
Pyracantha coccinea 'Lalandei'	23	-5.0
Cornus florida	22	-5.6
Euonymus patens	22	-5.6
Ilex crenata 'San Jose'	22	-5.6
Magnolia stellata	22	-5.6
Cotoneaster dammeri 'Skogholmen'	20	-6.7
Leucothoe catesbaei	20	-6.7
Rhododendron prunifolium	20	-6.7
Viburnum plicatum tomentosum	20	-6.7
Rhododendron 'Hino-Crimson'	19	-7.2
Euonymus alatus	19	-7.2
Stephanandra incisa	18	-7.8
Rhododendron Exbury hybrids	17	-8.3
Cotoneaster horizontalis	17	-8.3
Cryptomeria japonica	17	-8.3
Taxus media hicksii	17	-8.3
Cytisus X praecox	16	-8.9
Ilex glabra	16	-8.9
Koelreuteria paniculata	16	-8.9
Viburnum carlesii	15	-9.4
Acer palmatum 'Atropurpureum'	15	-9.4
Euonymus fortunei carrierei	15	-9.4
Euonymus fortunei 'Argenteo-marginatus'	15	-9.4
Hedera helix baltica	15	-9.4
Kalmia latifolia	15	-9.4

continued on next page

Table A-9, continued

Plant	°F	°C
Pachysandra terminalis	15	-9.4
Pieris japonica	15	-9.4
Rhododendron schlippenbachi	15	-9.4
Rhododendron 'Purple Gem'	15	-9.4
Vinca minor	15	-9.4
Cotoneaster adpressa praecox	12	-11.1
Juniperus conferta	12	-11.1
Juniperus horizontalis 'Plumosa'	12	-11.1
Juniperus squamata	12	-11.1
Taxus X media 'Nigra'	12	-11.1
Mahonia aquifolia	10	-12.2
Rhododendron X 'Gibraltar'	10	-12.2
Rhododendron X 'Hinodegiri'	10	-12.2
Thuja occidentalis	10	-12.2
Euonymus fortunei coloratus	5	-15.0
Leucothoe fontanesiana	5	-15.0
Pieris floribunda	5	-15.0
Juniperus horizontalis 'Douglasii'	0	-17.8
Rhododendron carolinianum	0	-17.8
Rhododendron catawbiense	0	-17.8
Picea glauca	-9	-23.3
Picea omorika	-9	-23.3
Potentilla fruticosa	-9	-23.3
Rhododendron P.J.M. hybrids	-9	-23.3

*Temperatures that will injure primary and possibly secondary roots but will not result in 100 percent kill of the root systems in moist soils.

SOURCE: Francis R. Gouin, Cooperative Extension Service, University of Maryland. Temperature data from: J. R. Havis, "Root Hardiness of Woody Ornamentals," *Horticultural Science* 11, no. 4 (1976):385–86; P. L. Steponokus, G. L. Good, and S. C. Wiest, "Root Hardiness of Woody Plants," *American Nurseryman* 144, no. 6 (1976):16.

CONVERSION FACTORS

Multiply	by	to obtain
acres	.404687	hectares
	.00404687	square kilometers
ares	1076.39	square feet
board feet	144 sq. in. X 1 in.	cubic inches
	.0833	cubic feet
centimeters	.0328083	feet
	.3937	inches
cubic centimeters	.0000353145	cubic feet
	.06102	cubic inches
cubic feet	28,317	cubic centimeters
	.028317	cubic meters
	28.317	liters
cubic inches	16.38716	cubic centimeters
cubic meters	35.3145	cubic feet
	1.30794	cubic yards
cubic yards	.764559	cubic meters
degrees Celsius	1.8	(minus 32) degrees Fahrenheit
degrees Fahrenheit (minus 32)	.5556	degrees Celsius
foot pounds	.13826	kilogram meters
feet	30.4801	centimeters
	.304801	meters
	304.801	millimeters
gallons, U.S.	.13368	cubic feet
	231	cubic inches
	3.78543	liters
grams	.00220462	pounds
hectares	2.47104	acres
	10,7638.7	square feet
	.00386191	square miles
inches	2.54001	centimeters
	.0254001	meters
	25.4001	millimeters
kilograms	2.20462	pounds
kilogram meters	7.233	foot pounds
kilograms per meter	.671972	pounds per foot
kilograms per square centimeter	14.2234	pounds per square inch
kilograms per square meter	.204817	pounds per square foot
kilograms per square millimeter	1,422.34	pounds per square inch
kilograms per cubic meter	.0624283	pounds per cubic foot
kilometers	.62137	miles
liters	.26417	gallons
	.0353145	cubic feet

continued on next page

Multiply	by	to obtain
meters	3.28083	feet
	39.37	inches
	1.09361	yards
miles	1.60935	kilometers
millimeters	.00328083	feet
	.03937	inches
pounds	453.592	grams
	.453592	kilograms
pounds per foot	1.48816	kilograms per meter
pounds per square foot	4.88241	kilograms per square meter
pounds per square inch	.07031	kilograms per square centimeter
	.0007031	kilograms per square millimeter
pounds per cubic foot	16.0184	kilograms per cubic meter
square centimeters	.155	square inches
square feet	.00000929034	hectares
	.0929034	square meters
square inches	6.45163	square centimeters
	645.163	square millimeters
square kilometers	247.104	acres
	.3861	square miles
square meters	10.7639	square feet
	1.19599	square yards
square miles	259	hectares
	2.59	square kilometers
square millimeters	.00155	square inches
square yards	.83613	square meters
tons	907.185	kilograms
yards	.914402	meters

APPENDIX B

· · · · · · · · · · · ·

SOURCES OF SUPPLY AND INFORMATION

AMERICAN SUPPLIERS

DRAINS AND DRAINAGE MATERIALS

Akzo Nobel Geosynthetics Company
Sand Hill Road
P.O. Box 1057
Enka, NC 28728
ph. (704) 665-5050; (800) 365-7391
fax (704) 665-5009
Enkadrain and Enkamat drainage material

Bartron Corporation
441 South 48th Street, Suite 107
Tempe, AZ 85281
ph. (602) 921-4979; (800) 992-9949
fax (602) 829-6730
Grassroad Pavers Plus drainage pavers

Ewing Home and Industrial Plastics
3441 East Harbour Drive
Phoenix, AZ 85034
ph. (602) 437-9530
fax (602) 437-0446
Grass-Cel

Geotech Systems, Inc.
9912 Georgetown Pike, Suite D2
Great Falls, VA 22066
ph. (703) 759-0300
fax (703) 757-0119
Geotech drainage medium

JDR Enterprises, Inc.
292 South Main Street, Suite 200
Alpharetta, GA 30004
ph. (770) 442-1461; (800) 843-7569
fax (770) 664-7951
e-mail: service@j-drain.com
J-Drain drainage material

TC Mirafi
365 South Holland Drive
Pendergrass, GA 30606
ph. (706) 693-2226
fax (706) 693-4400
drainage material and filter fabric

PermaTurf Company, Inc.
Division of C. R. Products, Inc.
13 Dow Road
Bow, NH 03304
ph. (800) 498-4116
fax (603) 288-0707
drainage material

Jay R. Smith Manufacturing Company
P.O. Box 3237
Montgomery, AL 36109
ph. (334) 277-8520
fax (334) 272-7396
metal side-perforated drains

Varicore Technologies
Box 128
Prinsburg, MN 56281
ph. (320) 978-8007; (800) 978-8007
fax (320) 978-6607
e-mail: service@varicore.com
Multi-Flow drainage system

FERTILIZER EQUIPMENT

E-Z Grow Automatic Fertilization
8421 Auburn Boulevard, Suite 261
Citrus Heights, CA 95610
ph. (916) 723-7112
fax (916) 723-2750
automatic fertilization equipment

FILTER FABRIC

Fabriscape Inc.
3145 West Columbus Avenue
Chicago, IL 60652
ph. (773) 436-7400; (800) 992-0550
fax (773) 436-0335
filter fabric

TC Mirafi
365 South Holland Drive
Pendergrass, GA 30606
ph. (706) 693-2226
fax (706) 693-4400
drainage material and filter fabric

MOISTURE SENSORS

Glen-Hilton
P.O. Box 31614
Richmond, VA 23294
   or
2504 Grenoble Road
Richmond, VA 23294
ph. (804) 755-1101
fax (804) 755-1102
e-mail: miniclik@glenhilton.com
Mini-Clik moisture-sensing systems

Griswold Controls
2803 Barranca Parkway
Irvine, CA 92606
ph. (949) 559-6000
fax (949) 559-6088
Scanex moisture-sensing and solid-state controller system

MPC HydroPro Irrigation Products
2805 West Service Road
Eagan, MN 55121
ph. (800) 672-3331
fax (612) 681-8106
HydroPro moisture-sensing controller

PEDESTAL PAVING

Envirospec Inc.
Ellicot Station
P.O. Box 119
Buffalo, NY 14205
ph. (716) 689-8548
fax (716) 689-7309
PAVE-EL pedestal pavers

PLANT CONTAINERS

Planter Technology
4007 Transport Street
Palo Alto, CA 94303
ph. (800) 542-2282
fax (650) 493-0789
self-watering containers

Primescape Products Company
855 East Aptakisic Road
Buffalo Grove, IL 60089
ph. (847) 634-4125; (800) 872-4361
fax (847) 634-4126
U.S. distributor for Mona Plant System (MPS) for controlled irrigation

PROTECTION BOARD

James Hardie Building Products
26300 La Alameda, Suite 250
Mission Viejo, CA 92691
ph. (888) 4327-7343
fax (949) 367-1294
e-mail: info@jameshardie.com
protection board (Note: Proven acceptable to protect membrane during construction; never proven under planting medium)

ROOF AND GARDEN SYSTEMS

American Hydrotech, Inc.
303 East Ohio Street
Chicago, IL 60611
ph. (312) 337-4998; (800) 877-6125
fax (312) 661-0731
Garden Roof Assembly

Soprema Company
310 Quadral Drive
Wadsworth, OH 44281
ph. (330) 334-0066; (800) 356-3521
fax (330) 334-4289
e-mail: sales@sopremaworld.com
Sopranature roof and garden system

SOIL AMENDMENTS

Carolina Stalite Company
205 Klumac Road
Salisbury, NC 28145-1037
ph. (704) 637-1515
fax (704) 638-0742
e-mail: info@stalite.com
PermaTill rotary-kiln expanded slate

Davisson Golf, Inc.
200-F Penrod Court
Glen Burnie, MD 21061
ph. (410) 590-2133; (800) 613-6888
fax (410) 590-2135
Isolite soil amendment

Eagle Picher Minerals, Inc.
6110 Plumas Street
Reno, NV 89509
ph. (702) 824-7600
diatomaceous earth

Industrial Services International, Inc.
P.O. Box 10834
Bradenton, FL 34282-0834
ph. (800) 227-6728
fax (813) 758-1175
Terra-Sorb superabsorbent to hold water

Solite
P.O. Box 27211
Richmond, VA 23261
   or
2508 Chamberlayne Avenue
Richmond, VA 23222
ph. (804) 321-6761
lightweight aggregate

SOIL-LESS MEDIA

Grodan Inc.
316 Mount Evans Boulevard, Suite D
Pine Junction, CO 80470
ph. (303) 838-5015
fax (303) 838-5011
Grodan rockwool planting medium

WATERPROOF MEMBRANES

DuPont Packaging and Industrial Polymers
D-5100
1007 Market Street
Wilmington, DE 19892
ph. (302) 773-2002; (800) 438-7225
fax (302) 773-2004
single-ply synthetic rubber membranes

Sarnafil Inc.
Canton Commerce Center
100 Dan Road
Canton, MA 02021
ph. (800) 451-2504, ext. 229
fax (617) 828-5365
waterproof membranes

GERMAN SUPPLIERS

Paul Bauder GmbH and Co.
Postfach 31 11 51
D-70471 Stuttgart
ph. 0711/8807-0
fax 0777/8807-300

Oskar Brecht and Co. KG
Leonberger Strasse 29/1
Postfach 1126
7257 Ditzengen

Daku GmbH
Dachbegrünungs-Systeme
Galileo-Galilei Strasse 24-26
D-55129 Mainz-Hechtsheim
ph. 06131/529831
fax 0711/712571

Fränkische Rohrwerke
Hellinger Strasse
D-97486 Königsberg/Bayern
ph. (09525) 88-0
fax (09525) 88-411
e-mail: fraenkische@swin.baynet.de

Leca Deutschland GmbH and Co. KG
Nienhöfer Strasse 29-37
25421 Pinneberg

Optima Zentrale Süd
Marketing und Vertriebs GmbH
Am Birkenstock 19
D-72505 Krauchenwies-Göggingen
ph. 7576/771-0
fax 7576/771-49
e-mail: 100317.77@compuserve.com

Sarna Kunststoff GmbH
Henschelelring 6
Postfach 1243
8011 Kircheim/München

Technoflor Dachbegrünungssysteme GmbH
Stiffstrasse 24
D-42489 Wülfrath
ph. 2058/925370
fax 2058/925360
e-mail: info@technoflor.de

ZinCo GmbH
Grabenstrasse 33
D-72669 Unterensingen
ph. 07022/6003-0
fax 07022/6003-16
e-mail: contact@zinco.de

GLOSSARY OF GERMAN TERMS

· · · · · · · · · · · · · · · · · · · ·

Readers who wish to do additional research on roof gardens will find that much information is available only in German. The terms below are commonly used on German drawings.

befestigen 1m alle 1,5m: tied down every 1.5 meters with steel wire

Beton B 15: reinforced concrete

Betonfertigteil: prefabricated concrete unit

Betonplatten 50/50/5: concrete slabs

Bewässerungschicht: irrigation layer

Dachabdichtung: waterproofing

Dachdichtung: roof sealant or waterproofing

Dampfsperre: vapor barrier

Drainschicht: drainage course

Druckleitung mit Gefälle zum Entleeren: pressure pipe with fall for emptying

Durchlauf: profile

Erdsubstrat: topsoil mix

FF: fireproof

Filtermatte: filter membrane

Filterschichte: filter layer

Filtervlies: filter fabric

Folie an Anschlussbahn: joining membrane or film

Gefälle: fall or slope

Gefällebeton: sloping concrete

Gewegplatte: precast paving block or module paver

Hydroperl: expanded shale gravel

Klinker: brick

Kupferleitung: copper pipe

Leitungen isolieren: to insulate piping or conduits

Mörtel: grout or mortar

OK Rohr-Oberkante: upper-edge pipe

Ösenschraube für Baumverankerung: stainless-steel eyebolt for guying or cabling of trees

Pflanzsubstrat: planting mix

Pirelleplatte: pressure pipe with slope for drainage

Pro paneel: screwed in place

Punktfundament: point foundation or pier

Rollkies: round gravel or drain rock

Rollschicht Klinker: hard, burned brick laid on edge (normally on top of wall)

Schutzvlies: protective membrane or fabric

Styropor: Styrofoam

Tragkonstruktion: structural slab

Tramlage: sleeper

Trennvlies abdecken: covering of separation membrane

Vegetationschicht: (1) vegetation layer; (2) root zone layer

verklebt: glued

Wärmedämmung: insulation

Wasserstand: water level

Wurzel & Isolierschutz: root-proof and insulation layer

Wurzelschutzfolie: root-proof membrane

Wurzelschutzfolie an Schutz beton: concrete protective cone with root-protection membrane

Wurzelschutzsystem: root-proofing system

BIBLIOGRAPHY

· · · · · · · · · · · · · · · · · ·

American Concrete Institute. *Guide to the Use of Waterproofing, Dampproofing, Protective and Decorative Barrier Systems for Concrete.* ACI 515-IR-79, rev. Detroit: American Concrete Institute, 1985.

American Society for Testing Materials. *Standard Guide for Design of Built-Up Bituminous Membrane Waterproofing Systems for Building Decks.* ASTM C981-89. Philadelphia: American Society for Testing Materials, 1989.

———. *Standard Guide for Use of High Solids Content, Cold Liquid-applied Elastomeric Waterproofing Membrane with Separate Wearing Course.* ASTM C898-89. Philadelphia: American Society for Testing Materials, 1989.

Baker, Maxwell C. "New Roofing Systems." *Canadian Building Digest,* January 1964, 49.

———. *Roofs: Design, Application and Maintenance.* Montreal: Multiscience Publications, 1980

Bauer, Walter. "Terrace Parking in Stockholm's Center." *Landscape Architecture,* July 1967, 267–69.

Callender, J., ed. *Time-Saver Standards for Architectural Design Data.* 6th ed. New York: McGraw-Hill, 1982.

"Constitution Plaza, Hartford, Connecticut." *Anthos* 4 (1964).

"Construction: Roof Gardens." *The Architects' Journal* (London), 27 February 1980.

Darbourne, John. "Roof Gardens for a Local Authority." *The Architects' Journal* (London), 18 September 1968, 587–89.

Dines, Nicholas, and Charles W. Harris, ed. *Time Saver Standards for Landscape Architecture.* 2d ed. New York: McGraw Hill, 1997.

Durr, A. *Dachbegrünung: Ein ökologischer Ausgleich.* Wiesbaden and Berlin: Bauverlag, 1994.

Ernst, W. *Dachabdichtung, Dachbegrünung. Mit Zusammenfassungen in Englisch und Französisch.* Bochum: Kleffman Verlag, 1992.

Finkel, Irving L. "The Hanging Gardens of Babylon." In *The Seven Wonders of the Ancient World* by Peter A. Clayton and Martin J. Price, 38–58. New York: Dorset Press, 1989; London: Routledge, 1988.

Friedberg, P. M. "Roofscape." *Architectural and Engineering News,* September 1969, 24–37.

Giedion, Sigfried. *Space, Time and Architecture.* Cambridge, MA: Harvard University Press, 1941.

Gollwitzer, Gerda, et al. *Dachflachen bewohnt, belebt, bepflanzt.* Munich: G. D. W. Callwey, 1971.

"Grosse Schanze." *Anthos* 2 (1964): 16–18.

Hicks, Phillip. "Landscape on Top of Underground Garages." *Landscape Design,* November 1965, 16–18.

"The Inverted Roof: Technical Study." *The Architects' Journal* (London), 14 May 1975, 1047–61.

Jashenski, Wilhelmina F. *The Gardens of Pompeii.* New Rochelle, NY: Caratzas Brothers, 1979.

Jellicoe, Sir Geoffrey, and Susan Jellicoe. *The Landscape of Man.* London: Thames and Hudson, 1975.

Jellicoe, Sir Geoffrey, Susan Jellicoe, Patrick Goode, and Michael Lancaster. *The Oxford Companion to Gardens.* Oxford: Oxford University Press, 1986.

Johnson, Steven Bruge. *The Roof Gardens of Broadway Theaters, 1883–1942.* Ann Arbor, MI: University of Michigan Research Press.

Kahn, Eve. "A Vase of Country Flowers." *Landscape Architecture,* September 1992.

Kaiser, Helmut. "Ein Versuch, Dachflachen mit wenig Aufwand zu begrünen" (An attempt at low-cost planting; English translation included). *Garten + Landschaft,* January 1981.

Kolb, Walter, and Tassion Schwartz. "The Extensive Planting of Roofs." *Garten + Landschaft,* June 1984, 43–46.

Krupka, B. *Dachbegrünung: Pflanzen und Vegetationsanwendung an Bauwerken.* Stuttgart: Verlag Eugen Ulmer, 1992.

Levinson, Nancy. "Cure for the Common Condo." *Landscape Architecture,* September 1992.

———. "Instant Gratification Extended." *Landscape Architecture,* September 1992.

Liesecke, Hans-Joachim, et al. *Grundlagen der Dach begrünung.* Berlin and Hannover: Patzer Verlag, 1989.

MacDonald, Ken. "Suspended Deck Used in Roof-top Design." *Landscape Design and Construction,* July 1963, 12–13.

Masson, Georgina. *Italian Gardens.* New York: Harry N. Abrams, 1961.

Morgan, William. "Buildings as Landscape: Five Current Projects by William Morgan." *Architectural Record,* September 1972, 129–56.

"New Rooftop Garden in Downtown Oakland." Sunset, May 1961, 220–22.

Osmundson, Theodore. "Roof and Deck Landscapes." In *Time Saver Standards for Landscape Architecture,* edited by Nicholas Dines and Charles W. Harris. 2d ed. New York: McGraw-Hill, 1997.

———. "Kaiser Center Roof Garden." *Landscape Architecture,* October 1962.

———. "The Changing Technique of Roof Garden Design." *Landscape Architecture,* September 1979, 494–503.

Packard, Robert T., ed. *Architectural Graphic Standards.* 7th ed. New York: John Wiley and Sons, 1981.

Patton, George. "Lawn Tops Library's Growth." *Landscape Architecture,* April 1968, 220–21.

Pellet, H. "Use of Aboveground Containers in Landscaping Problems Associated with Winter Soil Temperatures." Miscellaneous Report 111. Chaska, MN: The Landscape Arboretum, University of Minnesota Agricultural Experiment Station, 1976.

Penningsfeld, F., P. Kurtzmann, F. Kalthoff, and P. Fischer. "Tests on Various Protective Membranes for Roof Gardens." *Garten + Landschaft,* August 1981, 639–46.

Penningsfeld, F., et al. "Richtlinien für die Planung, Ausfuhrung und Pflege von Dachbegrünungen." Bonn: FLL (Colmanstrasse 32, 53115 Bonn, Germany).

"Planted Sloping Roof: Polar Building, Tokyo, Japan." *The Architects' Journal* (London), 24 October 1973, 1001–1002.

Powell, Kevin. "It Feels Like This Is Earth." *Landscape Architecture,* September 1992.

Prescott, William H. *The History of the Conquest of Mexico.* 1843. Reprint (abridged). Chicago: University of Chicago Press, 1966.

Raalte, Dirk van. *Dach und Balkongarten.* Berlin and Hamburg: Verlag Paul Parey, 1976.

Robinette, Gary O. "Plants: The Natural Air Conditioner." *Landscape Design and Construction,* March 1968.

———. *Roofscape: Rooftop Landscape Development.* Reston, VA: Environmental Design Press, 1976.

———. *Plants, People, and Environmental Quality.* Prepared for the U.S. Department of the Interior, National Parks Service. Washington, DC: U.S. Government Printing Office, No. 2405-0479.

Rogers, Richard H. "Rooftop Development." In *Handbook of Landscape Architectural Construction,* edited by Jot D. Carpenter, 1–12. Washington, DC: Landscape Architecture Foundation, 1974.

Rooftop Oasis Project: Tenants' Guide to Organizing a Rooftop Project. New York: Haus Rucker Inc., 1976.

San Francisco Beautiful. *Roof Gardens: From Conception to Construction.* San Francisco: San Francisco Beautiful, 1997.

Scalise, J. W., ed. *Earth Integrated Architecture.* Tempe, AZ: College of Architecure, Arizona State University, 1975.

Schild, Erich, et al. *Flachdächer, Dachterrassen, Balkone.* Wiesbaden: Bauverlag, 1976.

Schonholzer, P. "Roof Gardens in Industry." *Anthos* 2 (1968).

Scott, Geraldine Knight. "Horticulture on the Roof." *California Horticultural Journal,* January 1969, 23–26.

Scrivens, Stephen. "Suffolk Hospital: Roof Gardens." *The Architects' Journal* (London), 16 April 1980, 781–82.

———. "Willis Faber and Dumas: Roof Gardens." *The Architects' Journal* (London), 17 September 1980, 611–16.

———. "Kantonsspital, Basle: Roof Gardens." *The Architects' Journal* (London), 17 February 1982, 65–73.

———. "Vetlinof, Zurich: Roof Gardens." *The Architects' Journal* (London), February 1982, 63–64.

———. "Design Guide: Roof Gardens." *The Architects' Journal* (London), 17 March 1982.

———. "Scottish Widows: Roof Gardens." *The Architects' Journal* (London), September 1982, 611–16.

Scrivens, Stephen, and P. Cooper. "Irrigation 1." *Architects' Journal* Technical Study: General Principles. *The Architects' Journal* (London) 171, no. 11 (12 March 1980): 537–40.

———. "Irrigation 2." *Architects' Journal* Information Sheet 1: Drip Emitters. *The Architects' Journal* (London) 171, no. 11 (12 March 1980): 541–43.

———. "Irrigation 3." *Architects' Journal* Information Sheet 3: Pop-up Sprinklers and Spray Heads. *The Architects' Journal* (London) 171, no. 12 (19 March 1980): 583–85.

———. "Irrigation 4." *Architects' Journal* Information Sheet 3: Irrigation. *The Architects' Journal* (London) 171, no. 12 (19 March 1980): 587–88.

Sitta, Vladimir. "A Living Epidermis for the City." *Landscape Australia,* April 1983, 277–86.

Southard, Tony. "Living off the Ground." *The Architects' Journal* (London), 18 September 1968, 587–89.

———. "Roof Gardens." Information Sheet Landscape 42, 10 March 1971. London: *The Architects' Journal* Information Library, 1971.

Stifter, Roland. *Dachgarten: Grüne Inseln in der Stadt.* Stuttgart: Ulmer, 1988.

Sutro, Dirk. "Bloom Service." *Landscape Architecture,* September 1992.

Swerdlow, Joel L. "Under New York." *National Geographic* 191, no. 2 (February 1997): 110–31.

Teasdale, Pierre. *Roof Decks Design Guidelines.* Ottawa, Canada: Canada Mortgage and Housing Corporation, 1979.

"The Terrace Landscaping at Oakland's New Park-museum." *Sunset,* September 1969, 186–89.

Titova, Nina. "Rooftop Gardens." *Science in the U.S.S.R.* (Moscow), 1990, 20–25.

Truex, Phillip. "Conifers in the Winter Roof Garden." *Horticulture,* January 1969, 44–45.

"Two-Acre Bonaventure 17 Stories Up." *Landscape Architecture,* April 1968, 230–32.

"U. C. Soil Mix: The New Artificial Soil." *Sunset,* June 1960, 211–12.

Underground Space Center, University of Minnesota. *Earth Sheltered Community Design.* New York: Van Nostrand Reinhold, 1981.

———. *Earth Sheltered Residential Design.* New York: Van Nostrand Reinhold, 1982.

U.S. Department of Energy. Assistant Secretary, Conservation and Renewable Energy. Office of Building and Community Systems. "Controlling Summer Heat Islands." In *Proceedings of the Workshop on Saving Energy and Reducing Atmospheric Pollution by Controlling Summer Heat Islands.* Berkeley, California, 23–24 February 1989. LBL-27872.

U.S. Department of the Navy. *Earth Sheltered Buildings.* Design Manual 1.4, NAVFAC DM-1.4. Alexandria, VA: Naval Engineering Facilities Command, 1984.

Wagoner, John van. "Protected Membrane Roofs." In *Roofing and Waterproofing Manual.* 4th ed. Rosemont, IL: National Roofing Contractors Association, 1998.

Welsch, Roger. *Sodwalls.* Lincoln, NE: J. and L. Lee Company, 1991.

Whalley, John Mason. "The Landscape of the Roof." *Landscape Design* (London), May 1978, 7–24.

Wing, Franklin. "Rampant High-rises Put Cars under Cover." *Landscape Architecture,* July 1967, 265–67.

Wirth, Thomas E. "Landscape Architecture above Buildings." *Underground Space,* August 1977, 333–46.

———. "Landscape Architecture above Ground." In *Conference on Underground Space,* Harvard University, 1976, vol. 1. London: Pergamon Press, 1976.

Woess, Friedrich, Horst Zeitlberger, and Hans Loidl. *Dachgarten und Pflanztröge.* Vienna: Wohnen, Bauen, und Planen.

Zion, Robert. *Trees for Architecture and Landscape.* New York: Van Nostrand Reinhold, 1986.

INDEX

· · · · · · · · · · · ·

(Page numbers in *italic* refer to illustrations.)